# TABLE OF CONTENTS

Mometrix
TEST PREPARATION

# GACE

# Special Education General Curriculum/Elementary Education Secrets Study Guide

# DEAR FUTURE EXAM SUCCESS STORY

First of all, **THANK YOU** for purchasing Mometrix study materials!

Second, congratulations! You are one of the few determined test-takers who are committed to doing whatever it takes to excel on your exam. **You have come to the right place.** We developed these study materials with one goal in mind: to deliver you the information you need in a format that's concise and easy to use.

In addition to optimizing your guide for the content of the test, we've outlined our recommended steps for breaking down the preparation process into small, attainable goals so you can make sure you stay on track.

We've also analyzed the entire test-taking process, identifying the most common pitfalls and showing how you can overcome them and be ready for any curveball the test throws you.

Standardized testing is one of the biggest obstacles on your road to success, which only increases the importance of doing well in the high-pressure, high-stakes environment of test day. Your results on this test could have a significant impact on your future, and this guide provides the information and practical advice to help you achieve your full potential on test day.

**Your success is our success**

**We would love to hear from you!** If you would like to share the story of your exam success or if you have any questions or comments in regard to our products, please contact us at **800-673-8175** or **support@mometrix.com**.

Thanks again for your business and we wish you continued success!

Sincerely,
The Mometrix Test Preparation Team

**Need more help? Check out our flashcards at:**
**http://MometrixFlashcards.com/GACE**


Written and edited by the Mometrix Exam Secrets Test Prep Team
Printed in the United States of America

# Introduction

**Thank you for purchasing this resource**! You have made the choice to prepare yourself for a test that could have a huge impact on your future, and this guide is designed to help you be fully ready for test day. Obviously, it's important to have a solid understanding of the test material, but you also need to be prepared for the unique environment and stressors of the test, so that you can perform to the best of your abilities.

For this purpose, the first section that appears in this guide is the **Secret Keys**. We've devoted countless hours to meticulously researching what works and what doesn't, and we've boiled down our findings to the five most impactful steps you can take to improve your performance on the test. We start at the beginning with study planning and move through the preparation process, all the way to the testing strategies that will help you get the most out of what you know when you're finally sitting in front of the test.

We recommend that you start preparing for your test as far in advance as possible. However, if you've bought this guide as a last-minute study resource and only have a few days before your test, we recommend that you skip over the first two Secret Keys since they address a long-term study plan.

If you struggle with **test anxiety**, we strongly encourage you to check out our recommendations for how you can overcome it. Test anxiety is a formidable foe, but it can be beaten, and we want to make sure you have the tools you need to defeat it.

# Secret Key #1 – Plan Big, Study Small

There's a lot riding on your performance. If you want to ace this test, you're going to need to keep your skills sharp and the material fresh in your mind. You need a plan that lets you review everything you need to know while still fitting in your schedule. We'll break this strategy down into three categories.

## Information Organization

Start with the information you already have: the official test outline. From this, you can make a complete list of all the concepts you need to cover before the test. Organize these concepts into groups that can be studied together, and create a list of any related vocabulary you need to learn so you can brush up on any difficult terms. You'll want to keep this vocabulary list handy once you actually start studying since you may need to add to it along the way.

## Time Management

Once you have your set of study concepts, decide how to spread them out over the time you have left before the test. Break your study plan into small, clear goals so you have a manageable task for each day and know exactly what you're doing. Then just focus on one small step at a time. When you manage your time this way, you don't need to spend hours at a time studying. Studying a small block of content for a short period each day helps you retain information better and avoid stressing over how much you have left to do. You can relax knowing that you have a plan to cover everything in time. In order for this strategy to be effective though, you have to start studying early and stick to your schedule. Avoid the exhaustion and futility that comes from last-minute cramming!

## Study Environment

The environment you study in has a big impact on your learning. Studying in a coffee shop, while probably more enjoyable, is not likely to be as fruitful as studying in a quiet room. It's important to keep distractions to a minimum. You're only planning to study for a short block of time, so make the most of it. Don't pause to check your phone or get up to find a snack. It's also important to **avoid multitasking**. Research has consistently shown that multitasking will make your studying dramatically less effective. Your study area should also be comfortable and well-lit so you don't have the distraction of straining your eyes or sitting on an uncomfortable chair.

The time of day you study is also important. You want to be rested and alert. Don't wait until just before bedtime. Study when you'll be most likely to comprehend and remember. Even better, if you know what time of day your test will be, set that time aside for study. That way your brain will be used to working on that subject at that specific time and you'll have a better chance of recalling information.

Finally, it can be helpful to team up with others who are studying for the same test. Your actual studying should be done in as isolated an environment as possible, but the work of organizing the information and setting up the study plan can be divided up. In between study sessions, you can discuss with your teammates the concepts that you're all studying and quiz each other on the details. Just be sure that your teammates are as serious about the test as you are. If you find that your study time is being replaced with social time, you might need to find a new team.

# Secret Key #2 – Make Your Studying Count

You're devoting a lot of time and effort to preparing for this test, so you want to be absolutely certain it will pay off. This means doing more than just reading the content and hoping you can remember it on test day. It's important to make every minute of study count. There are two main areas you can focus on to make your studying count.

## Retention

It doesn't matter how much time you study if you can't remember the material. You need to make sure you are retaining the concepts. To check your retention of the information you're learning, try recalling it at later times with minimal prompting. Try carrying around flashcards and glance at one or two from time to time or ask a friend who's also studying for the test to quiz you.

To enhance your retention, look for ways to put the information into practice so that you can apply it rather than simply recalling it. If you're using the information in practical ways, it will be much easier to remember. Similarly, it helps to solidify a concept in your mind if you're not only reading it to yourself but also explaining it to someone else. Ask a friend to let you teach them about a concept you're a little shaky on (or speak aloud to an imaginary audience if necessary). As you try to summarize, define, give examples, and answer your friend's questions, you'll understand the concepts better and they will stay with you longer. Finally, step back for a big picture view and ask yourself how each piece of information fits with the whole subject. When you link the different concepts together and see them working together as a whole, it's easier to remember the individual components.

Finally, practice showing your work on any multi-step problems, even if you're just studying. Writing out each step you take to solve a problem will help solidify the process in your mind, and you'll be more likely to remember it during the test.

## Modality

*Modality* simply refers to the means or method by which you study. Choosing a study modality that fits your own individual learning style is crucial. No two people learn best in exactly the same way, so it's important to know your strengths and use them to your advantage.

For example, if you learn best by visualization, focus on visualizing a concept in your mind and draw an image or a diagram. Try color-coding your notes, illustrating them, or creating symbols that will trigger your mind to recall a learned concept. If you learn best by hearing or discussing information, find a study partner who learns the same way or read aloud to yourself. Think about how to put the information in your own words. Imagine that you are giving a lecture on the topic and record yourself so you can listen to it later.

For any learning style, flashcards can be helpful. Organize the information so you can take advantage of spare moments to review. Underline key words or phrases. Use different colors for different categories. Mnemonic devices (such as creating a short list in which every item starts with the same letter) can also help with retention. Find what works best for you and use it to store the information in your mind most effectively and easily.

# Secret Key #3 – Practice the Right Way

Your success on test day depends not only on how many hours you put into preparing, but also on whether you prepared the right way. It's good to check along the way to see if your studying is paying off. One of the most effective ways to do this is by taking practice tests to evaluate your progress. Practice tests are useful because they show exactly where you need to improve. Every time you take a practice test, pay special attention to these three groups of questions:

- The questions you got wrong
- The questions you had to guess on, even if you guessed right
- The questions you found difficult or slow to work through

This will show you exactly what your weak areas are, and where you need to devote more study time. Ask yourself why each of these questions gave you trouble. Was it because you didn't understand the material? Was it because you didn't remember the vocabulary? Do you need more repetitions on this type of question to build speed and confidence? Dig into those questions and figure out how you can strengthen your weak areas as you go back to review the material.

Additionally, many practice tests have a section explaining the answer choices. It can be tempting to read the explanation and think that you now have a good understanding of the concept. However, an explanation likely only covers part of the question's broader context. Even if the explanation makes perfect sense, **go back and investigate** every concept related to the question until you're positive you have a thorough understanding.

As you go along, keep in mind that the practice test is just that: practice. Memorizing these questions and answers will not be very helpful on the actual test because it is unlikely to have any of the same exact questions. If you only know the right answers to the sample questions, you won't be prepared for the real thing. **Study the concepts** until you understand them fully, and then you'll be able to answer any question that shows up on the test.

It's important to wait on the practice tests until you're ready. If you take a test on your first day of study, you may be overwhelmed by the amount of material covered and how much you need to learn. Work up to it gradually.

On test day, you'll need to be prepared for answering questions, managing your time, and using the test-taking strategies you've learned. It's a lot to balance, like a mental marathon that will have a big impact on your future. Like training for a marathon, you'll need to start slowly and work your way up. When test day arrives, you'll be ready.

Start with the strategies you've read in the first two Secret Keys—plan your course and study in the way that works best for you. If you have time, consider using multiple study resources to get different approaches to the same concepts. It can be helpful to see difficult concepts from more than one angle. Then find a good source for practice tests. Many times, the test website will suggest potential study resources or provide sample tests.

# Practice Test Strategy

If you're able to find at least three practice tests, we recommend this strategy:

## Untimed and Open-Book Practice

Take the first test with no time constraints and with your notes and study guide handy. Take your time and focus on applying the strategies you've learned.

## Timed and Open-Book Practice

Take the second practice test open-book as well, but set a timer and practice pacing yourself to finish in time.

## Timed and Closed-Book Practice

Take any other practice tests as if it were test day. Set a timer and put away your study materials. Sit at a table or desk in a quiet room, imagine yourself at the testing center, and answer questions as quickly and accurately as possible.

Keep repeating timed and closed-book tests on a regular basis until you run out of practice tests or it's time for the actual test. Your mind will be ready for the schedule and stress of test day, and you'll be able to focus on recalling the material you've learned.

# Secret Key #4 – Pace Yourself

Once you're fully prepared for the material on the test, your biggest challenge on test day will be managing your time. Just knowing that the clock is ticking can make you panic even if you have plenty of time left. Work on pacing yourself so you can build confidence against the time constraints of the exam. Pacing is a difficult skill to master, especially in a high-pressure environment, so **practice is vital**.

Set time expectations for your pace based on how much time is available. For example, if a section has 60 questions and the time limit is 30 minutes, you know you have to average 30 seconds or less per question in order to answer them all. Although 30 seconds is the hard limit, set 25 seconds per question as your goal, so you reserve extra time to spend on harder questions. When you budget extra time for the harder questions, you no longer have any reason to stress when those questions take longer to answer.

Don't let this time expectation distract you from working through the test at a calm, steady pace, but keep it in mind so you don't spend too much time on any one question. Recognize that taking extra time on one question you don't understand may keep you from answering two that you do understand later in the test. If your time limit for a question is up and you're still not sure of the answer, mark it and move on, and come back to it later if the time and the test format allow. If the testing format doesn't allow you to return to earlier questions, just make an educated guess; then put it out of your mind and move on.

On the easier questions, be careful not to rush. It may seem wise to hurry through them so you have more time for the challenging ones, but it's not worth missing one if you know the concept and just didn't take the time to read the question fully. Work efficiently but make sure you understand the question and have looked at all of the answer choices, since more than one may seem right at first.

Even if you're paying attention to the time, you may find yourself a little behind at some point. You should speed up to get back on track, but do so wisely. Don't panic; just take a few seconds less on each question until you're caught up. Don't guess without thinking, but do look through the answer choices and eliminate any you know are wrong. If you can get down to two choices, it is often worthwhile to guess from those. Once you've chosen an answer, move on and don't dwell on any that you skipped or had to hurry through. If a question was taking too long, chances are it was one of the harder ones, so you weren't as likely to get it right anyway.

On the other hand, if you find yourself getting ahead of schedule, it may be beneficial to slow down a little. The more quickly you work, the more likely you are to make a careless mistake that will affect your score. You've budgeted time for each question, so don't be afraid to spend that time. Practice an efficient but careful pace to get the most out of the time you have.

# Secret Key #5 – Have a Plan for Guessing

When you're taking the test, you may find yourself stuck on a question. Some of the answer choices seem better than others, but you don't see the one answer choice that is obviously correct. What do you do?

The scenario described above is very common, yet most test takers have not effectively prepared for it. Developing and practicing a plan for guessing may be one of the single most effective uses of your time as you get ready for the exam.

In developing your plan for guessing, there are three questions to address:

- When should you start the guessing process?
- How should you narrow down the choices?
- Which answer should you choose?

## When to Start the Guessing Process

Unless your plan for guessing is to select C every time (which, despite its merits, is not what we recommend), you need to leave yourself enough time to apply your answer elimination strategies. Since you have a limited amount of time for each question, that means that if you're going to give yourself the best shot at guessing correctly, you have to decide quickly whether or not you will guess.

Of course, the best-case scenario is that you don't have to guess at all, so first, see if you can answer the question based on your knowledge of the subject and basic reasoning skills. Focus on the key words in the question and try to jog your memory of related topics. Give yourself a chance to bring the knowledge to mind, but once you realize that you don't have (or you can't access) the knowledge you need to answer the question, it's time to start the guessing process.

It's almost always better to start the guessing process too early than too late. It only takes a few seconds to remember something and answer the question from knowledge. Carefully eliminating wrong answer choices takes longer. Plus, going through the process of eliminating answer choices can actually help jog your memory.

**Summary**: Start the guessing process as soon as you decide that you can't answer the question based on your knowledge.

## How to Narrow Down the Choices

The next chapter in this book (**Test-Taking Strategies**) includes a wide range of strategies for how to approach questions and how to look for answer choices to eliminate. You will definitely want to read those carefully, practice them, and figure out which ones work best for you. Here though, we're going to address a mindset rather than a particular strategy.

Your odds of guessing an answer correctly depend on how many options you are choosing from.

| **Number of options left** | 5 | 4 | 3 | 2 | 1 |
|---|---|---|---|---|---|
| **Odds of guessing correctly** | 20% | 25% | 33% | 50% | 100% |

You can see from this chart just how valuable it is to be able to eliminate incorrect answers and make an educated guess, but there are two things that many test takers do that cause them to miss out on the benefits of guessing:

- Accidentally eliminating the correct answer
- Selecting an answer based on an impression

We'll look at the first one here, and the second one in the next section.

To avoid accidentally eliminating the correct answer, we recommend a thought exercise called **the $5 challenge**. In this challenge, you only eliminate an answer choice from contention if you are willing to bet $5 on it being wrong. Why $5? Five dollars is a small but not insignificant amount of money. It's an amount you could afford to lose but wouldn't want to throw away. And while losing $5 once might not hurt too much, doing it twenty times will set you back $100. In the same way, each small decision you make—eliminating a choice here, guessing on a question there—won't by itself impact your score very much, but when you put them all together, they can make a big difference. By holding each answer choice elimination decision to a higher standard, you can reduce the risk of accidentally eliminating the correct answer.

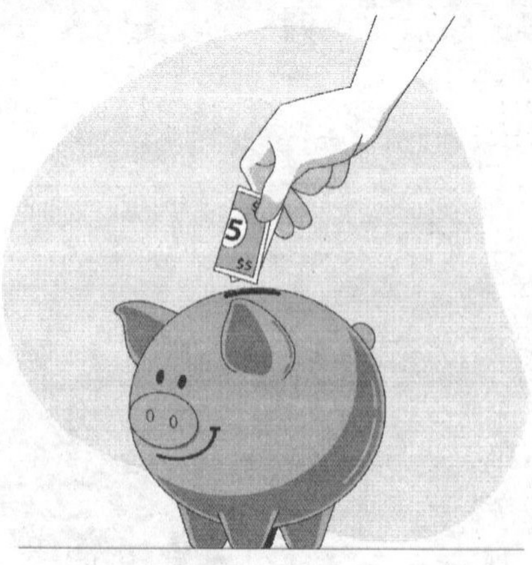

The $5 challenge can also be applied in a positive sense: If you are willing to bet $5 that an answer choice *is* correct, go ahead and mark it as correct.

**Summary**: Only eliminate an answer choice if you are willing to bet $5 that it is wrong.

## Which Answer to Choose

You're taking the test. You've run into a hard question and decided you'll have to guess. You've eliminated all the answer choices you're willing to bet $5 on. Now you have to pick an answer. Why do we even need to talk about this? Why can't you just pick whichever one you feel like when the time comes?

The answer to these questions is that if you don't come into the test with a plan, you'll rely on your impression to select an answer choice, and if you do that, you risk falling into a trap. The test writers know that everyone who takes their test will be guessing on some of the questions, so they intentionally write wrong answer choices to seem plausible. You still have to pick an answer though, and if the wrong answer choices are designed to look right, how can you ever be sure that you're not falling for their trap? The best solution we've found to this dilemma is to take the decision out of your hands entirely. Here is the process we recommend:

**Once you've eliminated any choices that you are confident (willing to bet $5) are wrong, select the first remaining choice as your answer.**

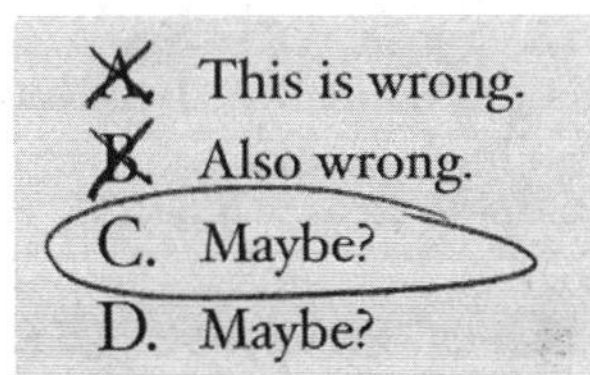


Whether you choose to select the first remaining choice, the second, or the last, the important thing is that you use some preselected standard. Using this approach guarantees that you will not be enticed into selecting an answer choice that looks right, because you are not basing your decision on how the answer choices look.

This is not meant to make you question your knowledge. Instead, it is to help you recognize the difference between your knowledge and your impressions. There's a huge difference between thinking an answer is right because of what you know, and thinking an answer is right because it looks or sounds like it should be right.

**Summary**: To ensure that your selection is appropriately random, make a predetermined selection from among all answer choices you have not eliminated.

# Test-Taking Strategies

This section contains a list of test-taking strategies that you may find helpful as you work through the test. By taking what you know and applying logical thought, you can maximize your chances of answering any question correctly!

It is very important to realize that every question is different and every person is different: no single strategy will work on every question, and no single strategy will work for every person. That's why we've included all of them here, so you can try them out and determine which ones work best for different types of questions and which ones work best for you.

## Question Strategies

### READ CAREFULLY

Read the question and the answer choices carefully. Don't miss the question because you misread the terms. You have plenty of time to read each question thoroughly and make sure you understand what is being asked. Yet a happy medium must be attained, so don't waste too much time. You must read carefully and efficiently.

### CONTEXTUAL CLUES

Look for contextual clues. If the question includes a word you are not familiar with, look at the immediate context for some indication of what the word might mean. Contextual clues can often give you all the information you need to decipher the meaning of an unfamiliar word. Even if you can't determine the meaning, you may be able to narrow down the possibilities enough to make a solid guess at the answer to the question.

### PREFIXES

If you're having trouble with a word in the question or answer choices, try dissecting it. Take advantage of every clue that the word might include. Prefixes can be a huge help. Usually, they allow you to determine a basic meaning. *Pre-* means before, *post-* means after, *pro-* is positive, *de-* is negative. From prefixes, you can get an idea of the general meaning of the word and try to put it into context.

### HEDGE WORDS

Watch out for critical hedge words, such as *likely, may, can, often, almost, mostly, usually, generally, rarely*, and *sometimes*. Question writers insert these hedge phrases to cover every possibility. Often an answer choice will be wrong simply because it leaves no room for exception. Be on guard for answer choices that have definitive words such as *exactly* and *always*.

### SWITCHBACK WORDS

Stay alert for *switchbacks*. These are the words and phrases frequently used to alert you to shifts in thought. The most common switchback words are *but, although*, and *however*. Others include *nevertheless, on the other hand, even though, while, in spite of, despite*, and *regardless of*. Switchback words are important to catch because they can change the direction of the question or an answer choice.

### FACE VALUE

When in doubt, use common sense. Accept the situation in the problem at face value. Don't read too much into it. These problems will not require you to make wild assumptions. If you have to go beyond creativity and warp time or space in order to have an answer choice fit the question, then you should move on and consider the other answer choices. These are normal problems rooted in reality. The applicable relationship or explanation may not be readily apparent, but it is there for you to figure out. Use your common sense to interpret anything that isn't clear.

# Answer Choice Strategies

## ⊘ Answer Selection

The most thorough way to pick an answer choice is to identify and eliminate wrong answers until only one is left, then confirm it is the correct answer. Sometimes an answer choice may immediately seem right, but be careful. The test writers will usually put more than one reasonable answer choice on each question, so take a second to read all of them and make sure that the other choices are not equally obvious. As long as you have time left, it is better to read every answer choice than to pick the first one that looks right without checking the others.

## ⊘ Answer Choice Families

An answer choice family consists of two (in rare cases, three) answer choices that are very similar in construction and cannot all be true at the same time. If you see two answer choices that are direct opposites or parallels, one of them is usually the correct answer. For instance, if one answer choice says that quantity $x$ increases and another either says that quantity $x$ decreases (opposite) or says that quantity $y$ increases (parallel), then those answer choices would fall into the same family. An answer choice that doesn't match the construction of the answer choice family is more likely to be incorrect. Most questions will not have answer choice families, but when they do appear, you should be prepared to recognize them.

## ⊘ Eliminate Answers

Eliminate answer choices as soon as you realize they are wrong, but make sure you consider all possibilities. If you are eliminating answer choices and realize that the last one you are left with is also wrong, don't panic. Start over and consider each choice again. There may be something you missed the first time that you will realize on the second pass.

## ⊘ Avoid Fact Traps

Don't be distracted by an answer choice that is factually true but doesn't answer the question. You are looking for the choice that answers the question. Stay focused on what the question is asking for so you don't accidentally pick an answer that is true but incorrect. Always go back to the question and make sure the answer choice you've selected actually answers the question and is not merely a true statement.

## ⊘ Extreme Statements

In general, you should avoid answers that put forth extreme actions as standard practice or proclaim controversial ideas as established fact. An answer choice that states the "process should be used in certain situations, if..." is much more likely to be correct than one that states the "process should be discontinued completely." The first is a calm rational statement and doesn't even make a definitive, uncompromising stance, using a hedge word *if* to provide wiggle room, whereas the second choice is far more extreme.

## ⊘ Benchmark

As you read through the answer choices and you come across one that seems to answer the question well, mentally select that answer choice. This is not your final answer, but it's the one that will help you evaluate the other answer choices. The one that you selected is your benchmark or standard for judging each of the other answer choices. Every other answer choice must be compared to your benchmark. That choice is correct until proven otherwise by another answer choice beating it. If you find a better answer, then that one becomes your new benchmark. Once you've decided that no other choice answers the question as well as your benchmark, you have your final answer.

### ⊘ Predict the Answer

Before you even start looking at the answer choices, it is often best to try to predict the answer. When you come up with the answer on your own, it is easier to avoid distractions and traps because you will know exactly what to look for. The right answer choice is unlikely to be word-for-word what you came up with, but it should be a close match. Even if you are confident that you have the right answer, you should still take the time to read each option before moving on.

## General Strategies

### ⊘ Tough Questions

If you are stumped on a problem or it appears too hard or too difficult, don't waste time. Move on! Remember though, if you can quickly check for obviously incorrect answer choices, your chances of guessing correctly are greatly improved. Before you completely give up, at least try to knock out a couple of possible answers. Eliminate what you can and then guess at the remaining answer choices before moving on.

### ⊘ Check Your Work

Since you will probably not know every term listed and the answer to every question, it is important that you get credit for the ones that you do know. Don't miss any questions through careless mistakes. If at all possible, try to take a second to look back over your answer selection and make sure you've selected the correct answer choice and haven't made a costly careless mistake (such as marking an answer choice that you didn't mean to mark). This quick double check should more than pay for itself in caught mistakes for the time it costs.

### ⊘ Pace Yourself

It's easy to be overwhelmed when you're looking at a page full of questions; your mind is confused and full of random thoughts, and the clock is ticking down faster than you would like. Calm down and maintain the pace that you have set for yourself. Especially as you get down to the last few minutes of the test, don't let the small numbers on the clock make you panic. As long as you are on track by monitoring your pace, you are guaranteed to have time for each question.

### ⊘ Don't Rush

It is very easy to make errors when you are in a hurry. Maintaining a fast pace in answering questions is pointless if it makes you miss questions that you would have gotten right otherwise. Test writers like to include distracting information and wrong answers that seem right. Taking a little extra time to avoid careless mistakes can make all the difference in your test score. Find a pace that allows you to be confident in the answers that you select.

### ⊘ Keep Moving

Panicking will not help you pass the test, so do your best to stay calm and keep moving. Taking deep breaths and going through the answer elimination steps you practiced can help to break through a stress barrier and keep your pace.

## Final Notes

The combination of a solid foundation of content knowledge and the confidence that comes from practicing your plan for applying that knowledge is the key to maximizing your performance on test day. As your foundation of content knowledge is built up and strengthened, you'll find that the strategies included in this chapter become more and more effective in helping you quickly sift through the distractions and traps of the test to isolate the correct answer.

Now that you're preparing to move forward into the test content chapters of this book, be sure to keep your goal in mind. As you read, think about how you will be able to apply this information on the test. If you've already seen sample questions for the test and you have an idea of the question format and style, try to come up with questions of your own that you can answer based on what you're reading. This will give you valuable practice applying your knowledge in the same ways you can expect to on test day.

**Good luck and good studying!**

# English Language Arts

## Print-Rich Classrooms

In early childhood classrooms, print-rich environments contain books and texts of different genres and topics, including both audio and digital texts. Walls and shelves have signs and labels to help with classroom procedures and organization. Posters display information related to content students have been studying. Reading, writing, and listening centers are available for students to explore during center time. Puppet theaters and flannel boards are present to encourage oral language and storytelling. There are also many literacy-related materials, such as letter tiles and sight word cards. Word walls are posted.

In **print-rich environments**, students are encouraged to share and display texts they have created. They may add their own stories to the classroom libraries or hang up signs they have made. Materials created during shared and interactive reading and writing experiences may also be displayed.

In classrooms for older students, signs and posters are displayed containing academic vocabulary, content students have been studying, and classroom procedures. Written and digital texts from a range of genres are present. There are also ample resources available for students to use to locate and share information, such as computers, tablets, dictionaries, and thesauri.

## Promoting Literacy Development with Dramatic Play Centers

**Dramatic play centers** are common in early childhood classrooms. These centers allow children to act out realistic situations through play. Examples include pretend restaurants, homes, veterinary clinics, and grocery stores. While engaging in dramatic play, children read, write, listen, and speak for authentic purposes.

As children role-play and interact with other children in dramatic play centers, they develop oral language skills. They engage in conversations and practice using language to accomplish tasks, such as ordering in restaurants. They also listen to peers and follow directions, such as when they are pretending to be restaurant servers.

Children also engage in reading activities in dramatic play centers. Labels and realistic print materials can be included. For example, pretend restaurants may include labeled cabinets and menus. Children can practice writing through dramatic play. For example, children who are pretending to be servers may write down orders on notepads.

## Building Literacy Activities into Daily Routines and Activities

Teachers can plan reading, writing, listening, and speaking activities across all subject areas. This can include a mixture of independent literacy activities and shared and interactive reading and writing experiences. Texts focusing on topics that are being studied in all content areas can be accessible in the classroom. Students can also write in all subject areas. For example, they can write the processes used to solve problems in math and create travel brochures in social studies.

Teachers of early childhood and elementary students can plan morning meetings in which daily written messages are read and discussed. Students can share current events and topics of interest with their classmates during these meetings, while other students listen and ask questions.

Early childhood and elementary teachers can also incorporate oral language and listening into daily routines. For example, they may recite specific chants or songs during transitions.

## Chapter Quiz

Ready to see how well you retained what you just read? Scan the QR code to go directly to the chapter quiz interface for this study guide. If you're using a computer, simply visit the online resources page at **mometrix.com/resources719/gacesegcelemed** and click the Chapter Quizzes link.

# Mathematics

## PREMATHEMATICAL LEARNING EXPERIENCES

Preschool children do not think in the same ways as older children and adults do, as Piaget observed. Their thinking is strongly based upon and connected to their sensory perceptions. This means that in solving problems, they depend mainly on how things look, sound, feel, smell, and taste. Therefore, preschool children should always be given concrete objects that they can touch, explore, and experiment with in any learning experience. They are not yet capable of understanding abstract concepts or manipulating information mentally, so they must have real things to work with to understand **premath** concepts. For example, they will learn to count solid objects like blocks, beads, or pennies before they can count numbers in their heads. They cannot benefit from rote math memorization or "sit still and listen" lessons. Since young children "centrate" on one characteristic, object, person, or event at a time, adults can offer activities encouraging decentration/incorporating multiple aspects (e.g., not only grouping all triangles but grouping all red triangles separately from blue triangles).

## PROBLEM SOLVING SKILLS

Being able to solve problems is fundamental to all other components of mathematics. Children learn the concept that a question can have more than one answer and a problem can have more than one solution by participating in problem-solving activities. To solve problems, a child must be able to explore a problem, a situation, or a subject; think through the problem, situation, or subject; and use logical reasoning. These abilities are needed to not only solve routine, everyday problems but also novel or unusual ones. Using problem-solving skills not only helps children think mathematically but also promotes their language development and their social skills when they work together. Children are naturally curious about how to solve everyday problems. Adults can take advantage of this inherent curiosity by discussing everyday challenges, asking children to propose ways to solve them, and asking them to explain how they arrived at their solutions. Adults can also invite children to propose problems and ask questions about them. This helps them learn to analyze different types of problems and realize that many problems have multiple possible solutions.

### *COMMON STEPS THAT PREPARE CHILDREN TO LEARN MATH*

The process of solving problems often involves the following steps:

1. Understanding the problem
2. Coming up with a plan to solve the problem
3. Putting that plan into action, and, finally, observing the outcome
4. Reflecting on whether the solution was effective and whether the answer arrived at makes sense

Solving problems not only involves learning this series of steps but also requires children to develop the qualities needed to solve problems. Children who are able to solve problems have a number of characteristics. For example, children who are effective problem solvers are able to focus their attention on the problem and its individual component parts. They can formulate hypotheses about the problem/situation and then test them for veracity. They are willing to take risks within reason. They are persistent if they do not solve a problem right away and do not give up if their first attempt at solving a problem is unsuccessful. They maintain flexibility and experiment with alternate methods. They also demonstrate self-regulation skills.

### *USING PROBLEM SOLVING SKILLS IN DAILY LIFE*

Young children continually explore their environments to unravel mysteries about how things work. For example, preschoolers use math concepts to understand that they have three toys, to comprehend that three fingers equals three toys, or to understand that two cookies plus one more equals three cookies. To do abstract mathematics in the future, young children will need two major skills that are also used to solve problems:

being able to visualize a scenario and being able to apply common sense thinking. Thinking and planning to achieve goals within the constraints of the properties of the surrounding environment is a natural behavior for young children. They will persist in their efforts to get an older sibling to stop another activity to play with them, to repair broken toys with tape or chewing gum, to manipulate a puzzle or plastic building blocks to get one uncooperative piece to fit, etc. The great 20th-century mathematician and teacher George Polya stated that problem-solving is "the most characteristically human activity." He pointed out that problem-solving is a skill learned by doing, and that developing this skill requires a great deal of practice.

### *Games/Activities That Encourage the Use of Problem-Solving Skills*

One method that has been found to enhance children's reasoning skills is using adult-child conversations to play mental mathematics games. For example, once children are able to count beyond five, adults can give them basic oral story problems to solve (e.g., "If you have two plums and I give you two more, how many will you have?"). Using children's favorite foods in story problems, which takes advantage of their ready ability to envision these foods, is a good place to start. Thereafter, adults can add story problems involving pets, toys, cars, shopping, and other familiar objects, animals, or activities. Experts advise adults not to restrict the types of problems presented to a child based solely on the child's grade level. Children can work with any situation if they can form mental imagery. Adults can sometimes insert harder tasks (e.g., problems involving larger numbers, problems involving division with remainders, or problems with negative number answers). Even toddlers can solve problems such as how to divide three cookies between two people. The division may not be fair, but it will likely be efficient. Adults should use the Socratic method, asking guiding questions to allow children to arrive at a solution to a problem themselves, rather than telling them a "right" answer.

### *Beneficial Practices of Playing Mental Math Games*

Adults can use children's favorite foods and toys to pose story problems to children that involve addition and subtraction. For example, they can ask them questions like "If I give you [this many] more, how many will you have?" or "If we take away [this many], how many are left?" It is better to ask children questions than to give them answers. It is important to use turn-taking. In this method, the adult poses a story problem to the child, and then the child gets to pose one to the adult. Adults must try to solve the problem, even if the child makes up numbers like "bazillion" or "eleventy." Games should be fun, not strictly factual like math tests. Adults can introduce age-appropriate story topics as children grow older. At the end of early childhood/around school age, children can handle the abstract algebraic concept of variables or unknown numbers (which some experts call "mystery numbers") and use this concept in games. Adults can pose riddles where $x$ or $n$ is the unknown number, and children must use an operation (e.g., $x + 4 = 7$) to solve the riddle.

**Review Video: Mathematical Operations**
Visit mometrix.com/academy and enter code: 208095

## Reasoning Skills

### *Communicating with Children to Promote Mathematical Reasoning Skills*

Adults should reciprocally talk to and listen to children during communication that is focused on using mathematical skills like problem-solving, reasoning, making connections, etc. To promote young children's understanding, adults can express mathematical concepts using pictures, words, diagrams, and symbols. Encouraging children to talk with their peers and adults helps them clarify their own thoughts and think about what they are doing. Communicating with children about mathematical thinking problems also develops their vocabularies and promotes early literacy and reading skills. Adults should listen to what children want to say and should have conversations with them. Communicating about math can also be accomplished through reading children's books that incorporate numbers and/or repetition or rhyme. In addition to talking, adults can communicate math concepts to children by drawing pictures or diagrams and using concrete objects (e.g., blocks, crayons, pieces of paper, fingers, etc.) to represent numbers and/or solve problems. Children also share their learning of math concepts through words, charts, drawings, tallies, etc. Even toddlers hold up fingers to tell others how old they are.

### *Using Reasoning to Apply Early Mathematical and Scientific Concepts*

A major component of problem-solving is **reasoning**. Children reason when they think through questions and find usable answers. They use reasoning skills to make sense of mathematical and scientific subject matter. Children use several abilities during the reasoning process. For example, they use logic to classify objects or concepts into groups. They follow logical sequences to arrive at conclusions that make sense. They use their analytical abilities to explain their own thought processes. They apply what they have learned about relationships and patterns to help them find solutions to problems. They also use reasoning to justify their mental processes and problem solutions. To support children's reasoning, adults can ask children questions, give them time to think about their answers, and listen to their answers. This simple tactic helps children learn how to reason. Adults can also ask children why something is as it is—letting them think for themselves rather than looking for a particular answer—and listen to the ideas they produce.

### Role of Representation Skills in Children's Learning

Young children develop an understanding of **symbolic representation**—the idea that objects, written letters, words, and other symbols are used to represent other objects or concepts—at an early age. This is evident in their make-believe/pretend play and in their ability to learn written language and connect it to spoken language. As children develop early math skills, representing their ideas and the information they acquire helps them organize, document, and share these ideas and facts with others. Children may count on their fingers; create tallies using checkmarks, tick marks, and/or words; draw pictures or maps; and, as they grow older, make graphs. Teachers must help children apply mathematical process skills as they use learning center materials. For example, when a child enjoys sorting rocks by color, the teacher can state that the child is classifying them, bridging informal math activities with math vocabulary. Asking the child how he or she is categorizing the rocks emphasizes math vocabulary. Asking the child after he or she finishes what other ways the rocks could be classified encourages problem-solving.

### Helping Children Transition from Intuitive to Formal Math Thinking

Children informally learn intuitive mathematical thinking through their everyday life experiences. They naturally apply mathematical concepts and reasoning to solve problems they face in their environment. However, one frequent problem among children when they begin formal education is that they can come to see academic mathematics as a collection of procedures and rules, instead of viewing it as a means of finding solutions to everyday, real-life problems. This view will interfere with children's ability to apply the formal mathematics they learn to their lives in a practical and useful way. Teachers can help prevent this outcome by establishing the connection between children's natural intuitive math and formal mathematics. They can do this by teaching math through the use of manipulative materials familiar to children. They can use mathematics vocabulary words when describing children's activities, which enables children to develop an awareness of the natural mathematical operations they use in their daily lives. When a teacher introduces a new mathematical concept to children, he or she can give illustrative examples that draw upon the children's actual life experiences.

### Relationship of Mathematics to Everyday Life and Other Academic Subjects

We use math throughout our lives during everyday activities. There are countless examples and combinations of various mathematical concepts in the real world. Additionally, math concepts inform other academic content areas, including music, art, and the sciences. Therefore, it is important for children not to view math as an isolated set of procedures and skills. Children comprehend math more easily when they can make connections, which involves applying common mathematical rules to multiple, varied functions, processes, and real-life activities. For example, adults can ask children to consider problems they encounter daily and solve them. When a parent asks a child to help put away groceries, the child practices sorting categories of foods and packages, and experiments with comparative package sizes and shapes. Parents need not be concerned with what specific mathematical processes are involved but should simply look for examples of math in everyday life and expose children to these examples on a regular basis. For example, pouring liquid into containers of various sizes and speculating which one will hold the most is an easy, fun activity that incorporates a number of skills and concepts, including estimation, measurement, spatial sense, and conservation of liquid volume.

### Patterns and Relationships

Patterns are generally defined as things that recur or are repeated regularly. Patterns can be found in images, sounds, numbers, events, actions, movements, etc. Relationships are generally defined as connections or associations between things that are identified and/or described using logic or reasoning. Being aware of patterns and relationships among aspects of the environment helps us comprehend the fundamental structure of these aspects. This awareness enables us to predict what will occur next in a series of events, even before it actually happens. This gives us more confidence in our environment and in our ability to interact with it. We find patterns and relationships in such areas of life as art, music, and clothing. Math-specific activities like counting numbers and working with geometrical shapes, lines, arcs, and curves also involve patterns and relationships. When children understand patterns and relationships, they can understand repetition, rhythm, categorization, and how to order things from smallest to biggest, from shortest to longest, etc.

Adults can help young children develop their understanding of patterns and relationships in life by looking at pictures and designs with them, encouraging and guiding them to identify patterns within drawings, paintings, and abstract designs such as prints on fabrics and other decorative designs. When children participate in movement activities, including dancing to music, running, skipping, hopping, playing simple musical instruments, etc., adults can help them identify patterns in their own and others' movements. Adults can encourage young children to participate in hands-on activities, such as stringing wood, plastic beads, or penne and other hollow dry pasta tubes onto pieces of string to make necklaces with simple patterns (e.g., blue-yellow-blue-yellow). As children grow older, adults can encourage them to create more complicated patterns. They can alternate a larger number of colors, and they can vary the numbers of each color in more complex ways (e.g., three blue, two yellow, one red, etc.).

### Contribution of Number Sense and Number Operations to Math Comprehension

Counting is one of the earliest numeracy skills that young children develop. Even before they have learned the names of all the numbers, young children learn to count to three, then to five, etc. However, **number sense** involves a great deal more than just counting. Number sense includes understanding the various applications of numbers. For instance, we use numbers as tools for conveying and manipulating information, as tools for describing quantities, and as tools for characterizing relationships between or among things. Children who have developed number sense are able to count with accuracy and competence. Given a specific number, they can count upward from that number. They can also count backward. They are able to break down a number and then reassemble it. They are able to recognize relationships between or among different numbers. When children can count, are familiar with numbers, and have good number sense, they can also add and subtract numbers. Being familiar with numbers and being able to count easily helps young children understand all other areas of mathematics.

### Activities to Help Develop Number Sense and Numeracy Skills

As children complete their daily activities, it is beneficial for adults to count real things with children and encourage them to count as well. This helps children understand numbers by using their own experiences with objects in the environment and gives them practice counting and using numbers. To help children understand that we use numbers to describe quantities and relationships, adults can ask children to sort objects by size, shape, or color similarity. They can also ask children to sort objects according to their differences (e.g., which object is bigger/smaller). Adults can also discuss with children how numbers are used to find street addresses and apartment numbers and to keep score during games. To help children count upward and downward with efficiency and accuracy, adults can point out that counting allows us to determine how many items are in a group. Adults should point to each object as they count it. They can count on their fingers and encourage young children to do the same. Adults should also help children count without repeating or skipping any numbers.

### Counting

**Counting** is considered a math skill milestone for young children. Typical four-year-olds enjoy counting aloud. Experts identify three levels of counting. The first is counting from 1 to 12, which requires memorization. The second level is counting from 13 to 19, which requires not only memorization but also an understanding of the more unusual rules for "teen" numbers. The third level is counting from 20 on. This process is very consistent, and the numbers are ordered according to regular rules. Experts in math education believe that at this level of counting, children are discovering a regular mathematical pattern for the first time, which is base ten (i.e., 20, 30, 40, 50, etc. are 2 tens, 3 tens, 4 tens, 5 tens, etc., and after the base, a number between 1 and 9 is added). Researchers and educators in early childhood mathematics programs recommend encouraging children as young as four years old to learn to count up to 100. They find that doing this helps young children learn about and explore patterns in depth.

## Perceiving and Identifying Shapes

The three levels of perceiving shapes that children typically move through sequentially are seeing, naming, and analyzing. Very young children recognize simple shapes like circles, squares, and triangles. As their cognitive and language skills develop, they learn the names for these shapes and use these names to identify single shapes. The third level is analyzing each shape to understand its properties. Whereas identifying shapes visually is intuitive and based on association, analyzing their properties is more abstract, since a shape can have a number of different appearances. For example, three-year-olds can differentiate a triangle from other shapes. However, if you show them a very tall and skinny, short and wide, lopsided, or crooked triangle, they will have trouble identifying it as a triangle. At the analysis level, children realize that a triangle has three sides, which are not necessarily equal in length. An activity that young children enjoy is closing their eyes, reaching into a bag of assorted shapes, finding a triangle by touch, and explaining why it is a triangle. This involves both the second and third levels of naming and analysis.

## Spatial Sense and Geometry

**Spatial sense** is an individual's awareness of one's own body in space and in relation to the objects and other people around the individual. Spatial sense allows young children to navigate environmental spaces without colliding with objects and other people; to see and hear adequately and to be aware of whether others can see and hear them; and to develop and observe a socially and culturally appropriate sense of their own and others' personal space. Geometry is the area of mathematics involving space, sizes, shapes, positions, movements, and directions. Geometry gives descriptions and classifications of our physical environment. By observing commonplace objects and spaces in their physical world, young children can learn about solid objects and substances, shapes, and angles. Adults can help young children learn geometry by identifying various shapes, angles, and three-dimensional figures for them; asking them to name these shapes, angles, and figures when they encounter them in the future; and asking them to describe different shapes, draw them in the air with their fingers, trace drawings of the shapes with their fingers, and then draw the shapes themselves.

### *Activities to Help Develop Spatial Sense and Geometry*

Because it involves many physical properties like shape, line, and angle, as well as abstract concepts, young children learn geometry most effectively via hands-on activities. Learning experiences that allow them to touch and manipulate concrete objects, such as boxes, containers, puzzles, blocks, and shape sorters, usually work best. Everyday activities can also help children learn geometry concepts. For example, adults can cut children's sandwiches into various geometrical shapes and let children fit them together and/or rearrange them into new patterns. Children become better able to follow directions and navigate through space when they develop geometric knowledge and spatial sense. Adults can provide activities that promote the development of geometric knowledge and spatial sense. For example, they can let children get into and out of big appliance boxes, climb over furniture, and go into, on top of, out of, under, around, over, and through different objects and structures to allow children to experience the relationship between their bodies and space and solids. As they mature, children can play games in which they search for "hidden" shapes. Such shapes may be irregular, may lack flat bases, or may be turned in various directions.

## Measurement

**Measurement** is the process of determining how long, wide, and tall something is physically and how much it weighs by using measuring units such as inches, feet, yards, square feet, ounces, and pounds. Measurement is also used to quantify time using units like seconds, minutes, hours, days, weeks, months, years, centuries, and millennia. Measurement is not just a formal means of quantifying size, area, and time. It is also an important method for young children to seek and identify relationships between and among things they encounter outside of school in everyday life. When young children practice measuring things, they are able to understand not only the sizes of objects and beings but also their comparative sizes (i.e., how large or small something is compared to another object used as a reference). Furthermore, they are able to figure out how big or little something is on their own.

While it is obviously important for children to eventually learn standardized measurement units like inches, feet, and yards, adults can facilitate early development of measurement skills by letting children choose their own measurement units. For example, they might use their favorite toy to describe a playmate or sibling as "three teddy bears tall," or they might describe a room as "seven toy cars long." Similarly, when children are too young to know formal time measurements like minutes and hours, adults can support children's ability to quantify time using favorite TV shows. For example, four-year-olds can often relate to the idea of one episode of a show (whether it is 30 minutes or 60 minutes long) as a time measurement. Adults can apply this with statements like, "Daddy will be home in one episode." Numerous everyday activities, including grocery shopping, cooking, sewing, gardening, woodworking, and many others, involve measurement. Adults can ask children to help with these tasks and then discuss measuring with children as they participate.

### *Measurement of Time*

Younger children typically do not have an understanding of the abstract concept of time. However, adults can still help children understand that time elapses and that we count/measure this process. For example, adults can ask younger children simple questions, such as "Who can stand on one foot longer?" This comparison strategy helps children figure out which of two or more actions/activities takes a longer/the longest period of time. Even when children do not yet understand what "five minutes" means, adults should still make such references (e.g., "You can play for five minutes longer, and then we must leave."). Repeating such references will eventually help children understand that time passes. Adults can time various everyday activities/events and tell children how long they took. They can also count the second hand's ticks on a watch/clock (e.g., "one second...two seconds...three seconds..."). This familiarizes children with counting, and with using counting to track the passage of time. Until children are old enough to understand abstractions like today/yesterday/tomorrow, adults can use concrete references like "after lunch" or "before bedtime."

## Fractions

Fractions are parts or pieces of a whole. While adults understand this and likely do not remember ever not understanding it, very young children think differently in this regard. As Piaget showed, children in the preoperational stage of cognitive development cannot perform logical or mathematical mental operations. They focus on one property of an object rather than all of its properties, a practice he called centration. Hence, if you cut an apple into pieces, very young children see that there are more pieces than there were before, and they believe that several apple pieces are more than one apple. They cannot yet comprehend the logical sequence of dividing an apple into fractions. To comprehend fractions, children must know what a whole unit consists of, how many pieces the unit is divided into, and whether the pieces are of equal size. Adults can help children understand fractions through informal sharing activities, such as slicing up a pizza or a pan of brownies, and/or equally dividing household/preschool chores and play materials.

## Estimation

Estimation is making an educated or informed guess about a measurement when no actual measurement is available. Adults often make estimates about the sizes of objects when their exact measurements are unknown, about the amounts of substances that have not actually been measured, and about the numbers of small objects in large collections when the objects have not actually been counted. However, young children are in the process of learning the concepts of sizes and numbers. Children must comprehend concepts of comparison and relativity (e.g., larger, smaller, more, less, etc.) before they will be able to make accurate estimates. When children start to develop the ability to estimate amounts or sizes, this process helps them learn related math vocabulary words, such as *about* or *around*, and *more than* and *less than* [something else]. Through estimating, they also learn how to make appropriate predictions and arrive at realistic answers. It is important for young children to learn how to make estimates, to recognize when it is appropriate to apply the estimation method, and to recognize when their estimates are reasonable.

### *Activities to Help Develop Estimation*

During everyday activities like shopping or eating, adults can ask children to estimate amounts of foods, numbers of items, or lengths of time. Later, adults can help children compare the actual outcome with their original estimate. This process helps children learn to make realistic/reasonable estimates. Activities promoting estimation skills can be very simple. Adults can ask children, for example, to guess which of their friends is tallest and then test the accuracy of the guess using real measurements. When children grow older, adults can write down estimates and real measurements and can then repeat the exercise described above or present a similar one. With repetition, children will eventually begin making more accurate estimates. The goal is not for children to come up with exact measurements but ones that are close to actual amounts/numbers. Giving children opportunities to practice improves their estimating skills.

## Probabilities and Statistics

In general, when people work with statistics, they present them in graphs or charts to organize them, interpret them, and make it easier to see relationships among individual statistics. Graphs are visual alternatives that depict mathematical information and show relationships among individual statistics, especially changes over time. Graphs also allow for the comparison of different groups. Probabilities indicate the likelihood that something will happen. Adults use probabilities to predict things, such as people's risks of developing or dying from various diseases or medical conditions; the chances of accidents; children's risks of experiencing academic difficulties, dropping out, or developing emotional and behavioral disorders; and the chances that a certain area will receive rain or snow. Scientists use probabilities to predict the likelihood of various behaviors or outcomes they are studying. They use statistics to show the numbers and proportions of responses or results obtained in research studies. Calendars are one type of chart. Adults can help children use them to organize daily and weekly activities and to understand how we organize information.

## Charts and Graphs

According to experts, almost every daily activity can be charted in some way. For example, adults can help children peel the little stickers off of plums, bananas, etc. and stick them to a piece of paper/poster board divided into columns. After a week, they can count each column to determine how many pieces of each kind of fruit they ate. Similarly, adults can show children how to use removable stickers or color forms to document the number of times they performed any daily activity. For example, children could place a color form near the front door every time somebody comes in, goes out, and/or rings the doorbell or knocks. This enables children to count the number of times given events occur by recording them. Some children are better able to understand math by viewing and making graphs. This is because creating graphs involves representing quantities visually instead of just listing numbers.

## Rational Numbers and Irrational Numbers

In mathematics, **rational numbers** are numbers that can be written as ratios or fractions. In other words, a rational number can be expressed as a fraction that has a whole number as the numerator (the number on top) and the denominator (the number on the bottom). Therefore, all whole numbers are automatically rational numbers, because all whole numbers can be written as fractions with a denominator of 1 (e.g., $5 = 5/1$, $68 = 68/1$, $237 = 237/1$, etc.). Even very large, unwieldy fractions (e.g., 9,731,245/42,754,021) are rational numbers, because they can be written as fractions. **Irrational numbers** can be written as decimal numbers, but not as fractions, because the numbers to the right of the decimal point that are less than 1 continue indefinitely without repeating. For example, the value of pi ($\pi$) begins as 3.141592... and continues without end or the square root of 2, $\sqrt{2} = 1.414213 \ldots$, and so on. There are an infinite number of irrational numbers between 0 and 1. However, irrational numbers are not used as commonly in everyday life as rational numbers.

**Review Video: Rational and Irrational Numbers**
Visit mometrix.com/academy and enter code: 280645

## Cardinal, Ordinal, Nominal, and Real Numbers

- **Cardinal numbers** are numbers that indicate quantity. For example, when we say "seven buttons" or "three kittens," we are using cardinal numbers.
- **Ordinal numbers** are numbers that indicate the order of items within a group or a set. For example, when we say "first," "second," "third," etc., we are using ordinal numbers.
- **Nominal numbers** are numbers that name things. For example, we use area code numbers along with telephone numbers to identify geographical calling areas, and we use zip code numbers to identify geographical mailing areas. Nominal numbers, therefore, identify categories or serve as labels for things. However, they are not related to the actual mathematical values of numbers, and do not indicate numerical quantities or operations.
- **Real numbers** include all rational and irrational numbers. Rational numbers can always be written as fractions that have both numerators and denominators that are whole numbers. Irrational numbers cannot, as they contain non-repeating decimal digits. Real numbers may or may not be cardinal numbers.

## Integrating Math into Everyday Activities and Early Childhood Math Curricula

Integrating math into the context of everyday activities has been the philosophy of early childhood math education until recently. For example, when teachers have children line up, they ask them who is first, second, third, etc. to practice counting. When children play with blocks, teachers ask them to identify their shapes and whether one block is larger/smaller than another. During snack times, teachers help children learn 1:1 correspondence by having them place one snack on each plate. These activities are quite valuable. However, some educators maintain that they are insufficient when used on their own, because in larger classes, it is not always possible to take advantage of "teachable moments" with every child. Therefore, this educational approach cannot be applied systematically. These educators recommend that in addition to integration strategies, early childhood teachers should use a curriculum. The HighScope curriculum, the Creative Curriculum, and Big Math for Little Kids are just a few examples. Many teachers combine several curricula, selecting parts of different programs. Using a curriculum allows teachers to use a more planned approach to integrate math into all activities.

## Clinical Interview

### *Background, Method, and Advantages*

Clinical interviews have long been used by individual and family therapists, as well as by researchers. Piaget used them along with observations and case histories to understand young children's thinking as he formulated his cognitive developmental theory. Interviewers ask structured, semi-structured, and open-ended questions and listen to the responses, often recording them for accuracy. This method gives the interviewer a way to find out what the respondent is thinking and feeling inside, which cannot be determined by observing outward behaviors alone. In educational settings, a teacher might ask a child questions like, "How did you do this?" "What is happening now?" "Can you tell me more about this?" "Why are you doing this?" and "What are you thinking about now?". Flexible questioning helps uncover the child's thought process, which is what is leading him or her to engage in specific behaviors. Just observing the behaviors alone does not allow the child to express his or her knowledge. While fully interviewing each child in a classroom is not practical, teachers can adapt this method by asking clinical interview-type questions as part of their instruction.

### *Using Questioning*

Teachers can gain a lot of information and insight about how children are learning math concepts by observing their behaviors. For children to actually express their knowledge and thinking processes, however, teachers must ask them questions. For example, when a teacher introduces new shapes to young children, he or she can ask them the shapes' names, how they differ from one another, and why they think the shapes differ. Teachers can then use children's various responses to elicit further responses from them. This technique requires children to use language in significant ways during math activities. Therefore, these activities not only teach math skills but also promote literacy development. Asking clinical interview-type questions promotes children's development of math communication skills, one of the essential components of math education. Additionally, being able to put one's knowledge and thoughts into words is a skill that is very important in all areas of education, not just math education. Using clinical interview-type questions helps children learn to use language to explain their thinking, share ideas, and express themselves, promoting and strengthening children's awareness of the functions of mathematical language.

## Young Children's Thinking That Inform Early Childhood Math Curricula

Young children think in concrete ways and cannot understand abstract concepts, so effective early childhood math curricula typically use many concrete objects that children can see, feel, and manipulate to help them understand math concepts. Young children also naturally learn through exploring their environments, so good EC math curricula have many exploration and discovery activities that allow and encourage hands-on learning. In everyday life, young children start to observe relationships as they explore their surroundings. They match like objects, sort unlike objects, categorize objects, and arrange objects in simple patterns based on shared or contrasting properties. They start to understand words and phrases like *a little, a lot, more, less,* and *the same* [as...]. Preschoolers use available materials such as sticks, pieces of string, their feet, their hands, and their fingers as tools to measure objects. They also use rulers, measuring cups, and other conventional tools. They use their measurements to develop descriptions, sequences, and arrangements, and to compare various objects.

## Activities That Help Children Develop Spatial Awareness

When preschool children build structures with blocks and put together pieces of puzzles during play, they are not only having fun but are also developing spatial awareness. The relationships of objects to each other and within space are important concepts for children to learn, and serve as a foundation for the principles of geometry and physics that children will learn later. When they are moving around, preschoolers begin to notice how other people and objects are positioned in space and how their own bodies move through space in relationship to objects and other people. This type of spatial awareness supports children's developing gross motor skills, coordination, and social skills. Young children can and should learn a number of math concepts and skills, such as the ones recommended by preschool math curricula like the HighScope program's "Numbers Plus" preschool mathematics curriculum. These concepts and skills include number symbols and names, counting, shapes, spatial awareness, relationships of parts to the whole, measurement, units, patterns, and analyzing data.

## Activities and Games That Make Learning Fun

### *Button Board*

By gluing buttons of various sizes and colors to a piece of cardboard, teachers can initiate a number of activities that help preschoolers learn math concepts while having fun. Preschoolers are commonly learning shapes and how to draw them. Teachers can give children lengths of string, twine, or yarn or long shoelaces and show them how to wrap them around different buttons to form shapes like rectangles, triangles, and squares. To practice counting and 1:1 correspondence, teachers can ask children to wrap their string around a given number of buttons. Preschoolers need to learn the concept that spoken number words like *five* can equate to a group of five concrete objects (such as buttons), and this activity promotes that learning. The button board is also useful for giving preschool children practice with sorting or classifying objects into groups based on a common characteristic. For example, the teacher can ask children to wrap their pieces of string around all the big buttons, all the little buttons, only the red buttons, only the blue buttons, etc.

### Beanbags and Hopscotch

Teachers can encourage preschool children's counting and number development by creating a grid on the floor with the numbers 1 to 10 using masking tape, construction paper, and markers. Teachers could also draw the grid outdoors by drawing on pavement with chalk. The teacher arranges the numbers in ascending order within the grid of 10 squares and asks the children if they can name these numbers. The teacher provides beanbags. Each child gets a chance to throw a beanbag into any one of the numbered squares, which allows them to see how far they can throw and/or practice their aim. Each child names the number inside the square where his or her beanbag lands. The children then play a version of hopscotch by hopping from numbered square to square, collecting their beanbags, and then hopping back. If desired, the teacher can write the number each child's beanbag lands on onto a "scoreboard" graph. Teachers can review learning after the game to assess whether children can count using number words, name selected numbers, and throw accurately with consistency.

### Reusing Sectioned Plastic Trays

A teacher can wash and reuse the compartmentalized plastic trays from the grocery store that are used for vegetables and fruit to create a preschool counting activity. The teacher supplies beads, pennies, erasers, or other small objects, as well as about a dozen sticky notes, writing a number on each note. For older preschoolers, the teacher can write the numeral and the word (e.g., "7" and "seven"). For younger children, the teacher can write the numeric symbol ("7," for example) plus seven dots or other marks as a clue to that number symbol. The teacher puts one numbered note in each compartment and the supply of small objects in the central dip compartment. Then, he or she guides each child to transfer the correct number of each small object to the correct compartment. The child should count aloud while transferring each small object and should repeat this process until all compartments with a numbered sticky note have the correct number of objects. Children can then repeat the process to practice and perfect their counting, or the teacher can place notes with different numbers in the tray's compartments.

### Fishing for Numbers

Teachers can help preschoolers practice identifying numbers and counting by creating a fun "fishing for numbers" game. Teachers cut 10 fish shapes that are about 6 inches long from pieces of construction paper that are different colors. Teachers then write a single number between 1 and 10 on each "fish." Near each fish "mouth," the teacher punches a hole and inserts a paper clip through it. The teacher makes "fishing rods" by tying strings to dowels and gluing a magnet to each string. After spreading out the fish so the children can easily see the numbers, the teacher assigns each child a number, and they "fish" for it, picking up the fish by bringing the magnet close to the paper clip. The children then "reel in" their catches. This gives children practice correctly identifying number names. The game can be adapted for more advanced math concepts as well. For example, the teacher can cut out fish shapes of various sizes and have children "fish" for larger or smaller fish. The activity can also be adapted to promote literacy development. The teacher can write letters instead of numbers on the fish to give students practice with alphabet recognition, or teacher can write a Dolch word/sight word on each fish to give students practice recognizing and identifying important vocabulary words.

### Collages

Fundamental math skills that prepare preschoolers for kindergarten include shape recognition. To introduce children to an activity they will view as fun rather than as work, teachers can show children how to make a collage of a familiar figure. This will also give children the opportunity to experiment with an artistic process. For example, they can create a Santa Claus or an Easter Bunny as a holiday art project. They can make **collages** of other imaginary or real people for various events, seasons, or topics. Teachers cut out paper templates, including circles for heads, triangles for hats, squares for bodies, and narrow rectangular strips for limbs. First, they help children name each shape. They have each child trace the template shapes onto paper and cut them out with child-safe scissors. The teacher then instructs the children to arrange their cutout shapes on a piece of cardboard or construction paper. Once they are in the correct positions, the children glue the shapes in place. Teachers can subsequently teach additional shapes (octagons, ovals, etc.), challenging children to make new, different collages.

### *Grab Bag*

Young children learn to name numbers in a way that is similar to how they learn to recite alphabet letters. However, learning to associate number symbols with concrete objects in the real world environment is a major advance in their cognitive development. The concept of 1:1 correspondence entails matching number symbols to the quantities they represent, an essential early math skill. Teachers can support the development of this math skill with a simple "grab bag" game youngsters enjoy. The teacher writes a number from 1 to 10 on each of the 10 cards, folding each card in half and putting them into a paper lunch bag. The teacher provides each child with a handful of pennies, play coins, buttons, or little blocks to use as counting tokens. Each child takes a turn closing his or her eyes and pulling a card out of the bag. The child reads the number on the card, counts out the corresponding number of pennies/tokens, and puts them with the card. As children learn, teachers can place additional and/or different numbers (e.g., 11 to 20) in the grab bag. To promote the development of early literacy skills, teachers can also include the name of the number on each card.

### *Pattern Resist Art*

A significant mark of progress in early math skills development is the ability to not only identify various shapes but also to draw them. Once young children develop this ability, they typically want to practice it all the time. Teachers can encourage this by helping children make pattern resist paintings. The teacher tapes white paper to children's tables/trays, gives them crayons, and invites them to fill the paper with drawings of different shapes of various sizes and colors. Teachers can introduce young children to new shapes (e.g., ovals, stars, crescent moons, etc.) by drawing them on separate pieces of paper for children to look at and copy. Then, the teacher replaces the crayons with water, watercolor paints, and brushes; shows the children how to dip brushes into paint and water to dilute the colors; and allows them to paint over their crayoned shapes, covering all the white paper with color. The children see the shapes show through the paint, creating the pattern resist. Dipping brushes and diluting various colors also develop children's color recognition skills and their hand-eye coordination.

### *Ice Cube Necklaces*

In hot weather, making ice cube necklaces is a fun activity that helps young children cool off while learning to sequence objects. The activity also helps children develop their manual motor skills and learn about liquid and solid states of matter. Regular ice cube trays are fine; those with "fun-shaped" compartments are even better. The teacher cuts plastic drinking straws so that they will fit into each ice cube compartment. The children participate, watching and/or helping pour water into trays and adding various food colorings/fruit juices. The teacher places one straw clipping into each compartment. While putting the trays into the freezer, the teacher tells the children that 32° Fahrenheit/0° Celsius is the temperature at which water freezes. Children practice making scientific observations by noting how long the water takes to freeze. They empty the cubes into a big bowl. The children put on bathing suits or other clothing that can get wet, and the class goes outdoors. The teacher provides strings that are knotted at one end, and calls out a color pattern (e.g., one blue cube, then a yellow cube, etc.). Children follow the teacher's instructions to create color-patterned necklaces they can tie, wear, and watch melt.

### *Red Rover*

Red Rover is a good game for groups of children who are attending parties or playing outdoors at parks or playgrounds. Two teams take turns calling and roving. The child called runs to the other team and tries to fit into its line. If successful, he or she gets to call another player to bring back to his or her home team. If not, the child joins the opposite team. The game continues until one team has no more members. Teachers can adapt this game to teach shape recognition by cutting out various shapes from construction paper of different colors and pinning a shape to each child's shirt. In large groups, more than one child can have the same shape or color. Instead of children's names, the teacher instructs players to use shapes and colors when calling (e.g., "Red Rover, Red Rover, blue circles come over!"). This supports the development of shape and color recognition skills. Teachers can vary action verbs (e.g., "...hop over/jump over/skip over") to support vocabulary development and comprehensive skills. When children perform such movements, they are also practicing and developing gross motor skills.

### COUNTING ON FINGERS

A common practice among preschool children is counting on their fingers. Young children learn concretely before they develop abstract thought, so they must have concrete objects to work with to understand abstract mathematical concepts. They use their fingers to count because fingers are concrete. A simple activity that allows children to continue finger counting while removing additional visual support is "blind finger counting." Using eyesight to count objects we can see is relatively easy. However, when children cannot see objects, they must learn to count mentally instead. This allows them to take another step in their progress from concrete to abstract thinking. To count mentally without visual reinforcement takes practice. Teachers can tape a shoebox lid to the box and cut a small hole in it. Children can fit a hand through the hole, but cannot see inside. Children close their eyes; the teacher drops several small objects into the box; and each child reaches in, counting the objects using only touch. Varying objects and quantities maintains the fun of this activity.

### SORTING AND CATEGORIZATION

One of the major learning accomplishments of young children is being able to identify similarities and differences among objects. Developing this ability enables children to sort like objects into groups and to place objects into categories based on their differences. When preschoolers compare and contrast objects, they demonstrate an important early step in the development of critical thinking, analytical, and problem-solving skills. For an easy, entertaining guessing game, adults can select assorted household items familiar to children and put them into a bag/pillowcase. They then give children various clues (e.g., "I stir lemonade with this...," "It's made of wood," "We keep it in the kitchen drawer...," etc.) and ask them to guess which items are in the bag. It is important to give young children one to two minutes to consider each clue before they make a guess. Adults repeat clues when children guess incorrectly. If children guess correctly, they are allowed to look inside the bag. Children greatly enjoy seeing that the object they guessed is actually inside the bag. Adults can gradually make the game more challenging by beginning with very common objects and then eventually progressing to more unusual ones.

### BAKING COOKIES

Young children are typically curious about adult activities like baking. They usually want to know more about the process and often ask many questions. They also love to be included and to participate, frequently offering/asking to help. Letting them help builds their self-esteem and self-efficacy (i.e., their confidence in their competence to accomplish a task). Adults can allow children to help while also providing instruction and practice with shape recognition, measurement, sorting, and categorization. The adult prepares a favorite cookie recipe. Some children can help measure ingredients, which helps develop the math skill of measurement. With the dough rolled out, children use cookie cutters of various shapes. Recognizing, naming, and selecting the shapes promote the development of shape recognition skills. Adults "shuffle"/mix the baked cookie shapes and have children separate cookies with like shapes into groups, which promotes sorting skills. Having children identify similar/different shapes, sizes, and colors promotes categorization skills. Arranging cookie shapes into patterns for children to identify promotes pattern recognition skills, which are necessary for the development of math skills and many other skills. Giving each child a cookie to eat afterward is naturally reinforcing.

### CREATIVE CRAFTS

Prerequisite abilities that young children need in order to develop early math skills include the ability to identify, copy, expand, and create patterns, as well as the ability to count. Adults can promote the development of these skills by giving children a craft project and introducing them to an interactive game they can play using their crafts. First, the children paint six ping pong balls red on one side to make red-and-white balls.

Then, the children paint six ping pong balls blue on one side to make blue-and-white balls. Once the paint dries, the adult puts several balls into an egg carton so that one color is face up. The adult starts making a simple pattern (e.g., two white, then two red, then two blue) and asks each child to continue the pattern. Then, the adult allows each child to create his or her own original color patterns. Once a child masters creating patterns using solid colors, he or she can then use both the white and colored sides of the balls to create more complex patterns. Children can design an infinite number of patterns, which are often quite artistic.

### *Shape Matching Games*

In one type of shape matching game, early childhood teachers help children make a game board out of construction paper that is shaped like a tree. Teachers first help the children cut a treetop and leaf shapes from green paper. They discuss children's preferences for tall/short and thick/thin trunks, giving them practice using descriptive vocabulary words, particularly ones related to size. This step builds both general and math concept vocabulary. Children cut trunks from brown paper and glue them on the treetops. While out of the children's sight, the teacher cuts 5 to 10 (or more) pairs of shapes per child/tree from different colors of construction paper. Pairs should not match exactly (e.g., a blue square can be paired with a red square). The teacher glues one of each pair of shapes to each child's tree while the child is not looking. The teacher then gives each child the rest of the shapes and invites children to see how quickly they can match each shape to its "partner" on the tree. The teacher can provide "warmer/cooler" distance clues and should provide reinforcement each time a child correctly matches a pair of shapes. Teachers can make this activity more challenging by using more shapes and/or getting students to match shapes that are different sizes (e.g., children can be asked to match smaller diamonds to larger diamonds).

### *Homemade Beanbag Game*

Young children enjoy tossing objects and practicing their aim. Adults can make a beanbag game that helps children learn numbers and identify sets, while also allowing them to construct their own game rules. First, the adult should cover five big, equally-sized coffee (or similar) cans with paper that is adhesive on one side. The adult should then use markers to write a number from 1 to 5 and draw the corresponding number of dots on each can. The next step is to fill 15 tube socks with beans and knot/tie/sew them shut. The following numerals and the corresponding number of dots should be written on each homemade beanbag using markers: the number 1 on five beanbags, the number 2 on four beanbags, the number 3 on three beanbags, the number 4 on two beanbags, and the number 5 on one beanbag. Next, the adult should attach the cans to the floor with tape or Velcro. Then, the adult should mark a line on the floor that children must stand behind, and should direct children ONLY to toss the beanbags into the cans. Children will devise various games/rules. First, they may simply toss the beanbags into the cans; then, some may try to toss beanbags into a can that has the same number as the one marked on the beanbag. Eventually, some may throw three beanbags into the "3" can. They may or may not keep score. Allowing children to determine the details and rules gives them an opportunity to develop their imagination and decision-making skills, and to create their own games while learning number and set identification.

### *Guessing Game*

Adults can adapt the format of "20 Questions," "I Spy," and other similar guessing games to focus on numbers and help children learn number concepts. For example, adults could say, "I'm thinking of a number from 1 to 10...." and then give children 10 guesses. Adults give children cues as they guess, such as "higher" and "lower," to help them narrow down the number of possible correct answers. As children improve, adults can increase the number range (e.g., from 0 to 50) or use larger numbers (e.g., from 20 to 40). As children's skills and self-confidence develop, adults can reverse roles, having children think of numbers and give clues while adults guess. Young children enjoy the fun of guessing, getting closer using clues, deducing correct answers, and fooling adults with their own clues. Concurrently, they learn to describe numbers, compare them, and sequence them. Adults can make the game more difficult by limiting the number of guesses allowed and/or setting time limits. They can make it easier by providing a written number line for children to reference. This game requires no materials (or just a basic number line), is a great way to pass time, and entertains children while helping to develop numeracy skills.

### ARTS AND CRAFTS

According to the US Department of Agriculture, preschoolers need three ½-cup servings of fruit and three ½-cup servings of vegetables daily. However, many young children are picky/resistant. Adults can motivate them to eat produce with a "food rainbow" project. Adults show children a picture of a rainbow and discuss its colors and their sequence (teaching some earth science, optics, and color theory). A fun art project is allowing students to color their own rainbows, which improves fine motor skills. Then, adults can have children cut out pictures from grocery circulars and name each food. The adult can help children find one healthy fruit/vegetable for each color, gluing each food to its corresponding stripe on the rainbow. Adults can then help children pull apart cotton balls and glue them to their rainbow pictures to represent clouds. Children can then post their food rainbows on refrigerators as artwork and as healthy eating reminders. At the bottom, children can draw and color one box (bottom-up) for each food they eat (e.g., blue for blueberries, orange for carrots, red for apples, etc.) to create a bar graph. Children should try to "eat" the entire rainbow every week. This activity gives children the opportunity to produce colorful art, eat better, track and document their diets, and develop graphing skills.

**Review Video: Data Interpretation of Graphs**
Visit mometrix.com/academy and enter code: 200439

### TREASURE HUNT

A treasure hunt is an ideal outdoor activity for young children and can also be adapted for indoor fun. The treasure can be anything such as a small toy, play money, chocolate "coins," or rocks spray painted gold or silver. The adult should put the treasure in a paper bag marked with a large X. The adult should hide it somewhere where it is not visible but will not be overly difficult for children to find. Then, the adult should make a treasure map, using few words and many pictures, sketching landmark objects in the area (e.g., trees and houses if the activity will be done outdoors, and furniture and walls if the activity will be done indoors). The adult should ensure the map is developmentally appropriate for young children and that they will be able to read it independently. Adults with time and motivation can make the map look authentic by soaking it in tea/coffee, drying it in a 200° F oven, or even charring its edges. Adults should include a dotted line on the map that reinforces the simple directions and indicates the path to the treasure, which is indicated on the map by a large X. Children have fun, use their imaginations, make connections between symbols and images to corresponding real-world physical objects, and begin learning to read maps.

### PASTA NECKLACE

Stringing beads/noodles is an activity that helps young children develop hand-eye coordination, which they will need for writing and other everyday activities that require fine motor coordination. Noodles are typically the perfect size for young children's hands. They are inexpensive, usually costing less than comparably-sized beads. Moreover, pasta is non-toxic, an advantage when working with children who put things in their mouths. Hollow, tubular noodles like penne, ziti, and wagon wheels are ideal. Fishing line, craft beading string, and other stiff string is best; soft, limp string/yarn is harder for young children to manipulate. Using multicolored vegetable pasta removes the need to use markers or dye to add color. If using white pasta, children can color the noodles with markers, but adults should keep in mind that the ink can bleed onto skin/clothes even when it is dry. Adults should cut pieces of string that are long enough to allow children to easily slip the necklaces on and off after they are tied. Adults should also use a knot to secure a noodle to one end of the string. By providing more than one noodle shape, adults can invite children to string the noodles to create patterns, which develops pattern recognition and pattern creation abilities. These abilities also inform repetition, rhythm, categorization, and sequencing skills, which are important in math, music, art, literature, and clothing design.

### NUMBER DASH

A game for young children that some educators call "Number Dash" (Miller, ed. Charner, 2009) builds foundational math concepts and skills while providing physical activity. It can involve small or large groups (the referenced authors say "the more the merrier"). Help children write large numbers on a paved area with sidewalk chalk. Make sure numbers are spread far enough apart so children will not collide while running. There should be one of each number for each child (e.g., six 1s, 2s, 3s, etc. if there are six children). Use chalk colors that contrast with the pavement color to ensure the numbers will be highly visible. Tell children to run ("dash") to whichever number you call out and stand on it until you call another number. Call out numbers randomly. Encourage children who have located the number to help their classmates/playmates. This game develops gross motor skills, number writing skills, and number recognition skills. It also provides experience with playing organized games, following rules, following directions, and cooperating with and helping others. This game can also be played with letters, colors, and/or shapes.

## Introducing Standard Measurement Using a Ruler

A teacher is introducing standard measures to her class as part of a unit on measurement, one of the early math skills. She shows the children a ruler, explaining that it is one foot long and that we can use it to measure inches and parts of inches. She demonstrates placing the ruler on paper to measure a given length, explaining that the ruler can also be used as a straight edge for drawing lines. One child asks, "How come you started with zero? Why don't you start with one like when we count?" The teacher responds, "That's a very good question! Zero means none/nothing. When we count, we start with one because we already have at least one of something. When you were born, you were not one year old; your age began at zero. After a year, on your first birthday, you were one year old. We also begin measuring distances at zero/none/nothing. The first unit of measurement is one, not two. The distance from zero to one is equal to one. To get to one inch, for example, we need to start at zero."

## Learning About Geometric Shapes and Their Properties

A teacher has been working with students to help them develop their shape identification skills. They can recognize shapes by sight and have also learned the defining properties of different shapes (number of sides, etc.). The teacher shows the class this figure:

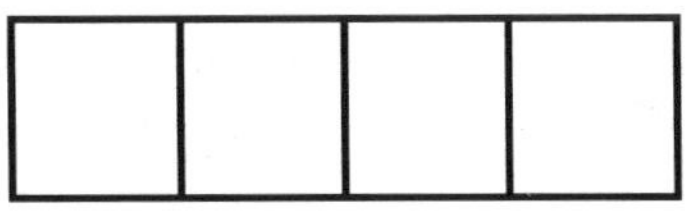

She asks how many rectangles they can find in the figure. One student answers, "There is one rectangle," which is incorrect because a square is a rectangle; this figure has four rectangles that are squares. Moreover, the entire figure is itself a rectangle. Another student therefore says, "There are five rectangles." This response is also incorrect. Two adjacent squares also form a rectangle; this means there are three additional rectangles. Three adjacent squares also form a rectangle; this means there are two additional rectangles. Thus, the figure has a total of 10 rectangles. Solving this puzzle requires the use of many skills, including analyzing visual information, synthesizing visual information, recognizing patterns, recognizing shapes, and identifying the properties of shapes.

## Collecting, Organizing, and Displaying Data Using Sticky Notes and Charts

A preschool teacher is teaching her group of ten children about basic data collection, data arrangement, and data display. She shows children yellow, blue, and green sticky notes, and has each child select his or her favorite color. Five children choose yellow notes, three select blue, and two choose green. By choosing one of three colors, each child has participated in data collection. The teacher draws lines to divide a sheet of paper into three columns, and labels each column with one of the colors. She helps the children place their chosen sticky notes in the correct columns. By arranging the colored sticky notes into columns, the teacher and children have organized the data they gathered. Once all notes are in their proper color columns, the completed chart is an example of how collected, organized data can be displayed.

| | Yellow sticky note | |
|---|---|---|
| | Yellow sticky note | |
| Blue sticky note | Yellow sticky note | |
| Blue sticky note | Yellow sticky note | Green sticky note |
| Blue sticky note | Yellow sticky note | Green sticky note |
| **BLUE** | **YELLOW** | **GREEN** |

The teacher asks the children which color was chosen the most. Seeing five yellow notes, they answer, "yellow." She asks which color was chosen the least, and they say, "green." She asks them to use numbers to arrange the color choices from most popular to least popular. They arrive at, "five yellow, three blue, and two green." Together, the teacher and the children point to and count 10 children. She tells them 5 equals half of 10, and asks which color half of the children chose. Together, they figure out it was yellow. These are examples of analyzing and interpreting data.

## Chapter Quiz

Ready to see how well you retained what you just read? Scan the QR code to go directly to the chapter quiz interface for this study guide. If you're using a computer, simply visit the online resources page at **mometrix.com/resources719/gacesegcelemed** and click the Chapter Quizzes link.

# Science

## Science Concepts Young Children Learn During Everyday Activities

Science entails asking questions, conducting investigations, collecting data, and seeking answers to the questions asked by analyzing the data collected. Natural events that can be examined over time and student-centered inquiry through hands-on activities that require the application of problem-solving skills are most appropriate for helping young children learn basic science. In their everyday lives, young children develop concepts of 1:1 correspondence through activities like fitting pegs into matching holes or distributing one item to each child in a class. They also develop counting concepts by counting enough items for each child in the group or counting pennies in a piggy bank. They develop classification concepts when they sort objects into separate piles according to their shapes or some other type of category (e.g., toy cars vs. toy trucks). When children transfer water, sand, rice, or other substances from one container to another, they develop measurement concepts. As they progress, children will apply these early concepts to more abstract scientific ideas during grade school.

## Science Concepts Infants and Toddlers Learn in Normal Processes

Infants use their senses to explore the environment and are motivated by innate curiosity. As they develop mobility, children gain more freedom, allowing them to make independent discoveries and think for themselves. Children learn size concepts by comparing the sizes of objects/persons in the environment to their own size and by observing that some objects are too large to hold, while others are small enough to hold. They learn about weight when trying to lift various objects. They learn about shape when they see that some objects roll away while others do not. Babies learn temporal sequences when they wake up wet and hungry, cry, and have parents change and feed them. They also learn this concept by playing, getting tired, and going to sleep. As soon as they look and move around, infants learn about space, including large and small spaces. Eventually, they develop spatial sense through experiences like being put in a playpen or crib in the middle of a large room. Toddlers naturally sort objects into groups according to their sizes, shapes, colors, and/or uses. They experiment with transferring water/sand among containers of various sizes. They learn part-to-whole relationships by building block structures and then dismantling them.

## Naturalistic, Informal, and Structured Learning Experiences

Children actively construct their knowledge of the environment through exploring it.

- During **naturalistic learning**, young children's learning experiences are spontaneously initiated by the child during everyday activities and the child controls his or her choices and actions.
- **Informal learning experiences** also allow the child to choose his or her actions and activities, but they include adult intervention at some point during the child's engagement in naturalistic pursuits.
- In **structured learning experiences**, the adult chooses the activities and supplies some direction as to how the child should perform the associated actions.

One consideration related to early childhood learning that teachers should keep in mind is that within any class or group of children, there are individual differences in learning styles. Additionally, children from different cultural groups have varying learning styles and approaches. Early childhood teachers can introduce science content in developmentally appropriate ways by keeping these variations in mind.

### *Naturalistic Learning Experiences*

Motivated by novelty and curiosity, young children spontaneously initiate naturalistic experiences during their everyday activities. Infants and toddlers in Piaget's sensorimotor stage learn by exploring the environment through their senses, so adults should provide them with many objects and substances they can see, hear, touch, smell, and taste. Through manipulating and observing concrete objects/substances, preschoolers in Piaget's preoperational stage begin learning concepts that will enable them to perform mental operations later on. Adults should observe children's actions and progress and should give positive reinforcement in the form of looks, facial expressions, gestures, and/or words encouraging and praising the child's actions. Young children need adult feedback to learn when they are performing the appropriate actions. For example, a toddler/preschooler selects a tool from the toolbox, saying, "This is big!" and the mother responds, "Yes!" A four-year-old sorting toys of various colors into separate containers is another example of a naturalistic experience. A five-year-old who observes while painting that mixing two colors yields a third color is yet another example.

### *Informal Learning Experience*

Informal learning experiences involve two main components. First, the child spontaneously initiates naturalistic learning experiences during everyday activities to explore and learn about the environment. Second, the adult takes advantage of opportunities during naturalistic experiences to insert informal learning experiences. Adults do not plan these in advance but take advantage of opportunities that occur naturally. One way this happens is when a child is on the right track to solve a problem but needs some encouragement or a hint from the adult. Another way is when the adult spots a "teachable moment" during the child's naturalistic activity and uses it to reinforce a basic concept. For example, a three-year-old might hold up three fingers, declaring, "I'm six years old." The parent says, "Let's count fingers: one, two, three. You're three years old." Or, a teacher asks a child who has a box of treats if he or she has enough for the whole class, and the child answers, "I don't know." The teacher then responds, "Let's count them together," and helps the child count.

### *Structured Learning Experiences*

Naturalistic learning experiences are spontaneously initiated and controlled by children. Informal learning experiences involve unplanned interventions by adults during children's naturalistic experiences, which is when adults offer suitable correction, assistance, and support. Structured learning experiences differ in that the adult pre-plans and initiates the activity/lesson and provides the child with some direction. For example, a teacher who observes a four-year-old's need to practice counting can give the child a pile of toys and then ask him or her how many there are. To develop size concepts, a teacher can give a small group of children several toys of different sizes and then ask the children to inspect them and talk about their characteristics. The teacher holds up one toy, instructing children to find one that is bigger or smaller. If a child needs to learn shape concepts, the teacher might introduce a game involving shapes, giving the child instructions on how to play the game. Or, a first-grade teacher, recognizing the importance of the concept of classification to the ability to organize scientific information, might ask students to bring in bones to classify during a unit on skeletons.

## Kindergarten Activity for Collecting and Organizing Data

Preschoolers and kindergarteners continue their earlier practices of exploration to learn new things, and they apply fundamental science concepts to collect and organize data in order to answer questions. To collect data, children must have observation, counting, recording, and organization skills. One activity kindergarteners and teachers enjoy is growing bean sprouts. For example, the teacher can show children two methods: one using glass jars and paper towels saturated with water, the other using cups of dirt. The children add water daily as needed, observe developments, and report to the teacher, who records their observations on a chart. The teacher gives each child a chart that they add information to each day. The children count how many days their beans took to sprout in the glass jars and in the cups of dirt. They then compare their own results for the two methods, and they compare their results to those of their classmates. The children apply concepts of counting, numbers, time, 1:1 correspondence, and comparison of numbers. They also witness the planting and growing process.

## Science Process Skills

**Science process skills** include observation (using the senses to identify properties of objects/situations), classification (grouping objects/situations according to their common properties), measurement (quantifying physical properties), communication (using observations, classifications, and measurements to report experimental results to others), inference (finding patterns and meaning in experiment results), and prediction (using experimental experience to formulate new hypotheses). Inferences and predictions must be differentiated from objective observations. Classification, measurement, and comparison are basic math concepts that, when applied to science problems, are called process skills. The other science process skills named, as well as defining and controlling variables, are equally necessary to solve both science and math problems. For example, using ramps can help young children learn basic physics concepts. Teachers ask children what would happen if two balls were rolled down a ramp at the same time, if two balls were rolled down a ramp of a different height/length, if two ramps of different heights/lengths were used, etc. In this activity, children apply the scientific concepts of observation, communication, inference, and prediction, as well as the concepts of height, length, counting, speed, distance, and comparison.

## Scientific Method

Children are born curious and naturally engage in problem-solving to learn. Problem-solving and inquiry are natural child behaviors. Early childhood teachers can use these behaviors to promote children's scientific inquiry. Scientific inquiry employs the **scientific method**. The first step in the method is to ask a question, which is another natural child behavior. Just as adult scientists formulate research questions, the first step of the scientific method for children is asking questions they want to answer. Next, to address a question, both adults and children must form a hypothesis (an educated guess about what the answer will be). The hypothesis informs and directs the next steps: designing and conducting an experiment to test whether the hypothesis is true or false. With teacher instruction/help, children experiment. For example, they might drop objects of different weights from a height to see when each lands, as Galileo did. Teachers help record outcomes. The next steps are deciding whether the results support or disprove the hypothesis and reporting the results and conclusions to others.

**Review Video: The Scientific Method**
Visit mometrix.com/academy and enter code: 191386

## Physical Science and Matter

**Physical science** is the science of the physical universe surrounding us. Everything in the universe consists of matter (i.e., anything that has mass and takes up space) or energy (i.e., anything that does not have mass or occupy space, but affects matter and space). The three primary states of matter are solid, liquid, and gas. Solids preserve their shape even when they are not in a container. Solids have specific, three-dimensional/crystalline atomic structures and specific melting points. Liquids have no independent shape outside of containers but have specific volumes. Liquid molecules are less cohesive than solid molecules but more cohesive than gas molecules. Liquids have flow, viscosity (flow resistance), and buoyancy. Liquids can undergo diffusion, osmosis, evaporation, condensation, solution, freezing, and heat conduction and convection. Liquids and gases are both fluids, and they share some of the same properties. Gases have no shape, expanding and spreading indefinitely outside of containers. Gases can become liquid and solid through cooling, compression, or both. Liquids and solids can become gaseous through heating. Vapor is the gaseous form of a substance that is solid/liquid at lower temperatures. For example, when water is heated, it becomes steam, a vapor.

**Review Video: States of Matter**
Visit mometrix.com/academy and enter code: 742449

## Particle Arrangement in Phases of Matter

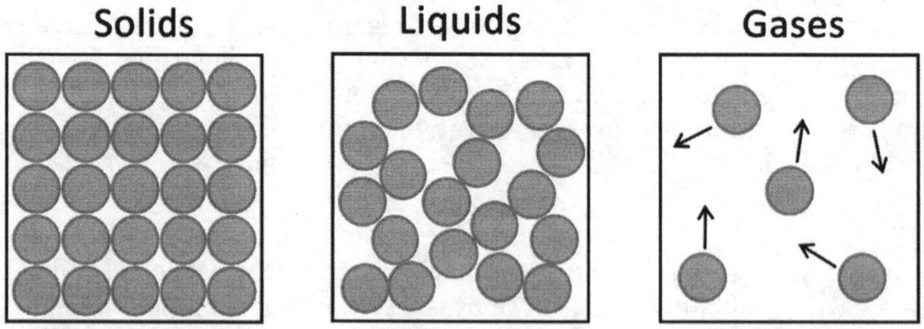


Solids: Particles are packed tightly together in a fixed arrangement. Particles can vibrate but not move.

Liquids: Particles are close together with no distinct arrangement. Particles can move and slide around each other.

Gases: Particles are free-floating with no distinct arrangement. Particles move and collide with each other.

### LIQUIDS

Of the three states of matter—solid, liquid, and gas—liquids have properties that fall somewhere in between those of solids and gases. The molecules of solids are the most cohesive (i.e., they have the greatest mutual attraction). Gas molecules are the least cohesive, and liquid molecules are in between. Liquids have no definite shape, while solids do. Liquids have a definite volume, whereas gases do not. The cohesion of liquid molecules draws them together, and the molecules below the surface pull surface molecules down, creating surface tension. This property can be observed in containers of water. Liquid molecules are also attracted to other substances' molecules (i.e., adhesion). Surface tension and adhesion combined cause liquids to rise in narrow containers, a property known as capillarity. Liquids are buoyant (i.e., they exert upward force, so objects which have more buoyancy than weight float in liquids, while objects which have more weight than buoyancy sink in liquids). Liquids can be made solid by freezing and can be made gaseous by heating/evaporation. Liquids can diffuse, which means they can mix with other molecules. Liquid diffusion across semi-permeable membranes is known as osmosis.

### SOLIDS

Solids maintain their shape when they are not inside of containers, whereas liquids and gases acquire the shapes of containers holding them. Containers also prevent liquids and gases from dispersing. Of the three forms of matter, solids have the most cohesive molecules. Solid molecules are most attracted to each other, and solid molecules are held together most strongly. Solid atoms are organized into defined, three-dimensional, lattice-shaped patterns (i.e., they are crystalline in structure). Solids also have specific temperatures at which they melt. Some substances that seem solid, such as plastic, gel, tar, and glass, are actually not true solids. They are amorphous solids because their atoms do not have a crystalline structure but are amorphous (i.e., the positions of their atoms have no long-range organization). They also have a range of melting temperatures rather than specific melting points.

### GASES

Gases have the least cohesive (i.e., mutually attracted) molecules of the three states of matter, while solids have the most cohesive molecules. Gases do not maintain a defined shape, while solids do. If not contained within a receptacle, gases spread and expand indefinitely. Gases can be elementary or compound. An elementary gas is composed of only one kind of chemical element. At normal temperatures and pressures, 12 elementary gases are known: argon, chlorine, fluorine, helium, hydrogen, krypton, neon, nitrogen, oxygen, ozone, radon, and xenon. Elementary gases can be either monatomic or diatomic, meaning they are either made of single atoms like argon (Ar), or bound pairs of atoms like oxygen ($O_2$). Compound gases have molecules containing atoms of more than one kind of chemical element. Carbon monoxide (which contains one carbon and one oxygen atom) and ammonia (which contains nitrogen and hydrogen atoms) are common compound gases.

## LIGHT

### *REFLECTION AND SCATTERING*

When a beam of light hits a smooth surface like a mirror, it bounces back off that surface. This rebounding is **reflection**. In physics, the law of reflection states that "the angle of incidence equals the angle of reflection." This means that when light is reflected, it always bounces off the surface at the same angle at which it hit that surface. When a beam of light hits a rough rather than a smooth surface, though, it is reflected back at many different angles, not just the angle at which it struck the surface. This reflection at multiple and various angles is scattering. Many objects we commonly use every day have rough surfaces. For example, paper may look smooth to the naked eye but actually has a rough surface. This property can be observed by viewing paper through a microscope. Because light waves striking paper are reflected in every direction by its rough surface, scattering enables us to read words printed on paper from any viewing angle.

### *ABSORPTION*

When light strikes a medium, the light wave's frequency is equal or close to the frequency at which the electrons in the medium's atoms can vibrate. These electrons receive the light's energy, making them vibrate. When a medium's atoms hang on tightly to their electrons, the electrons transmit their vibrations to the nucleus of each atom. This makes the atoms move faster and collide with the medium's other atoms. The energy the atoms got from the vibrations is then released as heat. This process is known as **absorption** of light. Materials that absorb light, such as wood and metal, are opaque. Some materials absorb certain light frequencies but transmit others. For example, glass transmits visible light (and therefore appears transparent to the naked eye), but absorbs ultraviolet frequencies. The sky looks blue because the atmosphere absorbs all colors in the spectrum except blue, which it reflects. Only blue wavelengths/frequencies bounce back to our eyes. This is an example of subtractive color, which we see in paints/dyes and all colored objects/materials. Pigments absorb some frequencies and reflect others.

### *REFRACTION*

When light moves from one transparent medium to another (e.g., between water and air/vice versa), the light's speed changes, bending the light wave. It bends either away from or toward the normal line, an imaginary straight line running at right angles to the medium's surface. We easily observe this bending when looking at a straw in a glass of water. The straw appears to break/bend at the waterline. The angle of refraction is the amount that the light wave bends. It is determined by how much the medium slows down the light's speed, which is the medium's refraction index. For example, diamonds are much denser and harder than water and thus have a higher refraction index. They slow down and trap light more than water does. Consequently, diamonds sparkle more than water. Lenses, such as those in eyeglasses and telescopes, rely on the principle of refraction. Curved lenses disperse or concentrate light waves, refracting light as it both enters and exits, thus changing the light's direction. This is how lenses correct (eyeglasses) and enhance (telescopes) our vision.

## MAGNETISM

**Magnetism** is the property some objects/substances have of attracting other materials. The form of magnetism most familiar to us is certain materials attracting iron. Magnets also attract steel, cobalt, and other materials. Generators supplying power include magnets, as do all electric motors. Loudspeakers and telephones contain magnets. Tape recorders use magnets. The tape they play is magnetized. Magnets are used in compasses to determine the location of north and various corresponding directions. In fact, the planet Earth is itself a giant magnet (which is why compasses point north). Hence, like the Earth, all magnets have two poles: a north/north-seeking pole and a south/south-seeking pole. Opposite poles attract and like poles repel each other. Magnets do not need to touch to attract or repel each other. A magnet's effective area/range is its magnetic field. All materials have some response to magnetic fields. Magnets can turn nearby magnetic materials into magnets, by a process known as magnetic induction. Materials that line up parallel to magnetic force field lines are paramagnetic, while materials that line up perpendicular to magnetic force field lines are diamagnetic.

### Modern Theory of Magnetism and What Scientists Do and Do Not Know

Scientists have known about the effects of magnetism for hundreds of years. However, they do not know exactly what magnetism is or what causes it. French physicist Pierre Weiss proposed a theory of magnetism in the early 20th century that is widely accepted. This theory posits that every magnetic material has groups of molecules—domains—that function as magnets. Until a material is magnetized, its domains have a random arrangement, so one domain's magnetism is canceled out by another's. When the material comes into a magnetic field—the range/area wherein a magnet is effective—its domains align themselves parallel to the magnetic field's lines of force. As a result, all of their north-seeking/north poles point in the same direction. Removing the magnetic field causes like poles to repel one another as they normally do. In easily magnetized materials, domains revert to random order. In materials that are harder to magnetize, domains lack sufficient force to disassemble, leaving the material magnetized. Later versions of Weiss's theory attribute domain magnetism to spinning electrons.

**Review Video: Magnets**
Visit mometrix.com/academy and enter code: 570803

### Insulation, Conduction, and the Flow of Electricity

The smallest units of all matter are atoms. The nuclei of atoms are orbited by negatively charged electrons. Some materials have electrons that are strongly bound to their atoms. These include air, glass, wood, cotton, plastic, and ceramic. Since their atoms rarely release electrons, these materials have little or no ability to conduct electricity and are known as electrical insulators. Insulators resist/block conduction. Metals and other conductive materials have free electrons that can detach from the atoms and move around. Without the tight binding of insulators, materials with loose electrons enable electric current to flow easily through them. Such materials are called electrical conductors. The movements of their electrons transmit electrical energy. Electricity requires something to make it flow (i.e., a generator). A generator creates a steady flow of electrons by moving a magnet close to a wire, creating a magnetic field to propel electrons. Electricity also requires a conductor (i.e., a medium through which it can move from one place to another).

### Movement of Electrical Currents by a Generator

Magnetism and electricity are related, and they interact with each other. Generators work by using magnets near conductive wires to produce moving streams of electrons. The agent of movement can range from a hand crank, to a steam engine, to the nuclear fission process. However, all agents of movements operate according to the same principle. A simple analogy is that a generator magnetically pushes electrical current the way a pump pushes water. Just as water pumps apply specific amounts of pressure to specific numbers of water molecules, generator magnets apply specific amounts of "pressure" to specific numbers of electrons. The number of moving electrons in an electrical circuit equals the current, or amperage. The unit of measurement for amperage is the ampere, or amp. The amount of force moving the electrons is the voltage. Its unit of measurement is the volt. One amp equals $6.24 \times 10^{18}$ electrons passing through a wire each second. For example, a generator could produce 1 amp using 6 volts when rotating 1,000 times per minute. Today's power stations rely on generators.

### Positions and Motions of Objects and Newton's Laws of Physics

Moving physical objects changes their positions. According **to Newton's first law of motion**, an object at rest tends to stay at rest, and an object in motion tends to stay in motion until a force changes the object's state of motion. For example, an object at rest could be a small rock sitting on the ground. If you kick the rock into the air, it moves through the air. The rock will continue to move, but when a force like gravity acts on it, it falls/stops moving. The resulting motion from kicking the rock illustrates Newton's third law of motion: for every action, there is an equal and opposite reaction. The acceleration or change in velocity ($a$) of an object depends on its mass ($m$) and the amount of force ($F$) that is applied to the object. Newton's second law of motion states that $F = ma$ (force equals mass times acceleration). Thus, moving objects maintain their speeds unless acted on by a force, like friction.

## HEAT

**Heat** is transmitted through conduction, radiation, and convection. Heat is transmitted within solids by conduction. When two objects at different temperatures touch each other, the hotter object's molecules are moving faster. They collide with the colder object's molecules, which are moving slower. As a result of the collision, the molecules that are moving more rapidly supply energy to the molecules that are moving more slowly. This speeds up the movement of the (previously) slower-moving molecules, which heats up the colder object. This process of transferring heat through contact is called thermal conductivity. An example of thermal conductivity is the heat sink. Heat sinks are used in many devices. Today, they are commonly used in computers. A heat sink transfers the heat building up in the computer processor, moving it away before it can damage the processor. Computers contain fans, which blow air across their heat sinks and expel the heated air out of the computers.

## ACOUSTICAL PRINCIPLES AND THE HUMAN HEARING PROCESS

When any physical object moves back and forth rapidly, this is known as **vibration**. The movements that occur during vibration disturb the surrounding medium, which may be solid, liquid, or gaseous. The most common sound conducting medium in our environment is gaseous: our atmosphere (i.e., the air). An object's vibratory movements represent a form of energy. As this acoustic energy moves through the air, it takes the form of waves, sound waves specifically. The outer ear receives and amplifies the sound and transmits it to the middle ear, where tiny bones vibrate in response to the sound energy and transmit it to the inner ear. The inner ear converts the acoustic energy into electrical energy. The electrical impulses are then carried by nerves to the brain. Structures in the brain associated with hearing receive these electrical signals and interpret them as sounds. The ears' reception of sound waves is auditory sensation, and the brain's interpretation of them is auditory perception.

## SOLAR SYSTEM

### *SOLAR SYSTEM'S LOCATION AND COMPONENTS*

The universe is composed of an unknown (possibly infinite) number of galaxies or star systems, such as the Spiral Nebula, the Crab Nebula, and the Milky Way. Our sun, Sol, is one of billions of stars in the Milky Way. The solar system's planets are held in position at varying distances (according to their size and mass) from the Sun by its gravitational force. These planets orbit or revolve around the Sun. From the closest to the Sun to the farthest away, the solar system's planets are Mercury, Venus, Earth, Mars, Jupiter, Saturn, Uranus, and Neptune. Pluto was historically included as the ninth planet but was demoted to a "dwarf planet" by the International Astronomical Union in 2006. Due to angular momentum, planets rotate on their axes, which are imaginary central lines between their north and south poles. One complete Earth rotation equals what we perceive as one 24-hour day. As the Earth turns, different portions face the Sun. These receive daylight, while the portions turned away from the Sun are in darkness. One complete revolution of the Earth around the Sun represents one calendar year.

### *PLUTO*

Since more powerful observatories have enabled greater detection and measurement of celestial objects, the International Astronomical Union has defined three criteria for defining a planet. First, it must orbit the Sun. Pluto meets this criterion. Second, it must have enough gravitational force to shape itself into a sphere. Pluto also meets this criterion. Third, a planet must have "cleared the neighborhood" in its orbit. This expression refers to the fact that as planets form, they become the strongest gravitational bodies within their orbits. Therefore, when close to smaller bodies, planets either consume these smaller bodies or repel them because of their greater gravity, clearing their orbital area or "neighborhood." To do this, a planet's mass must sufficiently exceed the mass of other bodies in its orbit. Pluto does not meet this criterion, having only 0.07 times the mass of other objects within its orbit. Thus, astronomers reclassified Pluto as a "dwarf planet" in 2006 based on its lesser mass and the many other objects in its orbit with comparable masses and sizes.

### *EARTH*

Earth is roughly spherical in shape. Its North and South Poles at the top and bottom are farthest away from and least exposed to the Sun, so they are always coldest. This accounts for the existence of the polar ice caps. The Equator, an imaginary line running around Earth at its middle exactly halfway between the North and South Poles, is at 0° latitude. Sunrises and sunsets at the Equator are the world's fastest. Days and nights are of virtually equal length at the Equator, and there is less seasonal variation than in other parts of the world. The equatorial climate is a tropical rainforest. Locations close to the North Pole, like Norway, are at such high latitudes that their nights are not dark in summertime, hence the expression "Land of the Midnight Sun." They also have very little light in wintertime. As Earth revolves around the Sun over the course of a year, the distance and angle of various locations relative to the Sun change, so different areas receive varying amounts of heat and light. This is what accounts for the changing seasons.

## ROCKS FOUND ON THE EARTH'S SURFACE

### *SEDIMENTARY ROCKS*

Earth's rock types are sedimentary, igneous, and metamorphic. These categories are based on the respective processes that form each type of rock. Igneous rocks are formed from volcanoes. Metamorphic rocks are formed when igneous and sedimentary rocks deep inside the Earth's crust are subjected to intense heat and/or pressure. **Sedimentary rocks** are formed on Earth's surface and characteristically accumulate in layers. Erosion and other natural processes deposit these layers. Some sedimentary rocks are held together by electrical attraction. Others are cemented together by chemicals and minerals that existed during their formation. Still others are not held together at all but are loose and crumbly. There are three subcategories of sedimentary rock. Clastic sedimentary rocks are made of little rock bits—clasts—that are compacted and cemented together. Chemical sedimentary rocks are frequently formed through repeated flooding and subsequent evaporation. The evaporation of water leaves a layer of minerals that were dissolved in the water. Limestone and deposits of salt and gypsum are examples. Organic sedimentary rocks are formed from organic matter, such as the calcium left behind from animal bones and shells.

### *METAMORPHIC ROCKS*

Sedimentary rocks are formed on the Earth's surface by layers of eroded material from mountains that were deposited by water, minerals like lime, salt and gypsum deposited by evaporated floodwater, and organic material like calcium from animal bones and shells. Igneous rocks are formed from liquid volcanic rock—either magma underground or lava on the surface—that cools and hardens. **Metamorphic rocks** are formed from sedimentary and igneous rocks. This happens when sedimentary and/or igneous rocks are deep inside the Earth's crust, where they are subjected to great pressure or heat. The process of metamorphism does not melt these rocks into liquid, which would happen inside a volcano. Rather, the pressure and/or heat change the rocks' molecular structure. Metamorphic rocks are thus more compact and denser than the sedimentary or igneous rocks from which they were formed. They also contain new minerals produced either by the reconfiguration of existing minerals' structures or by chemical reactions with liquids infiltrating the rock. Two examples of metamorphic rocks are marble and gneiss.

### *IGNEOUS ROCKS*

**Igneous** or volcanic rocks are formed from the magma emitted when a volcano erupts. Magma under the Earth's surface is subject to heat and pressure, keeping it in liquid form. During a volcanic eruption, some magma reaches the surface, emerging as lava. Lava cools rapidly in the outside air, becoming a solid with small crystals. Some magma does not reach Earth's surface, but is trapped underground within pockets in other rocks. Magma cools more slowly underground than lava does on the surface. This slower cooling forms rocks with larger crystals and coarser grains. The chemical composition and individual cooling temperatures of magma produce different kinds of igneous rocks. Lava that cools rapidly on the Earth's surface can become obsidian, a smooth, shiny black glass without crystals. It can also become another type of extrusive rock, such as andesite, basalt, pumice, rhyolite, scoria, or tuff (formed from volcanic ash and cinders). Magma that cools slowly in underground pockets can become granite, which has a coarse texture and large, visible mineral grains. It can also become another type of intrusive rock, such as diorite, gabbro, pegmatite, or peridotite.

## EROSION

**Erosion** is a natural process whereby Earth's landforms are broken down through weathering. Rain and wind wear away solid matter. Over time, rain reduces mountains to hills. Rocks break off from mountains and, in turn, disintegrate into sand. Weathering and the resulting erosion always occur in downhill directions. Rain washes rocks off mountains and down streams. Rains, rivers, and streams wash soils away, and ocean waves break down adjacent cliffs. Rocks, dirt, and sand change their form and location through erosion. They do not simply vanish. These transformations and movements are called mass wasting, which occurs chemically (as when rock is dissolved by chemicals in water) or mechanically (as when rock is broken into pieces). Because materials travel as a result of mass wasting, erosion can both break down some areas and build up others. For example, a river runs through and erodes a mountain, carrying the resulting sediment downstream. This sediment gradually builds up, creating wetlands at the river's mouth. A good example of this process is Louisiana's swamps, which were created by sediment transported by the Mississippi River.

## WEATHER, CLIMATE, AND METEOROLOGY

**Meteorology** is the study of the atmosphere, particularly as it pertains to forecasting the weather and understanding its processes. **Weather** is the condition of the atmosphere at any given moment. Most weather occurs in the troposphere and includes changing events such as clouds, storms, and temperature, as well as more extreme events such as tornadoes, hurricanes, and blizzards. **Climate** refers to the average weather for a particular area over time, typically at least 30 years. Latitude is an indicator of climate. Changes in climate occur over long time periods.

## WINDS AND GLOBAL WIND BELTS

**Winds** are the result of air moving by convection. Masses of warm air rise, and cold air sweeps into their place. The warm air also moves, cools, and sinks. The term "prevailing wind" refers to the wind that usually blows in an area in a single direction. Dominant winds are the winds with the highest speeds. Belts or bands that run latitudinally and blow in a specific direction are associated with convection cells. Hadley cells are formed directly north and south of the equator. The Farrell cells occur at about 30° to 60°. The jet stream runs between the Farrell cells and the polar cells. At the higher and lower latitudes, the direction is easterly. At mid-latitudes, the direction is westerly. From the North Pole to the south, the surface winds are Polar High Easterlies, Subpolar Low Westerlies, Subtropical High or Horse Latitudes, North-East Trade winds, Equatorial Low or Doldrums, South-East Trades, Subtropical High or Horse Latitudes, Subpolar Low Easterlies, and Polar High.

## RELATIVE HUMIDITY, ABSOLUTE HUMIDITY, AND DEW POINT TEMPERATURE

**Humidity** refers to water vapor contained in the air. The amount of moisture contained in air depends upon its temperature. The higher the air temperature, the more moisture it can hold. These higher levels of moisture are associated with higher humidity. **Absolute humidity** refers to the total amount of moisture air is capable of holding at a certain temperature. **Relative humidity** is the ratio of water vapor in the air compared to the amount the air is capable of holding at its current temperature. As temperature decreases, absolute humidity stays the same and relative humidity increases. A hygrometer is a device used to measure humidity. The **dew point** is the temperature at which water vapor condenses into water at a particular humidity.

## PRECIPITATION

After clouds reach the dew point, **precipitation** occurs. Precipitation can take the form of a liquid or a solid. It is known by many names, including rain, snow, ice, dew, and frost. **Liquid** forms of precipitation include rain and drizzle. Rain or drizzle that freezes on contact is known as freezing rain or freezing drizzle. **Solid or frozen** forms of precipitation include snow, ice needles or diamond dust, sleet or ice pellets, hail, and graupel or snow pellets. Virga is a form of precipitation that evaporates before reaching the ground. It usually looks like sheets or shafts falling from a cloud. The amount of rainfall is measured with a rain gauge. Intensity can be measured according to how fast precipitation is falling or by how severely it limits visibility. Precipitation plays a major role in the water cycle since it is responsible for depositing much of the Earth's fresh water.

### CLOUDS

**Clouds** form when air cools and warm air is forced to give up some of its water vapor because it can no longer hold it. This vapor condenses and forms tiny droplets of water or ice crystals called clouds. Particles, or aerosols, are needed for water vapor to form water droplets. These are called **condensation nuclei**. Clouds are created by surface heating, mountains and terrain, rising air masses, and weather fronts. Clouds precipitate, returning the water they contain to Earth. Clouds can also create atmospheric optics. They can scatter light, creating colorful phenomena such as rainbows, colorful sunsets, and the green flash phenomenon.

### LIVING ORGANISMS

All **living organisms** have fundamental needs that must be met. For example, plants that grow on land need light, air, water, and nutrients in amounts that vary according to the individual plant. Undersea plants may need less/no light. They need gases present in the water but not in the air above the water. Like land plants, they require nutrients. Like plants, animals (including humans) need air, water, and nutrients. They do not depend on light for photosynthesis like most plants, but some animals require more light than others, while others need less than others or none at all. Organisms cannot survive in environments that do not meet their basic needs. However, many organisms have evolved to adapt to various environments. For example, cacti are desert plants that thrive with only tiny amounts of water, and camels are desert animals that can also go for long periods of time with little water. Penguins and polar bears have adapted to very cold climates. Internal cues (e.g., hunger) and external cues (e.g., environmental change) motivate and shape the behaviors of individual organisms.

### TYPES OF ANIMAL LIFE CYCLES

Most animals, including mammals, birds, fish, reptiles, and spiders, have simple life cycles. They are born live or hatch from eggs, and then grow to adulthood. Animals with simple life cycles include humans. Amphibians like frogs and newts have an additional stage involving a metamorphosis, or transformation. After birth, they breathe through gills and live underwater during youth (e.g., tadpoles). By adulthood, they breathe through lungs and move to land. Butterflies are examples of animals (insects) that undergo complete metamorphosis, meaning they change their overall form. After hatching from an embryo/egg, the juvenile form, or larva, resembles a worm and completes the majority of feeding required. In the next stage, the pupa does not feed, and is typically camouflaged in what is called an inactive stage. Mosquito pupae are called tumblers. The butterfly pupa is called a chrysalis and is protected by a cocoon. In the final stage, the adult (imago) grows wings (typically) and breeds. Some insects like dragonflies, cockroaches, and grasshoppers undergo an incomplete metamorphosis. There are egg, larva, and adult stages, but no pupa stage.

### ECOLOGY

**Ecology** is defined as the study of interactions between organisms and their environments. **Abiotic factors** are the parts of any ecosystem that are not alive but which affect that ecosystem's living members. Abiotic factors also determine the locations of particular ecosystems that have certain characteristics. Abiotic factors include the sunlight; the atmosphere, including oxygen, hydrogen, and nitrogen; the water; the soil; the temperatures within a system; and the nutrient cycles of chemical elements and compounds that pass among living organisms and their physical environments. **Biotic factors** are the living organisms within any ecosystem, which include not only humans and animals but also plants and microorganisms. The definition of biotic factors also includes the interactions that occur between and among various organisms within an ecosystem. Sunlight determines plant growth and, hence, biome locations. Sunlight, in turn, is affected by water depth.

Ocean depths where sunlight penetrates, called photic zones, are where the majority of the photosynthesis on Earth occurs.

**Review Video: Photosynthesis**
Visit mometrix.com/academy and enter code: 227035

## Organism Reproduction

A few examples of the many ways in which organisms reproduce include binary fission, whereby the cells of prokaryotic bacteria reproduce; budding, which is how yeast cells reproduce; and asexual reproduction. The latter occurs in plants when they are grafted, when cuttings are taken from them and then rooted, or when they put out runners. Plants also reproduce sexually, as do humans and most other animals. Animals, including humans, produce gametes (i.e., sperm or eggs) in their gonads through the process of meiosis. Gametes are haploid, containing half the number of chromosomes found in the body's cells. During fertilization, the gametes combine to form a zygote, which is diploid. It has the full number of chromosomes (half from each gamete), which are arranged in a genetically unique combination. Zygotes undergo mitosis, reproducing their gene combination with identical DNA sequences in all new cells, which then migrate and differentiate into organizations of specialized organs and tissues. These specialized organs in biologically mature organisms, alerted by signals such as hormonal cues, undergo meiosis to create new haploid gametes, beginning the cycle again.

## Plant Reproduction

Most plants can reproduce asexually. For example, cuttings can be rooted in water and planted. Some plants put out runners that root new growths. Many plants can be grafted to produce new ones. Plants also reproduce sexually. Plants' sexual life cycles are more complex than animals', since plants alternate between haploid form (i.e., having a single set of chromosomes) and diploid form (i.e., having two sets of chromosomes) during their life cycles. Plants produce haploid cells called gametes (equivalent to sperm and egg in animals) that combine during fertilization, producing zygotes (diploid cells with chromosomes from both gametes). Cells reproduce exact copies through mitosis (asexual reproduction), becoming differentiated/specialized to form organs. Mature diploid plants called sporophytes—the plant form we usually see—produce spores. In sporophytes' specialized organs, cells undergo meiosis. This is part of the process of sexual reproduction, during which cells with half the normal number of chromosomes are produced before fertilization occurs. The spores produced by the sporophyte generation undergo mitosis, growing into a haploid plant of the gametophyte generation that produces gametes. The cycle then repeats.

## Ecological Relationships

Organisms interact, both with other organisms and their environments. Relationships wherein two differing organisms regularly interact so that one or both of them benefit are known as **ecological relationships**. In **mutualistic** relationships, both organisms benefit. For example, bacteria live in termites' digestive systems. Termites eat wood. However, they cannot digest the cellulose (the main part of plant cell walls) in wood. The bacteria in termites' guts break down the cellulose for them, releasing the wood's nutrients. Reciprocally, the termites as hosts give the bacteria a home and food. In **commensalistic** relationships, one organism benefits and the other one is unaffected. One example is barnacles attaching to whales. Barnacles, which are filter feeders, benefit from the whales' swimming, which creates currents in the water that bring the barnacles food. The whales are not disturbed by the barnacles. In **parasitic** relationships, the parasite benefits, but the host suffers. For example, tapeworms inside animals' digestive tracts get nutrients. The hosts lose the nutrients stolen by the worms and can sustain tissue damage because of the presence of the tapeworms.

## Chapter Quiz

Ready to see how well you retained what you just read? Scan the QR code to go directly to the chapter quiz interface for this study guide. If you're using a computer, simply visit the online resources page at **mometrix.com/resources719/gacesegcelemed** and click the Chapter Quizzes link.

# Social Studies

## Human Socialization and Major Socializing Agencies

**Socialization** is the process by which individuals learn their society's norms, values, beliefs, and attitudes and what behaviors society expects of them relative to those parameters. This learning is imparted by agencies of socialization. The family, peer groups, and leaders of opinion are considered primary socializing agencies. The family is probably the most important because it has the most significant influence on individual development. Families influence the self-concept, feelings, attitudes, and behaviors of each individual member. As children grow, they encounter peer groups throughout life, which also establish norms and values to which individual group members conform. Schools, workplaces, religions, and mass media are considered secondary socializing agencies. Schools dictate additional academic and behavioral norms, values, beliefs, and behaviors. Workplaces have their own cultures that continue, modify, and/or add to the values and behaviors expected of their members. Religions also regulate members' behavior through beliefs, values, goals, and norms that reflect moral principles within a society. Mass media communicate societal conventions (e.g., fashion/style), which enables individuals to learn and adopt new behaviors and/or lifestyles.

### *Influence of Institutions on Individual Identity, Relationships, Beliefs, and Behaviors*

Family is the first and most important socializing agent. Infants learn behavioral patterns from mothers. Their primary socialization is enabled through such early behaviors as nursing, smiling, and toddling. Babies soon interact with other family members. All the infant's physiological and psychological needs are met within the family. Babies learn their sleeping, eating, and toileting habits within the family environment. Babies' personalities also develop based on their early experiences, especially the amounts and types of parental love and affection they receive. School is also a critical socializing agent. Children extend family relationships to society when they go to school. Cognitive and social school experiences develop children's knowledge, skills, beliefs, interests, attitudes, and customs and help determine the roles children will play when they become adults. In addition to family relationships, receiving reinforcements at school and observing and imitating teachers influence personality development. Peer groups that are based on friendships, shared ideas, and common interests in music and sports teach children/teens about conforming to rules and being rejected for not complying with these rules. Mass media like TV profoundly influence children, both negatively and positively.

## Culture

While no single definition of culture is universally embraced, one from the cultural anthropology perspective is "...a system of shared beliefs, values, customs, behaviors and artifacts that members of society use to cope with their worlds and with one another, and that are transmitted from generation to generation through learning." (Bates and Fratkin, 2002) Cultural groups are based on a wide range of factors, including geographic location, occupation, religion, sexual orientation, and income. Individuals may follow the beliefs and values of more than one culture concurrently. For instance, recent immigrants often espouse values and beliefs from both their original and adopted countries. Traditionally, social systems like education and healthcare have approached cultural diversity by focusing on race/ethnicity and common beliefs about various racial/ethnic group customs. These are frequently generalizations (e.g., lumping Mexican, Cuban, and Puerto Rican cultures together and describing them as "Latino" culture). This type of practice can lead to oversimplified stereotypes and, therefore, to unrealistic behavioral expectations. Service professionals need more detailed knowledge of cultural complexities and subtleties to effectively engage and interact with families.

## Collectivism and Individualism

Certain world cultures are oriented more toward **collectivism**, while others are oriented more toward individualism. Native American, Latin American, Asian, and African cultures are more often collectivistic, focusing on interdependence, social interactions, relationships, and connections among individuals. North American, Canadian, European, and Australian cultures are more commonly individualistic, focusing on independence, uniqueness, self-determination, and self-actualization (realizing one's full potential). Individualism favors competition and distinguishing oneself as an individual, while collectivism favors cooperation that promotes and contributes to the harmony and well-being of the group. **Individualist** cultures value teaching young children object manipulation and scientific thinking, while collectivist cultures value social and relational behaviors. For example, adults in collectivist cultures may interpret a child's first steps as walking toward the adult, while adults in individualist cultures interpret them as developing motor skills and autonomy. These interpretations signify what each culture values most, forming the child's cultural orientation early in life. The planning and design of educational and other programs should be informed by a knowledge of these and other cultural differences.

## Cultural Competence

### *Culturally Competent Professionals*

A **culturally competent professional** demonstrates the ability to enable "...mutually rewarding interactions and meaningful relationships in the delivery of effective services for children and family whose cultural heritage differs from his or her own." (Shonkoff, National Research Council and Institute of Medicine, 2000) Providing interpreters and/or translators does not on its own constitute cultural competence. Hiring racially diverse educational staff in schools is also not enough. Culturally competent educators demonstrate highly developed self-awareness of their own cultural values and beliefs. They must also have and/or develop communication skills that allow them to elicit information from students and families regarding their own cultural beliefs. Further, they must be able to understand how diverse cultural views may affect a child's education, as well as how parents/families receive, comprehend, interpret, and respond to educators' communications. Therefore, educators must develop communication skills to meet educational goals.

### *Aspects of Cultural Competence*

It is important for educational professionals to acquire and demonstrate cultural competence at the individual level to effectively interact with individual children and their families. Moreover, cultural competence is also important at the program level, the school level, and the system level. According to the **National Center for Cultural Competence** (NCCC), system-level cultural competence is a continuing process that includes "...valuing diversity, conducting self-assessments (including organizational assessments), managing the dynamics of differences, acquiring and institutionalizing cultural knowledge, and adapting to the diversity and cultural contexts of the individuals and communities served." (Goode, 2001) Individual educational interactions are informed by a knowledge of cultural diversity and of the importance of such diversity in educational settings, an ability to adapt to the population's cultural needs, and a willingness to engage in ongoing self-reflection. This same set of knowledge and skills is also applied at the system level. Family engagement is important in early childhood care and education. This includes understanding the developmental needs of families as well as their children, especially when families and/or children speak different languages.

## Acculturation Versus Assimilation

**Acculturation** describes the process whereby people adapt or change their cultural traditions, values, and beliefs as a result of coming into contact with and being influenced by other cultures over time. Some cultures adopt certain characteristics from other cultures they are exposed to, and two or more separate cultures may sometimes virtually fuse. However, **assimilation**, wherein various ethnic groups unite to form a new culture, is different from acculturation. One dominant culture may assimilate others. A historical example is the Roman Empire, which forced many members of ancient Greek, Hebrew, and other cultures to abandon their own cultures and adopt Roman law, military allegiance, traditions, language, religion, practices, and customs (including dress). The extent of a diverse cultural group's acculturation influences how it interacts with social systems like education and healthcare. Groups that are strongly motivated to maintain their cultural identity may interact less with mainstream systems that significantly conflict with or vary from their own cultural beliefs.

### *Measuring the Acculturation of Immigrants and Diverse Cultural Groups in America*

Social scientists currently use indices such as people's country of birth, how long they have lived in America, their knowledge of the English language, and their level of English language use to study acculturation. However, these factors are measured not because they are the core elements of acculturation but because they are easier to validly and reliably measure than the underlying cultural beliefs, attitudes, and behaviors they reflect, which are harder to quantify. The interactions between American educators and culturally diverse families can be problematic on both sides. Educators have difficulty interacting, communicating, and collaborating with families that come from a variety of other countries, speak various other languages, and differ in their degree of acculturation to American culture. On the other hand, immigrant and culturally diverse families encounter a foreign language, different cultural customs and practices, and an unfamiliar educational system with different methods of assessment, placement, curriculum planning and design, instruction, and evaluation—not to mention different special education laws and procedures. Thus, the acculturation challenges related to interactions between American educators and culturally diverse families are bilateral.

**Review Video: Collaborating with Other Professionals**
Visit mometrix.com/academy and enter code: 100351

## Cultural Differences in Parents' Goals for Raising Their Children

Depending on their cultural group, parents have varying goals for their children and use different practices to achieve those goals. For example, research on four different cultural groups in Hawaii found the following differences related to what parents visualized when they pictured their children as successful adults:

- **Native Hawaiians** most wanted their children to have social connections, be happy in their social networks, and demonstrate self-reliance as adults.
- **Caucasian American** parents most valued self-reliance, happiness, spontaneity, and creativity as developmental outcomes for their children.
- **Filipino American** parents most valued the development of traits related to obedience, citizenship, respect for authority, and good conduct and manners in their children.
- **Japanese American** parents placed priority on their children's achievement, as well as their ability to live well-organized lives, stay in contact with family, and master the demands of life.

Such distinct, significant differences imply that these parent groups would vary in how they would respond to young children's assertive behaviors, in their disciplinary styles (e.g., permissive, authoritative, authoritarian), and in the emphasis they would place on activities focusing on physical and cognitive skill mastery vs. social competence and connection.

### *Educational Services Accessed by Different Cultures*

Parents in America have been found to show distinct preferences for the kinds of care and educational services they access for their children. For example, Caucasian parents in America are more likely to turn to preschool centers for help with their young children's care and instruction. This preference is influenced not only by custom but also by scientific evidence that center-based preschool experience improves children's skills and prepares them for school. Hispanic parents in America are more likely to use home-based and/or family-based care settings. This preference probably reflects the more collectivist Hispanic perspective, which places more importance on social relationships than on structured learning in early childhood. Educators can take a culturally competent approach to such cultural diversity by looking for ways in which young children's school readiness skills can be promoted in family and home-based child care settings.

### *Different Views on Care, Education, and the Nature of Their Cognitive Abilities*

Depending on their native culture, parents vary in terms of the early experiences they select for their young children. For example, Latino parents tend to prefer family-based/home-based care. White parents tend to prefer center-based daycare and education designed to promote school readiness. Another cultural difference is parental beliefs about children's learning capacities. For example, research in California found that the majority of Latino parents believed their children's learning capacity is set at birth; only a small minority of white parents held this belief. Parents subscribing to a transactional child development model view the complex interaction between child and environment as creating a dynamic developmental process. These parents are more likely to value the stimulation of early childhood development, seek/implement activities that will provide such stimulation, and access early intervention services for children with developmental delays/difficulties. Parents subscribing to a view of fixed, innate cognitive capacity are less likely to believe their children's cognitive abilities can be influenced by educational experiences, and may not see the benefits of or seek out early learning stimulation and intervention.

### *Cultural Influences and How Much Parents in America Read to Their Children*

Researchers analyzing national early childhood surveys have identified significant variations in how often white, Asian, and Hispanic parents read to their young children. This variation is not solely due to varying cultural values. Additional factors include parents' financial limitations; time limitations; familiarity and comfort with accessing libraries and other government resources, websites, etc.; and literacy levels in both English and their native languages. Educators must realize that trying to encourage or even teach parents to read to their children earlier and/or more often is unlikely to be successful if parents do not place value or priority on the benefits of being read to, or do not view the outcomes of reading aloud to children as benefits. Reading to children is known to promote school readiness and academic success. Educators should also understand that some children, despite not being read to in early childhood, become successful adults. Additionally, some cultures, including African Americans, emphasize oral learning traditions more than written ones, developing different skills, such as the basic understanding of story flow.

## Factors Affecting Parents Who Are Immigrants to America

Parents educated in other countries may not know a great deal about the American educational system and may not be aware of the educational demands made on their children, even in early childhood. Educators need to work with these parents to find common ground by identifying shared goals for children. While culturally diverse parents may disagree with some educators' goals, they can collaborate with educators to promote those on which they do agree. Immigrant parents may also be unaware of additional services available in America for children with developmental and/or learning problems. Educators can help parents by providing this information. Another consideration is that some other cultures have more paternalistic educational systems. Parents from such cultures, rather than vocally advocating for their children who need services, tend to wait for teachers/specialists to voice concerns before communicating any problems they have observed. Thus, they could miss out on the chance to obtain helpful services. Even worse, educators could misconstrue their behavior as a lack of interest in children's progress, or as resistance to confronting problems.

## Developmental Milestones Varying by Culture

Research has found that different cultures have different age expectations for many early childhood developmental milestones. For example, Filipinos expect children to eat using utensils at 32.4 months. Anglo families expect children to do this at 17.7 months, and Puerto Ricans expect children to reach this milestone at 26.5 months. Filipino cultures expect children to sleep all night by 32.4 months; Puerto Rican and Anglo cultures expect this at 14.5 and 14.4 months, respectively. Similarly, while Anglos expect children to sleep by themselves at around 13.8 months and Puerto Ricans at around 14.6 months, Filipinos do not expect this until 38.8 months. Filipinos expect children to eat solid food by 6.7 months, Anglos by 8.2 months, and Puerto Ricans by 10.1 months. In Anglo families, an 18-month-old not drinking from a cup could indicate developmental delay if parents introduced the cup when the child was one year old and regularly continued encouraging cup use. But, Filipino parents of an 18-month-old have likely not even introduced the child to a cup yet, so the fact that the child is not using a cup would not be cause for concern from a development standpoint.

When early childhood researchers investigated the average expectations of different cultural groups of when children would reach various developmental milestones, some of the milestones they examined included eating solid food, weaning from nursing, drinking from a cup, eating with the fingers, eating with utensils, sleeping alone, sleeping through the night, choosing one's own clothes, dressing oneself, and playing alone. They also looked at daytime and nighttime toilet training. Educators must become aware of different cultures' different socialization goals before assuming culturally diverse children have developmental delays. On the other hand, they must also avoid automatically attributing variations in milestone achievement to cultural child-rearing differences when full developmental assessments might be indicated. Family expectations and values influence the complex process of developmental assessment. When families and assessors share common cultures, it is more likely that valid data will be collected and interpreted. When their cultures differ, however, it is more likely that the assessment information will be misinterpreted. Employing early childhood teachers/care providers who are familiar with the child, family, and assessment setting as mediators can make developmental assessments more culturally competent.

## Essential Geographical Concepts

Ten concepts considered essential to the study of geography are as follows:

- **Location** identifies "where" a place is and examines the positive and negative properties of any place on the surface of the Earth. Absolute location is based upon latitude and longitude. Relative location is based upon changing characteristics of a region and is influenced by surrounding areas. For example, urban areas have higher land prices than rural ones.
- **Distance** identifies "how far" a place is, and is often described in terms of location. It is also related to the effort required to meet basic life needs. For example, the distance of raw materials from factories affects transportation costs and hence product prices. In another example, land costs less the farther it is from highways.
- **Achievability** identifies how accessible a geographical area is based on the conditions on the Earth's surface. For example, villages on beaches are easier to reach. Villages surrounded by forests or swamps are harder to reach. As its economy, science, technology, and transportation develop, a region's level of dependency on other areas changes.
- **Patterns** are found in geographical forms and in how geographical phenomena spread, which affects dependency on those phenomena. For example, in fold regions (areas where the folding of rocks forms mountains), the rivers typically form trellis patterns. Patterns are also seen in human activity that is based on geography. For example, in mountainous regions, settlements predominantly form spreading patterns.
- **Morphology** is the shape of our planet's surface resulting from inner and outer forces. For example, along the northern coast of Java, sugarcane plantations predominate in the lowlands.
- **Agglomeration** is defined as collecting into a mass and refers to a geographic concentration of people, activities, and/or settlements within areas that are most profitable and relatively narrow in size.
- **Utility value** refers to the existence and relative usefulness of natural resources. For example, fishermen find more utility value in the ocean than farmers do, and naturalists perceive more utility value in forests than academics would.
- **Interaction** is the reciprocal and interdependent relationship between two or more geographical areas, which can generate new geographical phenomena, configurations, and problems. For example, a rural village produces raw materials through activities like mining ores or growing and harvesting plant crops, while a city produces industrial goods. The village needs the city as a market for its raw materials and may also need the city's industrial products. The city needs the village for its raw materials to use in industrial production. This interdependence causes interaction.
- **Area differentiation** informs the study of variations among regional geographical phenomena. For example, different plants are cultivated in highlands vs. lowlands due to their different altitudes and climates. Area differentiation also informs the study of regional variations in occupation (farming vs. fishing, etc.).
- **Spatial interrelatedness** shows the relationship between/among geographic and non-physical phenomena, like rural and urban areas. The example above of village-city interaction also applies here.

## Geographical Maps

### General Features and Purposes

Maps can be drawn to show natural or man-made features. For example, some maps depict mountains, elevations (altitudes), average rainfall, average temperatures, and other natural features of an area. Other maps are made to depict countries, states, cities, roads, empires, wars, and other man-made features. Different types of maps are described according to their purposes. For example, political maps are made to depict countries, areas within a country, and/or cities. Physical maps are drawn to display natural features of the terrain in an area, such as rivers, lakes, and mountains. Thematic maps are drawn to focus on a more specific theme or topic, such as the locations and names of battles during a war or the average amounts of rainfall a country, state, or region receives in a given year or month. Some maps are made for more than one purpose and indicate more than one of the types of information described above.

### Basic Tools Supplied on Maps

On maps depicting local, national, and world geography, cartographers supply tools for navigating these maps. For example, the compass rose indicates the directions of north, south, east, and west. By looking at the compass, people can identify the locational relationships of places (e.g., in South America, Chile is west of Argentina). The scale of miles indicates how distances on a map correspond to actual geographical distances, enabling us to estimate real distances. For example, the scale might show that one inch is equal to 500 miles. By placing a piece of paper on the map, we can mark it to measure the distance between two cities (e.g., Washington, DC, in the USA and Ottawa in Canada) on the map, and then line the paper up with the scale of miles to estimate an actual distance of approximately 650 miles between the two cities. Map keys/legends identify what a map's symbols and colors represent.

### Grids

Maps show absolute geographic location (i.e., the precise "address" of any place on the planet) using a grid of lines. The lines running from east to west are called parallels or latitudes, and they correspond to how many degrees away from the equator a place is located. The lines running from north to south are called meridians or longitudes, and they correspond to how many degrees away from the prime meridian a place is located. To determine the absolute location of a place, we find the spot on the map where its latitude and longitude intersect. This intersection is the place's absolute location. For example, if we look at Mexico City on a map, we will find that its latitude is 19° north and its longitude is 99° west, which is expressed in cartography as 19° N, 99° W. Numbers of latitudes and longitudes like these are also referred to as coordinates.

## Reading and Analyzing a Special Purpose Map

First, read a map's title and look at the overall map. This provides a general idea of what the map shows. For example, a map entitled "Battles of the Punic Wars" would not be a good choice if someone was looking for the political boundaries of modern-day Greece, Italy, and Spain.

Next, read the map's legend/key to see what symbols and colors the map uses and what each represents. For example, some lines represent divisions between countries/states; some, roads; some, rivers; etc. Different colors can indicate different countries/states, elevations, amounts of rainfall, population densities, etc. These are not uniform across all maps, so legends/keys are necessary references.

Use the legend/key to interpret what the map shows. For example, by looking at colors representing elevations, one can determine which area of a country has the highest/lowest altitude.

Draw conclusions about what the map displays. For example, if a country map mainly has one color that indicates a certain elevation range, it can be concluded that this is the country's most common elevation.

## Graphs

Graphs display numerical information in pictorial forms, making it easier to view statistics quickly and draw conclusions about them. For example, it is easier to see patterns and trends like increases and decreases in quantities using visual graphs than columns of numbers. Line graphs, bar graphs, and pie charts are the most common types of graphs. Line graphs depict changes over time by plotting points for a quantity measured each day, week, month, year, decade, or century and connecting the points to make a line. For example, showing the population of a city each decade in a line graph reveals how the population has changed over time. Bar graphs compare quantities related to different times, places, people, and things. Each quantity is depicted by a separate bar, and its length corresponds to a number. Bar graphs make it easy to see which amounts are largest and smallest within a group (e.g., which of several countries has the largest population). Circle graphs (also called pie charts) divide a circle into segments (like slices of a pie) showing percentages or parts of a whole, which facilitates making comparisons between a few categories. For example, the department with the largest budget is the largest segment on a pie chart of company expenses.

**Review Video: Data Interpretation of Graphs**
Visit mometrix.com/academy and enter code: 200439

## Importance of Chronological Thinking to Understanding History

To see cause-and-effect relationships in historical events and explore and understand relationships among those events, students must have a solid grasp of when things happened and in what time sequence (chronology). Teachers can help students develop **chronological thinking** by using and assigning well-constructed/well-written narratives. These include histories written in the same style as stories, works of historical literature, and biographies. These hold students' attention, allowing them to focus on authors' depictions of temporal relationships among antecedents, actions, and consequences; of historical motivations and deeds of individuals and groups; and of the time structure of sequential occurrences. By middle school, students should have the skills needed to measure time mathematically (e.g., in years, decades, centuries, or millennia), interpret data displayed in timelines, and calculate time in BC and AD. High school students should be able to analyze patterns of historical duration (e.g., how long the US Constitutional government has lasted) and patterns of historical succession (e.g., the development of expanding trade and communication systems, from Neolithic times through ancient empires and from early modern times to modern global interaction).

## Reasons/Purposes for Our Country's Laws and Teaching Citizenship

Young children must understand the purposes of rules/laws: They identify acceptable/unacceptable citizen behaviors; make society and life predictable, secure, and orderly; designate responsibilities to citizens; and prevent persons in authority positions from abusing their roles by limiting their power. Understanding these functions of laws/rules enables children to realize that our government consists of individuals and groups authorized to create, implement, and enforce laws and manage legal disputes. Some creative early childhood teachers have used children's literature to illustrate these concepts. Children can relate personally to stories' characters, and story situations make the concepts real and concrete to children. Stories can be springboards for discussing rules and when they do or do not apply. One activity involves children in small groups making class rules (e.g., "No talking" and "Stay in your seat"), and then rewriting these to be more realistic (e.g., "Talk softly in class; listen when others talk" and "Sit down and get right to work"). When children consider issues of safety or fairness, they begin to develop an understanding of judicial and legislative roles.

## Introduction to Historiography

Historiography is the study of the methods and approaches that historians use to create histories. It involves examining how historical evidence is chosen, interpreted, evaluated, analyzed, and used in the writing of history. Historiography is not concerned with the events that make up history but rather the manner in which that history was recorded. The sources, techniques, and theoretical frameworks used to record the history of a certain subject constitute that subject's historiography.

## Common Terminology Used When Studying History

When studying history, it is important to have a clear understanding of various terms that can be used interchangeably. The term **time** refers to the continuous passing of events in the past, present, and future. Time is a scientific measure that conventionally uses minutes, hours, days, and years as its **standard**

**measures**. Time passes with or without significant events taking place. **History** is distinct from time as it is the record of **significant events** throughout the past. The term **chronology** refers to the arrangement of events in their correct order. As history contains uncertainty, the chronology of particular events is up for debate. Terms used to describe the ebb and flow of history are change and continuity. **Continuity** refers to periods of time that are relatively stable in history with no major changes, whereas times of **change** refer to rich periods in history with significant events that alter the common practices of that time, often leading into a new era. When describing what has changed for a civilization over time, it is common to focus on political, economic, social, and technological aspects. For instance, the United States government was established in 1776 and continues today. This demonstrates a change at the beginning of the timeline related the United States, but since then, there has been political continuity as it has existed for roughly 250 years. Other aspects of life in this period may have experienced other changes, such as the innovation of electricity, steam engines, and automobiles. When a portion of time has relatively stable conditions such that it can be summed up by a common characterization, it is called a **period of time**; this process of summing up time into periods is called **periodization**.

## Civilization, City-States, and Empires

Since history is the study of recorded events throughout time, it is naturally tied to organized society with a developed language to record the events. The development necessary to record history generally coincides with early civilization. A **civilization** is a human society that has established complex means of surviving as a group. These **functions** are developing a food supply, a social structure, a shared language, a culture, and technology. The first known complex civilization is Mesopotamia, which was more easily developed due to its fertile farmlands, access to water through an available river. Mesopotamia is a good example of a **city-state**, which is essentially an independently sovereign city that does not depend on another government. Mesopotamia, as an early civilization, was the central hub and government in its region. The model of city-states still exists today, though they are often comparatively less significant in size and economy compared to other nation-states. Examples of modern city-states include Monaco, Vatican City, and Singapore. As the early civilizations continued to develop, they would eventually grow into **empires**, which are larger sovereign states with multiple territories, though they are usually governed centrally by a monarch or emperor.

## Interpreting Timelines

Timelines are a useful tool for visualizing the chronology of events as well as a great method to map out periods and view changes or continuity throughout history. Timelines can focus on either small or large ranges and can be multifaceted so that one period or type of event can be compared with another. A key element of a timeline is having a consistent interval mapped out. For instance, if we wanted to construct a timeline to map the events that happened for a single day, we would likely use hours to plot out the continuum. One might start the timeline at 12am and end the timeline at 12am the next night to show the picture of the entire day. Each event or period, such as sleeping, waking up, eating, going to work, and special occurrences can be marked on the timeline to plot out the day. If someone wanted to compare multiple days, these timelines could be lined up and compared and contrasted to find what is common to all days and what is unique. These same concepts can be applied to historical timelines as well. Instead of mapping just one day, one might consider mapping the events leading up to and throughout a particular war. The significance of events should change with the focus of the timeline. Seeing events plotted on a steady continuum of time can be very helpful in understanding the pacing of events throughout history.

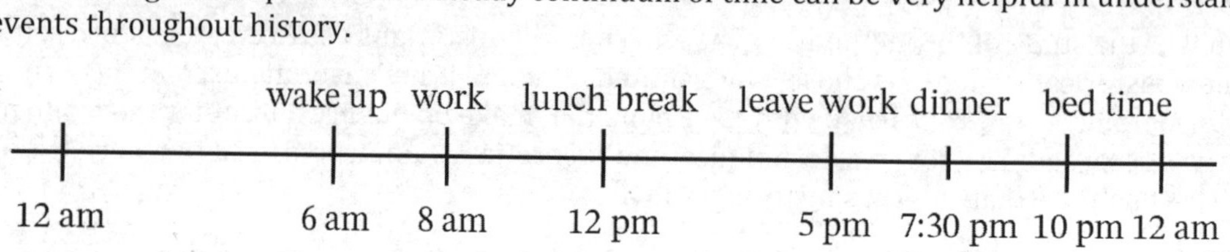


## Relationships Between Historical Events and Their Implications

As one aspect of society changes, it frequently proves to have significant effects on other parts of society. One of the easiest ways to see this effect is the innovation of new technologies. An example of a highly impactful technology is the printing press. Prior to this invention, all written documents had to be written by hand, which was time-consuming and costly. Books were very expensive and rare, which put the burden of education on mainly religious authorities and very wealthy classes of people. This new innovation allowed for more written works to be spread, which caused a need for literacy and education, ultimately evoking huge cultural and political changes. Technology tends to be a much quicker influencer of change in civilization, as it is sudden and can have dramatic impacts on how things are done. Cultural, political, and economic effects tend to move more gradually but likewise have strong effects that can change civilization forever.

## Primary and Secondary Sources of Historical Information

When studying history, it is important to consider the reliability, validity, and availability of sources of information. **Primary sources** are first-hand accounts of an event, such as a transcript of a speech, a recording, statistics, or a work of art. **Secondary sources** are indirect records, such as text books, newspapers, and other forms of reviews of the primary sources. Secondary sources of information can still be valid and useful, but are more open to **interpretation** and **bias**. Information from recent history, such as the election of a president in the 2010s is very reliable, as there are many sources of information that are in consensus about the objective event. Furthermore, many people still alive are primary sources since they were alive and witnessed the election. This is not true of less modern history, such as the election of Abraham Lincoln in 1860. There are still plentiful records of the information, but all witnesses to the election have passed away at this point. This event took place in an era where newspapers and legitimate documentation was widespread and available. The clarity and objectivity of sources are indisputable because they are so abundant. If, however, we only had political cartoons and election campaign brochures to go by, the reliability and accuracy of the information may be up for debate because the source materials are only secondary sources of information and are likely to contain biases. Generally, the further back in history one researches, the fewer sources are available due to lack of documentation, technological limitations, and language barriers. With fewer sources, and possibly conflicting information, historians must put together the most reasonable explanation of what took place during the period in question, given the amount of information available to them.

## Types of Sources of Information Used in Historical Research

- **Almanacs**—books that are published each year to express current information for consideration in the coming year. These often act as time capsules for that particular year and can give historians insight into economic and technological details of the time.
- **Encyclopedias**—resources that cover a variety of topics broadly for the purpose of giving the reader an overview. Wikipedia is an internet-based version of an encyclopedia that is useful for finding leads or obtaining general information about a topic.
- **Bibliographies**—a list of resources used in composing a scholarly work. These are usually primary and secondary sources that can be used to check an author's sources or to give leads on similar research. Similar concepts include works-cited pages and literature reviews.
- **Periodical Guides**—a series of publications over time, usually in the form of magazines or journals. These usually broach a more specific category of information, such as on research methods, psychology, or medical procedures, and are intended to help members of a particular field stay up-to-date with current research in their field.
- **Biographical Dictionaries**—a resource that contains a list of important names to know about the given subject and a description of how they contributed to the field. For instance, if one were interested in the Revolutionary War, a biographical dictionary would include information on each of the founding fathers and other significant individuals of the time.
- **Maps**—representations of land and territories that can display a variety of factors, including geographical features, political features, economics, demographics, and many more aspects. Digital maps can generally be manipulated to show multiple features at once.

## Uses and Limitations of Various Historical Source Materials

Historical source materials are a type of primary source material that offer historians the opportunity to study people, places, and events that occurred in the past. Unfortunately, there are limitations to what these materials can tell us. A limitation of **historical source materials** is that they may be biased by those who created them. For example, those who create historical documents such as letters may leave out details or exaggerate parts in order to make their points more convincing. Another limitation might be that some historical sources only provide evidence for certain points of view, as they were recorded by those with specific interests and perspectives.

- An **oral history** provides an account of an event that happened in the past, which is told by the person who was there when it happened. Oral histories are important because they allow us to learn about things that may not be written in books or recorded in documents.
- **Newspapers** are important source materials for scholars because they provide a detailed account of the past, which cannot be found in books or other sources. Newspapers are not always reliable as they may not be based on fact, while others might omit certain information or give undue weight towards one side of an issue at the expense of another.
- **Diaries** and personal **journals** can provide valuable information for historians because they are detailed histories of people's lives. However, the reliability of these accounts is always in question because they were created by just one person and aren't always written with the intention of sharing.
- **Artifacts** can be defined as objects created by humans, which can give hints at the peoples' material culture and intangible culture. Material culture includes things like buildings or furniture while intangible culture includes things like music or dance. The benefits of artifacts are that they can offer insights into how people lived in the past. They can also be used to shed light on the thoughts, feelings, fears, tensions, customs, rituals, and other social practices at that time.
- **Tax lists** and **census data** are useful sources of insight into how people lived during a certain time. They provide us with reliable information about the income, demographics, and beliefs of the people living in a particular time.
- **Personal correspondence** has been an important form of historical information for historians. It gives an insight into the lives and interactions of ordinary people. The main benefits of using personal correspondence as a source for history is that it provides an authentic portrayal of the author's thoughts and feelings during a time period or in response to significant events.

## Historical Interpretation and Biases

History is a discipline that relies on the interpretation of **facts** to create **narratives**. Due to the types and availability of sources, history tends to leave itself open to **subjectivity**. Often, this means that **biases** are introduced at either the source of information, the interpretation of the information, or at the explanation of the information. For instance, if the only **sources of information** about an event are newspapers, the author of these historical sources may have been biased, causing the **interpretation** of the actual events to be skewed from the start. Similarly, the person interpreting the source may have their own biases that they introduce or even **teach** to others in the process of communicating the historical narrative. Commonly described biases in modern interpretation of history generally revolve around sociopolitical issues such as Eurocentrism, popular political parties, economic biases, and cultural favoritism.

## Historical Revisionism

Historical revisionism is the act of reinterpreting a historical account through established historical methodologies. This is often done when new information is discovered or old information is reinterpreted in such a way that it warrants reconsidering the previously accepted history of an event or period. Historical revisionism is an essential and necessary process in creating accurate histories. Revisionism can, sometimes, be used incorrectly and in a way that leads to a less accurate interpretation of historical events. An example of this would be when the historical record is denied or deliberately distorted. This can involve using falsified records, purposefully misrepresenting the meaning of a piece of historical evidence, manipulating statistics, or unjustly denying the validity of historical evidence. A common example of this is Holocaust denial, which is an antisemitic theory that the Holocaust was either fabricated or greatly exaggerated.

## Chapter Quiz

Ready to see how well you retained what you just read? Scan the QR code to go directly to the chapter quiz interface for this study guide. If you're using a computer, simply visit the online resources page at **mometrix.com/resources719/gacesegcelemed** and click the Chapter Quizzes link.

# Health, Physical Education, and the Arts

## Health and Physical Education Foundations

### Human Health and Wellness and Disease Prevention

Healthy development and disease prevention both begin before birth. Expecting mothers need to be informed about good nutrition and the supplemental nutrition required for prenatal support of developing embryos and fetuses. Mothers should also get sufficient but not overly strenuous exercise, avoid undue stress, find effective coping skills to deal with unavoidable life stressors, and avoid exposure to environmental toxins, such as radiation, pollution, and chemicals. They should avoid alcohol, tobacco, and exposure to secondhand smoke, as well as most drugs—street, over-the-counter, herbal, and prescription—unless they are prescribed by obstetricians/other physicians who are aware of the pregnancy. Babies initially need their mother's colostrum to provide immunity, and subsequently require breast milk or approved infant formula. Babies must also be held, cuddled, and given attention and affection to ensure survival, growth, and health. Young children need smaller amounts of food than adults that is equally as nutritious; sufficient exercise; adequate sleep; and cognitive, emotional, and social stimulation and interaction. Appropriate nutrition and exercise, avoidance of alcohol/tobacco/other drugs, and positive relationships and interactions are essential for wellness and disease prevention at all ages.

### 2009 American Recovery and Reinvestment Act

**The 2009 American Recovery and Reinvestment Act** has allotted $650 million for preventing chronic disease. To apply these funds, the US Department of Health and Human Services (HHS) has designed a comprehensive initiative entitled Communities Putting Prevention to Work. This initiative aims to create sustainable positive health changes in American communities, prevent or delay chronic disease, reduce disease risk factors, and promote child and adult wellness. Obesity and tobacco use, considered the foremost preventable sources of disability and death, are targeted by this initiative's evidence-based research programs and strategies, which are intended to reinforce state abilities and mobilize community resources. The initiative's central, $373-million community program includes support from the Centers for Disease Control and Prevention in selected communities for attaining the prevention outcomes of increasing physical activity levels, improving nutrition, reducing the incidence of obesity and higher than optimal body weights, decreasing tobacco use, and decreasing secondhand smoke exposure. Through this initiative, HHS hopes to produce effective models that can be reproduced in states and communities nationwide.

### Environmental Health Risks

Children's body systems, unlike those of mature adults, are still developing. They eat, drink, and breathe more in proportion to their body sizes than adults do. Typical child behaviors expose children to more potentially toxic chemicals and organisms. Therefore, children can be more vulnerable to environmental health risks. To protect children, adults can prohibit smoking in homes and cars; keep homes free of dust, mold, pet dander, and pests that can trigger allergies; avoid outdoor activities on high-pollution/"ozone alert" days; and carpool and/or use public transportation. Adults can prevent lead poisoning by only giving children cold water to drink and using cold water to prepare infant formula and cook food; washing bottles, pacifiers, and toys frequently; and protecting children from lead-based paints in older buildings. Adults must ensure children do not have access to toxic chemicals. Maintaining furnaces, chimneys, and appliances; using outdoor gas appliances and tools properly; refraining from using gas appliances and tools indoors; and installing approved CO alarms can all help prevent carbon monoxide poisoning. Choosing fish carefully can help prevent mercury toxicity. Keeping infants out of direct sunlight, using sun-protective clothing, and applying sunscreen on young children are also important.

## Federal Executive Order 13045

Passed by President Clinton, **Executive Order 13045** declares a policy for identifying and assessing environmental health and safety risks that affect children disproportionately, and for addressing these risks through the policies, standards, programs, and activities of every independent federal regulatory agency. This order defines environmental health and safety risks as those that can be attributed to substances children ingest or contact (e.g., air they breathe; food they eat; water they drink, bathe in, and swim in; soil they live upon; and products they are exposed to or use). The order established a task force reporting to the president and consulting with the Domestic Policy Council, the National Science and Technology Council, the Council on Environmental Quality, and the Office of Management and Budget. The task force is co-chaired by the HHS secretary and the EPA administrator. The task force oversees a coordinated, integrated federal research agenda and reports relevant research/data biennially; issues principle, policy, and priority statements; recommends appropriate federal/state/local/tribal government, nonprofit, and private sector partnerships; makes public outreach/communication proposals; identifies related high-priority initiatives; and evaluates new legislation to determine whether it will meet the goals of Executive Order 13045.

## Circulatory System

The **circulatory system** continuously supplies blood containing oxygen and nutrients to all body tissue cells, exchanges oxygenated blood for the waste products produced during the metabolism process, and transports waste for elimination. Central to the vascular (vessel) system is the heart, which is located in the mediastinum within the thoracic cavity. The heart is encased and protected by the pericardium, a double-walled, tough fibrous sac. The heart has four chambers: two atria and two ventricles. A system of valves regulates opening and closing among the chambers, the aorta, the pulmonary artery, and the great vessels. The aorta, originating at the heart, is the body's largest artery. The pulmonary artery branches to the left and to the right and transports venous blood from the heart's lower right chamber to the lung for oxygenation. The pulmonary veins return oxygenated blood from the lung to the left atrium of the heart. The superior and inferior venae cavae are vessels that empty into the heart's right atrium.

## Integumentary and Musculoskeletal Systems

In the human body, the **integumentary system** consists of skin, hair, nails, and oil and sweat glands. The skin has three layers: the epidermis, the dermis, and subcutaneous tissues. Skin protects tissues underneath it from bacterial infections, blocks most chemicals from entering, prevents fluid loss, and reduces the probability of mechanical injury to underlying body structures. Skin regulates body temperature and synthesizes needed chemicals. It is also a sense organ, as it has sensory receptors for touch, pressure, heat, and pain. It also contains motor fibers that enable necessary reactions to these sensations and stimuli. The **musculoskeletal system** includes bones, joints, and three types of connective tissues: tendons, ligaments, and cartilage. It is responsible for our body shape and provides stability and support. It also protects our internal organs and enables locomotion. Bones store calcium and other minerals, and bone marrow produces required blood cells. Muscle fibers contract to enable movement. Depending on their innervation, muscles can have voluntary or involuntary (like the heart) movements. Muscles need blood supply and oxygen to work. Thus, the musculoskeletal system depends on other systems, including the circulatory, nervous, and respiratory systems.

**Review Video: Integumentary System**
Visit mometrix.com/academy and enter code: 655980

**Review Video: Skeletal System**
Visit mometrix.com/academy and enter code: 256447

## Lymphatic System

The **lymphatic system** includes lymph (a fluid), collection ducts, and tissues. Lymphatic tissues comprise the lymph nodes, the thymus gland, the tonsils, and the Peyer's patches of the intestinal tract. Lymphoid components are also present in the lungs, the mucosa in the stomach and the appendix, and the bone marrow. Microscopic capillaries merge to form lymph-collecting ducts. These ducts drain to specific centers of lymphatic tissue. The lymph system's functioning is supported by the spleen and thymus glands. While not all characteristics and functions of the lymphatic system are established, known functions include: return transportation of lymph, protein, and microorganisms to the cardiovascular system; production of lymphocytes by the lymph nodes; filtering of the blood by the lymph nodes; production of antibodies to enable immune response against infection; absorption of fats and fat-soluble substances from the intestine; formation of blood cells in response to some illnesses/conditions; and phagocytosis (i.e., the surrounding/swallowing/"eating" of infectious particles by cells lining the sinuses of the lymph nodes, spleen, and liver). The lymph system defends the body against infection and supports the veins by helping to return fluids to the bloodstream.

## RESPIRATORY SYSTEM

The **respiratory system** provides oxygen to the body and removes carbon dioxide, the waste product of respiration (breathing). In doing so, the respiratory system and many other body systems work together through complex interactions. Twelve thoracic vertebrae, twelve pairs of ribs, the sternum, the diaphragm, and the intercostal muscles comprise the thoracic cage containing the lungs. As one breathes in and out, the thoracic cage is always moving. The diaphragm, a muscular wall dividing the chest cavity and abdominal cavity, functions as a bellows for breathing and also plays a role in expelling feces and delivering babies. There are air pathways between the nose/mouth, pharynx, trachea, bronchi, bronchioles, and lungs. Alveoli, tiny air sacs in the lungs, exchange oxygen and carbon dioxide. During inspiration/inhalation, the ribs and sternum rise, the diaphragm contracts and lowers, the intercostal muscles contract, air pressure in the lungs decreases, and air enters the lungs. During exhalation, the intercostal muscles and diaphragm relax, the ribs and sternum return to a resting position, air pressure in the lungs increases, and air exits the lungs.

**Review Video: Respiratory System**
Visit mometrix.com/academy and enter code: 783075

## THE BRAIN

The brain is divided into five major parts: the cerebrum, the midbrain, the cerebellum, the pons, and the medulla oblongata. The cranial nerves are:

| ID | Name | Function |
|---|---|---|
| I | Olfactory | Controls the sense of smell |
| II | Optic | Controls vision |
| III | Oculomotor | Controls the movements of the eye muscles, the movements of the upper eyelids, and the pupillary reflexes (expanding and contracting to admit more/less light) |
| IV | Trochlear | Controls the movements of the superior oblique eye muscles |
| V | Trigeminal | Controls facial sensation, the eye's corneal reflex, and chewing |
| VI | Abducens | Controls the movements of the lateral rectus eye muscle |
| VII | Facial | Controls movement of the facial muscles and the taste sensation in the front two-thirds of the tongue |
| VIII | Vestibulocochlear | Controls equilibrium (balance) via the vestibular system in the inner ear, and hearing (the cochlea is in the inner ear) |
| IX | Glossopharyngeal | Controls the taste sensation in the rear one-third of the tongue |
| X | Vagus | Controls pharyngeal contraction (gag reflex), vocal cord movements, and soft palate movements |
| XI | Spinal accessory | Controls movement of the sternocleidomastoid and trapezius muscles |
| XII | Hypoglossal | Controls tongue movements |

**Review Video: Brain Anatomy**
Visit mometrix.com/academy and enter code: 222476

## Central Nervous System

Some main functions of the **central nervous system** (i.e., the brain and spinal cord) include controlling consciousness and all mental processes, regulating the functions and movements of the body, and sending and receiving nerve impulses to and from all parts of the body. For example, when we touch something hot, sensory nerve endings in our fingers send impulses to the brain, which interprets them as heat and sends a signal along motor nerves to pull our fingers away. The autonomic nervous system is automatic and involuntary. For example, it makes our heart beat. We cannot voluntarily start or stop our heartbeat. The voluntary nervous system is under our conscious control. For example, our brains use it to send impulses to our skeletal muscles when we want to sit, stand, or walk, and those muscles contract in response. The autonomic nervous system is divided into parasympathetic and sympathetic components. The parasympathetic portion stimulates muscular activity in the organs and gland secretion. The sympathetic portion stimulates heartbeat, vasoconstriction, and sweating. These two portions of the autonomic nervous system oppose/balance each other to regulate the system.

## Digestive System

The chief functions of the **digestive system** are to provide nutrition to the body's cells and eliminate waste products left after nourishment is extracted from foods. The process consists of three phases: ingestion (taking in foods and liquids), digestion (converting ingested nutrients through physical and chemical means into forms that the cells of the body tissues can absorb and distribute), and elimination (removing the byproducts of digestion—also known as waste—that cannot be utilized). Other body systems work with the digestive system to process nutrients. For example, the nervous system plays a role in appetite, which is a signal for us to eat. The central nervous system also stimulates the release and flow of digestive juices. The endocrine system supplies chemicals (e.g., juices from the pancreas) that aid in digestion. The circulatory system delivers digested and absorbed nutrients to the tissue cells and also picks up waste products produced as a result of the metabolism process.

During chewing, the teeth and tongue physically break down food. Glands secrete saliva to provide lubrication during chewing and swallowing, and provide digestive enzymes to begin the process of chemically breaking down the foods we eat. The pharynx delivers food to the esophagus, where muscular contractions (peristalsis) move food downward. The epiglottis closes the trachea (windpipe) during swallowing to prevent food from being aspirated into the lungs. Glands in the stomach lining secrete gastric fluid comprised of hydrochloric acid and other chemicals, which dissolve food into semiliquid chyme. Chyme gradually passes into the small intestine, where most digestion and absorption occur. The small intestine is made up of the duodenum, the jejunum, and the ileum. The pancreas secretes digestive juices, the gallbladder secretes bile, and the intestinal mucosa secretes other juices into the duodenum to digest chyme. Digested nutrients are absorbed through the intestinal walls into capillaries and lymphatic vessels to be distributed to body cells. The large intestine consists of the cecum, the colon (ascending, transverse, descending, and sigmoid), the rectum, and the anus. The colon completes digestion and absorption and delivers wastes to the rectum, which eliminates them through the anus.

**Review Video: Gastrointestinal System**
Visit mometrix.com/academy and enter code: 378740

## Urinary System

The function of the **urinary system** is to eliminate the liquid wastes produced through nutrient metabolism by excreting them from the body. The urinary system is made up of two kidneys, two ureters, the bladder, and the urethra. Behind the abdominal cavity at the thoracolumbar level are the kidneys, a pair of large bean-shaped glands. They continually remove water, salts, toxins, and nitrogenous wastes from the bloodstream and convert these substances into urine. Urine droplets flow from the kidneys into the ureters. The ureters are long, narrow tubes carrying urine to the bladder, which is a hollow, muscular, elastic organ. When enough urine collects in the bladder, nerves stimulate the body to empty it via urination. In human females, the urethra is about an inch and a half long and is located in the upper vaginal wall. In males, the urethra is about eight inches long and extends from the bladder through the prostate gland and the penis. Both urine and sperm pass through the male urethra, while the female urethra and vaginal canal are separate.

**Review Video: Urinary System**
Visit mometrix.com/academy and enter code: 601053

## ENDOCRINE SYSTEM

The human **endocrine system** is one of the most complex body systems. Scientists understand many of its functions but not all of them. It is a system of ductless, internally secreting glands (some necessary to life) that extract various substances from tissue fluids and the bloodstream to create completely new substances (i.e., hormones). Operating without ducts, endocrine glands secrete hormones directly into the blood and lymph circulatory systems for distribution to the organs. The endocrine system's main glands include the pituitary, thyroid, parathyroid, and adrenal glands; the Islets of Langerhans in the pancreas; and the gonads (male testes and female ovaries). Additionally, the pancreas is both an endocrine and an exocrine gland. Its endocrine (internal secretion) function is to secrete insulin to regulate sugar metabolism; its exocrine (external secretion) function is to secrete pancreatic juice into the duodenum to aid in digestion. If the pancreas produces insufficient insulin, type 1 diabetes results. If the body responds insufficiently to insulin, type 2 diabetes results.

**Review Video: Endocrine System**
Visit mometrix.com/academy and enter code: 678939

### *PITUITARY, THYROID, AND PARATHYROID GLANDS*

The **pituitary and thyroid glands** are both components of the endocrine system. The pituitary gland functions directly by regulating physical growth, development, and sexual maturation in children and adolescents; regulating the retention and excretion of fluid; regulating the balance of electrolytes (sodium, potassium, and chloride) in blood and tissues; and regulating new mothers' lactation (milk production). The pituitary is termed the hypophyseal "master" gland because it also regulates all other glands in the endocrine system. Therefore, it is involved in regulating food assimilation and metabolism through hydrating the thyroid gland; regulating body composition, adaptation, and resistance to stress through acting on the adrenal and parathyroid glands; regulating breathing, circulation, digestion, urine excretion, and muscular action through the collective activity of multiple hormones; and regulating sexual development, activity, and reproduction through acting on the gonads. The thyroid gland manufactures and secretes hormones that regulate child growth and development, as well as certain metabolic processes and their rates. It also stores iodine. The **parathyroid glands** secrete hormones that regulate blood calcium levels, phosphorus metabolism, and muscle and nervous system excitation.

## REPRODUCTIVE SYSTEM

### *MALE*

The scrotum and the penis are the external reproductive organs of the human male. The internal organs of the male reproductive system include two testes, two epididymides, two seminal ducts, two seminal vesicles, two ejaculatory ducts, two spermatic cords, the urethra, the prostate gland, and several other glands. The testes, which are glandular organs, hang on either side of the scrotum from spermatic cords. These cords contain the vas deferens, blood vessels, and supportive tissues. Male sperm cells and hormones are produced by the testes. Each testis has an epididymis connecting it to the vas deferens, an excretory seminal duct. The vas deferens travels upward inside the spermatic cords to the prostate gland, which is in front of the neck of the urinary bladder. There, the vas deferens joins with the pouch-like glands called seminal vesicles to form ejaculatory ducts. The prostate gland and seminal vesicles secrete substances into the semen that promote sperm motility. The ejaculatory ducts release semen into the urethra, and from here, the semen is ejected through the penis during sexual intercourse.

### *FEMALE*

The external female reproductive organs include the mons pubis, the labia majora, the labia minora, the clitoris, the vestibule, the hymen, the Bartholin's glands, and several other glands. The breasts/mammary glands can also be considered parts of the reproductive system, as they produce milk for infants following reproduction. Internal organs include the vagina, the two fallopian tubes, the uterus, and the two ovaries. Hormones stimulate either ovary to produce an ovum/egg roughly once a month. A follicle containing an egg cell forms. When the egg matures, the follicle ruptures, releasing the egg. This is known as ovulation. The ovum passes into a fallopian tube and travels toward the uterus. Hormones have meanwhile also stimulated the endometrium (uterine lining) to thicken and increase its blood supply. When the egg reaches the womb, it is implanted in the endometrium if it was fertilized in the fallopian tube by a male sperm. This is known as conception. If the egg was not fertilized, hormone signals subside, causing the endometrium to detach from the uterine wall. The sloughed-off endometrial tissue, the resulting blood, and the unfertilized egg exit the body. This process is known as menstruation.

**Review Video: Reproductive Systems**
Visit mometrix.com/academy and enter code: 505450

## Physical, Emotional, and Social Factors on Personal Physical Health

The parts of the body, including the brain, are connected, related, interactive, and interdependent. As humans also interact and are interdependent with their environment, both internal and external factors influence their health. For example, physical factors like exposure to air pollution or radiation can cause illnesses like asthma, other lung diseases, and various cancers. Too much or too little nutrition can cause obesity and diabetes or malnutrition. Too much or too little exercise can cause exhaustion and injuries or weakness, diabetes, and cardiovascular and pulmonary problems. Not exercising enough may also be a factor in being overweight or obese. Diabetes itself causes many related health problems, including blindness, circulatory deficiencies, amputation, and cardiovascular disease. Water and/or sleep deprivation ultimately cause death. Emotional factors like depression, anxiety, and irritability can cause a host of health problems, including insomnia, overeating, anorexia, high blood pressure, and heart disease. Social factors include family influences. According to the family systems theory, dysfunctional family dynamics can cause a child to develop a physical illness. Whether the source is family, society outside the home, or both, stress is a social influence with multiple negative health impacts.

## Effect of Nutrition on Development

Children must consume a full range of nutrients for their brains to work normally. They need protein for its amino acids, which enable the brain's neurotransmitters (chemical messengers) to fire and communicate with each other. They need fruit and vegetable sugars and other complex carbohydrates to supply fuel to power the brain's functioning. Children's nutrition begins before birth. Pregnant women who do not eat adequate nutrients, vitamins, and minerals have higher risks of delivering infants with low birth weights. Research has found that babies with low birth weights are more likely to experience hearing and vision problems and to need special education services in school at some point. Children in school who consume insufficient amounts of protein have been found to score lower on achievement tests than their peers who are getting enough protein. Children with iron deficiencies display fatigue and ADHD-like symptoms, including impaired concentration, shortened attention spans, and irritability. Children who miss breakfast consistently perform slower on problem-solving tests than those who do not. Their responses are also less accurate. Children who regularly miss meals have compromised immunity against illnesses and infections, and they miss more school.

## Motor Skills

**Motor skills** are the large and small movements of the body. These movements include such things as pushing, pulling, lifting, and carrying larger objects using the legs, arms, and back, as well as picking up, grasping, and manipulating smaller objects using the hands and fingers. The former are gross motor skills, and the latter are fine motor skills. To develop these, children must make effective use of their mind-body connection (i.e., getting the muscles and bones to perform the movements the mind intends). They must also have developed spatial awareness (i.e., an accurate sense of the relationship between their bodies and the surrounding space and other bodies/objects). Teaching children to move large and small muscles in time to rhythmic songs helps develop motor skills. Teaching directions like up, down, clockwise, and counterclockwise helps with motor planning development. When children find motor skills challenging to master, educators must provide them with frequent instruction, adequate re-teaching, and ample modeling that allows them to observe and imitate problematic movements.

## Fine Motor Movements

**Fine motor movements** use small muscles in the eyes, lips, tongue, wrists, fingers, and toes. Fine/small motor movements work together with gross muscle movements to develop movement skills and patterns. Fine motor skills are often used for purposes of functional and expressive communication, like using tools, creating artworks, and writing and typing language. Eye-hand coordination, eye-foot coordination, and manual and finger dexterity are required for the fine motor movements used in drawing, writing, and typing. Fine motor practice also develops children's tactile (touch) awareness and spatial awareness. Rolling dough/putty/clay into balls and/or hiding things inside them promote fine motor skills. Tearing and cutting paper along dotted lines and creating patterns teach accurate size and shape perception and formation. Stringing, lacing, and creating structures using plastic building blocks develop hand-eye coordination and skills needed to create color patterns. Flip cards, pegs, and stickers promote object placement skills. Writing skills are developed by writing letters/numbers in shaving cream, sand, pudding, and/or on chalkboards using wet makeup sponges/cotton swabs; using toothbrushes on dry erase boards; and practicing placement on cardboard using rice, beans, pasta or glitter.

## Gross Motor Skills

Sitting, standing, crawling, walking, running, galloping, jumping, catching, throwing, and kicking use **gross motor skills**. Activities that help young children develop their gross motor skills include standing on dots/marks on the floor; crawling under and climbing over things, including objects that are part of obstacle courses; and balancing on balance beams. These develop body control, coordination, laterality (using the left/right sides of the body separately), and synchronization of the body's left and right sides. Children develop body control and balance through hopping around objects. They develop coordination and overall gross motor skills through jumping over things like boxes, beanbags, lines, and strings and by kicking objects like balls and balloons of various sizes. Walking and running around, through, and/or over obstacles like tires and hoops and/or participating in relays develop gross motor skills. Organized games involving skipping around things to music with various rhythms, and activities requiring twisting, turning, and bending all develop gross motor skills, preparing children for lifelong engagement in sports activities.

## Newborn/Infant Motor Reflexes and Skills

Newborns exhibit the tonic reflex, adopting the "fencing position." In this position, the head is turned to one side, the arm on that side is in front of the eyes, and the other arm is flexed. This normally disappears by the time an infant is around four months old. It may serve as preparation for reaching voluntarily for things/people. The stepping reflex disappears at around two months of age, and prepares babies for walking voluntarily. The palmar grasping reflex on an adult finger disappears by the time an infant is around three to four months old, and prepares babies for grasping voluntarily. When held upright, a baby can typically hold his/her head steady and erect by about six weeks of age on average. About 90 percent of infants will develop this skill between the ages of three weeks and four months. Babies lift up from the prone position using their arms by the time they are about two months old. About 90 percent of infants will develop this skill between the ages of three weeks and four months. Babies can also roll from side to back by the time they are about two months old. About 90 percent of infants will develop this skill between the ages of three weeks and five months. An infant can grasp a cube by the age of three months and three weeks on average. About 90 percent of infants will develop this skill between the ages of two and seven months.

## Infant Motor Skills Milestones

By four and a half months on average, babies can roll from back to side. The range within which 90 percent of infants will be able to do this is two to seven months. Most babies can sit unsupported by seven months on average. The range within which 90 percent of infants will be able to do this is five to nine months. Most infants also crawl by seven months on average. The range within which 90 percent of infants will be able to do this is five to eleven months. Babies pull themselves up to a standing position by around eight months on average. The range within which 90 percent of infants will be able to do this is five to twelve months. Babies play "patty-cake" by nine months, three weeks on average. The range within which 90 percent of infants will be able to do this is seven to fifteen months. Babies/toddlers can stand alone by 11 months on average. The range within which 90 percent of infants will be able to do this is 9 to 16 months. Toddlers can walk unassisted by the age of 11 months, 3 weeks on average. The range within which 90 percent of infants will be able to do this is 9 to 17 months. Children can stack two cubes by the age of 13 months, 3 weeks on average. The range within which 90 percent of infants will be able to do this is 10 to 19 months. They scribble energetically by the age of 14 months on average. The range within which 90 percent of infants will be able to do this is 10 to 21 months. They can climb stairs with assistance by the age of 16 months on average. The range within which 90 percent of infants will be able to do this is 12 to 23 months. Normally developing children can typically can jump in place by the age of 23 months, 2 weeks on average. The range within which 90 percent of infants will be able to do this is 17 to 30 months.

## Salient Aspects of Typical Early Childhood Physical Development

Early childhood physical growth, while significant, is slower than infant growth. From birth to 2 years, children generally grow to four times their newborn weight and 2/3 their newborn length and height. From 2–3 years, however, children usually gain only about 4 lb. and 3.5 inches. From 4–6 years, growth slows more; gains of 5–7 lb. and 2.5 inches are typical. Due to slowing growth rates, 3- and 4-year-olds appear to eat less food but do not; they actually just eat fewer calories per pound of body weight. Brain growth is still rapid in preschoolers: brains attain 55 percent of adult size by 2 years, and 90 percent by 6 years. The majority of brain growth is usually by 4–4.5 years, with a growth spurt around 2 years and growth rates slowing significantly between 5 and 6 years. Larger brain size indicates not more neurons but larger sizes, differences in their organization, more glial cells nourishing and supporting neurons, and greater myelination (development of the sheath protecting nerve fibers and facilitating their efficient intercommunication).

## Nature-Nurture Interaction in Early Childhood Physical Development

The physical development of babies and young children is a product of the interactions between genetic and environmental factors. Also, a child's physical progress is equally influenced by environmental and psychological variables. For the body, brain, and nervous system to grow and develop normally, children must live in healthy environments. When the interaction of hereditary and environmental influences is not healthful, this is frequently reflected in abnormal patterns of growth. Failure to thrive syndrome is a dramatic example. When children are abused or neglected for long periods of time, they actually stop growing. The social environments of such children create psychological stress. This stress makes the child's pituitary gland stop releasing growth hormones, and growth ceases. When such environmental stress is relieved and these children are given proper care, stimulation, and affection, they begin growing again. They often grow rapidly enough to catch up on the growth they missed earlier. Normal body and brain growth—as well as psychological development—depend upon the collaboration of nature and nurture.

## Signs of Progress in Typical Motor Development

Genetics, physiological maturation, nutrition, and experience through practice combine to further preschoolers' motor skills development. Newborns' reflexive behaviors progress to preschoolers' voluntary activities. Also, children's perception of the size, shape, and position of the body and body parts becomes more accurate by preschool ages. In addition, increases in bilateral coordination of the body's two sides enhance preschoolers' motor skills. Motor skills development entails both learning new movements and gradually integrating previously learned movements into smooth, continuous patterns, as in learning to throw a ball with skill. Both large muscles (for gross-motor skills like climbing, running, and jumping) and small muscles (for fine-motor skills like drawing and tying knots) develop. Eye-hand coordination involves fine-motor control. Preschoolers use visual feedback, seeing whether they are making things go where and do what they want them to, in learning to manipulate small objects with their hands and fingers.

## Gender Differences in Motor Development

On average, preschool boys have larger muscles than preschool girls, so they can run faster, climb higher, and jump farther. Boys at these ages tend to be more muscular physically. Preschool girls, while less muscular, are on the average more mature physically for their ages than boys. While boys usually exceed girls in their large-muscle, gross-motor abilities like running, jumping, and climbing, girls tend to surpass boys in small-muscle, fine-motor abilities like buttoning buttons, using scissors, and similar activities involving the manipulation of small tools, utensils, and objects. While preschool boys exhibit more strength in large-muscle, gross-motor actions, preschool girls are more advanced than preschool boys in large-muscle, gross-motor skills that do not demand strength so much as coordination, like hopping, balancing on one foot, and skipping. While these specific gender differences in preschoolers' physical and motor development have been observed consistently in research, it is also found that preschool girls' and boys' physical and motor development patterns are generally more similar than different overall.

## Cephalocaudal and Proximodistal Development

Infant and child motor development follows the same developmental sequences as prenatal embryonic and fetal physical development. **Cephalocaudal** means head to tail. Just as the body develops from the head down before birth, babies and young children develop motor control of their heads before they develop control of their legs. **Proximodistal** means near to far (i.e., central to distant). Head, torso, and arm control develop prior to hand and finger control. Babies learn a lot about how things look, sound, and feel once they master gross motor skills for reaching and grasping. These then evolve toward fine motor skills. For example, at around three months of age, an infant's voluntary reaching gradually becomes more accurate. The infant will not need arm guidance, because he or she has spatial awareness of location and motion. Babies reach less by five months when they can move things within reach. By nine months, babies can redirect reaching to grasp objects moving in different directions. By six to twelve months, development of the pincer grasp enhances babies' capacities for object manipulation.

## Motor Skills Developing Between Ages 2 and 6

Children develop motor skills most quickly between the ages of two and six years. They demonstrate basic locomotion skills, first walking and then running, skipping, hopping, galloping, and jumping. They also develop ball-handling skills, fine motor eye-hand coordination, and—as an extension of previously developed creeping skills—climbing skills. By two years of age, children develop balance for basic kicking, which evolves into the ability to execute full kicks (including backswings) by six years of age. They try throwing by two to three years of age. They develop related skills—including taking a forward step—by the age of six. They develop the ability to shuffle by three years of age, which develops into the ability to skip by six years of age. By the age of three, children walk automatically. They try running, but they are clumsy and lack adequate control. This ability improves by between four and five years of age. By this time, children are also more skilled at executing starts, stops, and turns. By the age of five or six, children can run like adults. They develop climbing skills (ladders, etc.) between the ages of three and six. The ability to jump longer distances and hopping and galloping skills develop by age six. Children can catch a large ball while holding their arm straight by the age of three. They can catch a ball while holding their elbows out to the front by age four, and they can do this while holding their elbows at their sides by age six.

## How Cooking and Self-Care Activities Help Develop Fine Motor Skills

Young children are often fascinated by adults' cooking activities, want to participate, and offer to help. Involving them is not only beneficial to their self-esteem but also develops various skills. Measuring amounts of liquids and solids in different forms develops children's math skills. Mixing, stirring, and blending ingredients using different parts of their hands develop children's fine motor skills. Life skills include self-care skills, such as combing one's hair, brushing one's teeth, fastening and unfastening buttons and snaps on clothing, and lacing and unlacing shoes. Life skills also require being able to open and close drawers, doors, and jars; to clean a house; and to wash things. It is necessary to children's normal development that they learn to combine multiple fine motor skills. Children's development of fine motor skills also needs to be integrated with the development of various self-care and other life skills (such as those described above) that are required for normal activities of daily living.

## BENEFITS OF PHYSICAL ACTIVITY

When young children engage in physical activity, they learn new motor skills and reinforce, advance, and refine existing ones. They also learn important early math skills like spatial awareness. Whenever they attempt new activities, they encounter challenges, such as having to develop higher levels of coordination, control, precision, strength, speed, flexibility, and agility. They are also challenged to coordinate their mental and physical processes more closely and in a manner that is more complex. They learn to exert effort and to persevere in the face of difficulty. When they succeed at meeting these challenges, their self-esteem and self-efficacy (sense of competence to perform tasks) are enhanced. Since motor skills generally develop ahead of language skills, physical activity is a valuable means of direct self-expression. Young children learn many social skills through interacting with peers and adults during physical games, sports activities, etc. In addition to all these benefits, young children normally seek out physical activity, deriving a great deal of fun and enjoyment through moving, playing games/sports, and interacting physically with others.

## NATIONAL PHYSICAL EDUCATION STANDARDS

The National Association for Sport and Physical Education (NASPE) has developed six national physical education standards. These standards state that someone who is physically educated:

1. Shows the motor skills and patterns of movement competencies s/he needs to conduct various physical activities
2. Shows comprehension of the basic concepts, main principles, methods, and techniques of movement as they relate to learning and executing physical activities
3. Regularly engages in physical activity
4. Reaches and sustains a level of physical fitness that enhances health
5. Demonstrates behaviors, personally and socially, that reflect self-respect and respect for others within contexts of physical activity
6. Places value upon the benefits of physical activities and of being fit and active, such as the pleasure; the improvement and maintenance of health; the physical, personal, and social challenges; and the opportunities to interact socially and express oneself

## PHYSICAL, EMOTIONAL, AND SOCIAL FACTORS

Young children who have already become overweight/obese because of an improper diet and lack of exercise are more likely than children who are within a healthy weight range to find physical activity uncomfortable and avoid it. Even those who enjoy activity are more at risk of injury if they are overweight or lack physical conditioning. Exercise is more challenging for children with illnesses. For example, asthma interferes with breathing. Therefore, asthmatic children must be supervised and monitored when exercising. So must diabetic children, whose blood sugar can fluctuate excessively due to exercising. Their food intake must be monitored and coordinated with exercise. Children with physical disabilities may require adaptive equipment and/or alternative methods of physical instruction and exercising. Emotionally, children experiencing depression are likely to be apathetic and uninterested in movement. Hyperactive children (e.g., those with ADHD) are often overactive physically to the point of exhaustion. Children lacking adequate social skills, friends, and/or peer groups have fewer opportunities and are less likely to engage in physical games and sports with others, so their motor skills and physical fitness may suffer.

## AMOUNTS AND PROPORTIONS OF ENGAGEMENT IN PHYSICAL ACTIVITY

The **World Health Organization** (WHO) advises that children between the ages of 5 and 17 should engage in a minimum of 1 hour (continuously or incrementally) of moderate to vigorous physical activity per day.

According to the WHO, exercising for more than one hour daily (within reason) will confer additional health benefits. The majority of children's physical activity should be aerobic in nature. Aerobic exercise uses large muscle groups, is rhythmic and continuous, and works the heart and lungs so that the pulmonary and cardiovascular systems become more efficient at absorbing and transporting oxygen. Children should take part in exercises and/or activities that strengthen the muscles and bones through weight-bearing and other methods at least three times per week. Children's play activities that can fulfill bone-strengthening requirements include running, jumping, turning, and playing various games. Engaging in general play, playing games, playing sports, doing chores, using exercise as a means of transportation (e.g., walking, biking, etc.), participating in planned exercise sessions, and attending physical education classes are all activities available in family, community, and school settings that can allow children to meet physical activity and fitness requirements.

# Fine Arts Foundations and Creativity

## Learning Outcomes Achieved Through Visual Arts

The arts are just as important to include in curricula as language, math, science, social studies, health, and physical education. Early learning standards in many states now reflect the goal to integrate the arts into the overall curriculum. Teachers need to provide young children with activities that promote development of fine motor skills, exploration of art materials and processes, and symbolic representation of concepts through artworks. Early childhood educators should not merely assign isolated art activities. They can clarify many concepts and improve learning by providing art projects that fit into the overall curriculum and are relevant to individual learning units. Teachers should develop detailed, well-organized step lists for each activity. Clear directions not only maintain classroom order but also provide children with a structure within which to experiment with art and enhance their sequencing skills. Teachers should use process-oriented activities, both on their own and within lessons that require products. For example, painting pictures of animals combines product (representing an animal) with process (exploring paint use). Teachers should supply and explain rules/steps for process activities that explore the use of art materials and processes.

### *Viktor Lowenfeld*

**Viktor Lowenfeld** (1903–1960) taught art to elementary school students and sculpture to blind students. Lowenfeld's acquaintance with Sigmund Freud, who was interested in his work with people with visual impairments, motivated Lowenfeld to pursue scientific research. He published several books on using creative arts activities therapeutically. Lowenfeld was familiar with six stages previously identified in the growth of art. He combined these with principles of human development drawn from the school of psychoanalytic psychology founded by Freud. In his adaptation, he named the six stages reflecting the development of children's art as scribble, preschematic, schematic, dawning realism, pseudorealistic, and period of decision. Lowenfeld identified adolescent learning styles as haptic, focused on physical sensations and subjective emotional experiences, and as visual, focused on appearances, each demanding corresponding instructional approaches. Lowenfeld's book *Creative and Mental Growth* (1947) was the most influential text in art education during the later 20th century. Lowenfeld's psychological emphasis in this text gave scientific foundations to creative and artistic expression and identified developmentally age-appropriate art media and activities.

## STAGES OF GROWTH AND DEVELOPMENT IN ART

Austrian and German art scholars established six stages in art.

1. **Scribble stage:** from 2–4 years, children first make uncontrolled scribbles, then controlled scribbling, then progress to naming their scribbles to indicate what they represent.
2. **Preschematic stage:** From ages 4–6, children begin to develop a visual schema. Schema, meaning mental representation, comes from Piaget's cognitive-developmental theory. Without complete comprehension of dimensions and sizes, children may draw people and houses the same height; they use color more emotionally than logically. They may omit or exaggerate facial features, or they might draw sizes by importance (e.g., drawing themselves as largest among people or drawing the most important feature, such as the head, as the largest or only body part).
3. **Schematic stage:** from 7–9 years, drawings more reflect actual physical proportions and colors.
4. **Dawning realism:** from ages 9–11, drawings become increasingly representational.
5. **Pseudorealistic stage:** from ages 11–13, children reflect their ability to reason.
6. **Period of decision stage:** children ages 14+ reflect the adolescent identity crisis.

## CHARACTERISTICS IN ART REFLECTING DEVELOPMENT

Observations of young children find that while a 2½-year-old can grasp a crayon and scribble with it, by the age of 4 years, he or she can draw a picture we recognize as human. The typical 4-year-old drawing of a human being is called the "tadpole person" because it has no body, a large head, and stick limbs. Between the ages of 3 and 4 years, children typically make a transition from scribbling to producing tadpole person drawings. This development is enabled by greater development in motor control and eye-hand coordination, among other variables. Between the ages of 4 and 5 years, children make another transition by progressing from drawing tadpole persons to drawing complete figures with heads and bodies. Howard Gardner, psychologist and author of the theory of multiple intelligences, stated that children achieve a "summit of artistry" by the end of their preschool years. He describes their drawings as "characteristically colorful, balanced, rhythmic, and expressive, conveying something of the range and...vitality associated with artistic mastery." (1980)

## PLANNING ART ACTIVITIES OR PROJECTS

Early childhood teachers should first establish the concept they want to teach, the objectives they want to meet through planning and teaching the lesson/activity, and the learning objectives they want the children to meet through participating. Then, a teacher can construct a simple prototype for the project. This enables the teacher to estimate how long it will take the children to complete the activity and to explore and discover the optimal sequencing of steps for the activity. The teacher should then write down the plan, step-by-step. Steps should include those that need to be completed before the activity. These might include preliminary discussion, book reading/sharing related to the project, viewing related artworks and/or photos, etc. Steps should also include those that need to be completed while setting up the activity, such as dispensing paints and clay, assembling paintbrushes/other instruments, and passing out paper and other materials. Teachers do not need to be artistically proficient. Young children are not art critics, and teachers can find a great deal of information about art materials and processes by reading books and searching online. Available professional development courses focusing on art can also give teachers more ideas for lesson plans.

**Review Video: Learning Objectives**
Visit mometrix.com/academy and enter code: 528458

## Functions of Art

### Social Functions

Artworks can be created for physical, social, and personal purposes. When art focuses on the social lives of groups rather than on one individual's experiences or viewpoint, it serves social functions. Art carrying political stances/messages always performs social functions. Dadaist Oppenheim's hair-covered tea set did not perform any physical function but served social functions by politically protesting World War I and many other social/political issues. During the Great Depression, photographers like Dorothea Lange, Gordon Parks, Walker Evans, and Arthur Rothstein, commissioned by the Farm Security Administration, produced stark records of people's suffering. These depictions of social conditions also served social functions. Fine artists like Francisco Goya and William Hogarth, as well as cartoonists like Thomas Nast and Charles Bragg, created satirical works of art lampooning various social and political customs and situations. Satire is intended not only to provide comic relief, insight, and perspective but also to stimulate social change. Therefore, it serves social functions. Another social function is improving community status and pride through art treasures.

### Physical Functions

Ascertaining the function of a work of art requires considering its context. Half of the context involves the artist. Knowing the artist's country, the historical time period during which the artist lived, and the social and political culture of the time informs artwork and our ability to infer what the artist was thinking and intending when he or she was creating it. The other half of the context involves the viewer. Knowing what the artwork means to you in your own place and time informs your perception of and response to it. Taken within context, art serves physical, personal, and social functions. For example, architecture, industrial design, and crafts have physical functions. A raku pottery bowl made in Japan serves a physical function during a tea ceremony. However, a teacup covered with hair (paired with a hair-covered saucer and spoon) by Dada artist Meret Oppenheim (1936) makes an artistic statement but serves no physical function. When we view a tribal war club in a museum, regardless of the exquisite craftsmanship it may demonstrate, we realize it was made primarily for bludgeoning enemies.

### Personal Functions

Works of art can have physical, social, and personal functions. Of these three, the personal functions of art are the most variable. Artists' motivations to create works include the desire to express their feelings and ideas, to obtain gratification through producing art, to communicate messages to viewers, to enable both themselves and their viewers to have an aesthetic experience, and to simply entertain viewers. Some artists also claim that they sometimes create art for no particular reason and that the art produced has no meaning. Art can perform a personal function of control. For example, some artists use their work to give order to the world's apparent chaos. Others use art to create chaos in an overly orderly, boring environment. Art can be therapeutic for both artists and viewers. Much art has served the personal function of religion. Artworks with biological purposes, like cultural fertility symbols or bodily decorations designed to attract mates for procreation, are also examples of the personal functions of art.

## Learning Objectives

When children participate in teacher-designed art activities, they can fulfill learning objectives such as exploring various art materials and processes; developing awareness of visual art and its basic elements (e.g., line, shape, color, and texture); using art forms to represent feelings, thoughts, and/or stories; developing the skills of color recognition and discrimination; and even building their vocabularies and language skills, depending on the activities. Teachers can integrate such objectives with an overall theme for each art activity/project that they integrate with the current theme for their lesson or curriculum unit. For example, if space travel is the class theme one week, constructing model rocket ships is more appropriate than painting self-portraits. Even open-ended activities to explore art materials and processes can be integrated with thematic units. For example, teachers can apply activities exploring cutting and gluing processes to a theme of one specific color by providing various materials and textures that are all the same color. In this way, teachers can connect a learning concept to experimentation with artistic processes.

## Creating, Performing, and Responding

Three processes common to all branches of the arts—visual, musical, dance, dramatic, and performance art—are **creating**, **performing**, and **responding**. The first of these, creating, involves the genesis of the artistic product.

There are several steps in creating:

- **Imagining** is the step during which the artist develops his or her ideas and considers the concepts and feelings which he or she wants to communicate and express through the work.
- **Planning** is the step during which the artist researches, experiments with, and designs the means by which he or she will present ideas and emotions (e.g., the materials that will be used and how they will be manipulated to produce the desired effects).
- **Making, evaluating, and refining** is the step during which the artist applies his or her skills and various techniques to create an artistic product that will bring his or her ideas and feelings to life.
- **Presenting** is the step during which the artist exhibits visual art in a gallery, private exhibit, or another type of showing. The artist might also perform music, dance, theater, or performance art for an audience so that others can participate in and respond to the artwork.

## Processes Involved in the Production and Reception of Works of Art

In all branches of the arts, artists and their audiences (who may also be participants in the case of performance art) complete three basic artistic processes that are closely related: creation, performance, and response.

The performance process includes five steps:

- **Selecting** is the step during which the artist makes a choice about what to present. For example, musicians choose pieces to play. Dancers choose choreographic pieces to perform. Visual artists select which of their paintings, drawings, sculptures, and mobiles/stabiles to display. Theater producers, directors, and actors choose a play to perform.
- **Analyzing** is the step during which the performer researches the background of the chosen work and analyzes its structure to understand it and its import.
- **Interpreting** is the step during which the performer develops a personal idea about what the work should express or accomplish.
- **Rehearsing, evaluating, and refining** is the step during which the performer applies his or her skills and techniques to develop a personal interpretation that will enable his or her performance to make the work come alive. The artist then evaluates the performance and makes further refinements to subsequent presentations.
- **Presenting** is the final step, during which the artist performs the work for others.

## Fundamental Artistic Processes Common to All Branches of the Arts

The artistic process of responding to artwork includes four steps:

- **Selection** is the step during which the person(s) who will receive the artwork choose what they want to experience (possible choices include attending a gallery exhibit of paintings, drawings, or sculptures; going to see a theatrical play or a movie; attending a dance performance; attending/participating in a performance art show; or reading a book of poetry or prose).

- **Analysis** is the step during which the viewers, audience, participants, or readers see/hear and understand the components of the work and mentally bring these components together to perceive the work as a whole.
- **Interpretation** is the step during which those experiencing the work and/or its performance construct meaning from what they have witnessed, developing a personal response to the creator(s)' and performer(s)' expressions of concepts and emotions.
- **Evaluation** is the final step, during which the respondent(s) assess the quality of the artwork and of its performance.

## Facilitating Student Learning with Creating, Performing, and Responding

The artistic processes have many steps in common. This interrelatedness among the processes informs students' development of educated responses to artworks. For instance, when students learn the step of evaluating their own artworks, they learn to apply better critical approaches when interpreting the artworks created by others. They also use their experiences to direct their selection of works they want to witness and respond to in the future. When students learn how to evaluate and refine their own work, this facilitates their subsequent evaluation and selection of others' works to watch, to perform themselves, and/or to purchase. Teachers can promote this by encouraging students to transfer their learning from one artistic process to another. For example, teachers can introduce students to others' work while they are creating their own so they can transfer what they learn about the creation process to the responding process. When students are solving specific creative/artistic problems, teachers can expose them to other artists' solutions and encourage students to consider these solutions.

## Lines

In visual media, a line is the path of a moving point, the edge of a flat or two-dimensional shape, or the outline of a solid, three-dimensional object. Lines are longer than they are wide. The term *measure* refers to the width of a line. Lines can be straight, curved, wavy, angular, or zigzag. Lines can be horizontal (side to side), vertical (up and down), or diagonal (at an angle between vertical and horizontal). Lines can also be implied. In this case, they are not physically present, but the artist's arrangement of other elements suggests lines, which organize the picture and/or guide viewers' eyes. The movement a line follows/appears to show is called direction. Where and how a line is placed in a picture/design is called location. Lines define areas and imply or create open or closed shapes like circles, rectangles, etc. Lines combined with shapes create implied volume in paintings/drawings and actual volume in sculptures. Lines express various qualities by being jagged, loopy, bold, repetitive, etc., and evoke different emotional and mental viewer responses.

## Shape, Form, and Value

Shape refers to two-dimensional areas created by connecting lines to outline the contours of objects depicted in art. Shapes can be positive or negative (i.e., defined not by their own outlines but by the edges of surrounding shapes). Shapes may be biomorphic (i.e., shapes found in nature) or geometric. Variations in value, texture, or color can make shapes stand out in a piece. Form is the three-dimensional projection of shape. Form has dimension and volume. In paintings and drawings, form appears to have mass, while in sculptures, it actually does have mass. The term *form* can also be used to describe an artwork's overall structure. Value refers to the appearance and range of lights and darks seen in a visual work of art. Regardless of color, value varies between black and white, with an indefinite range of various shades of gray between these two absolutes.

## Texture and Space

Texture refers to how rough or smooth a surface appears or feels. Everyday materials have texture, as do works of art. An object or a work of art can look and/or feel spongy or glassy, wet or dry, soft or hard, etc. Texture can be real, as with sandpaper and other rough-textured materials used to create works of art, or it can be illusory, as when materials appear hard or soft but are really not. Space is defined as the measurable distance between predetermined points. It can be shallow or limited, with a foreground and a background, or it can be deep or extended, with a middle ground as well as a foreground and a background. Two-dimensional space has height and width; three-dimensional space has height and width, plus volume and time. Like negative shape (shape that is not defined by its own outlines but by the surrounding shapes and their outlines), negative space appears in art. It is the space around and between the positive objects or shapes depicted. This negative space forms its own shapes around positive subjects.

## Rhythm

In visual art, rhythm is achieved through repeating visual movement. Visual movement is created by arranging lines, shapes, and/or colors to give the viewer's eye a sense of motion and direction. Just as we hear rhythm in music through aural beats and varying note durations, we see rhythm in paintings through visual movement of lines, angles, shapes, and other elements. Just as Beethoven used repetition of musical phrases and themes to create mood, drama, and movement, artists use movement and repetition to create visual rhythm. For example, in "Nude Descending a Staircase, No. 2" (1912) by Marcel Duchamp, the artist depicts an abstracted human figure, repeating the figure using overlapping placements in a diagonal, downward pattern. The series of repeated shapes and angles gives the impression of viewing action in strobe lighting or via stop-action photography. The figures are physically still but visually convey the effect of moving down a staircase. By directionally repeating the figure, Duchamp shows movement and rhythm within the static medium of a painting.

## Color

Color refers to the wavelengths of light reflected by a surface. Some wavelengths are absorbed by paints and other visual art media/materials; we do not see these. Other wavelengths are reflected; these are the ones we see as colors. Primary colors are pure, individual colors that cannot be separated into other colors or produced by mixing colors. The three primary colors are red, blue, and yellow. Secondary colors are combinations of two primary colors (e.g., orange = red + yellow, green = blue + yellow, and violet = red + blue). Intermediate colors are produced by mixing a primary and a secondary color (e.g., red-orange, yellow-orange, blue-green, yellow-green, blue-violet, or red-violet). Colors are arranged on the color wheel. Analogous colors are adjacent to each other on the wheel. Examples of analogous colors include yellow and orange, orange and red, blue and green, and green and yellow. Complementary colors are opposite each other on the color wheel. Examples of complementary colors include blue and orange, yellow and purple, and red and green. Mixing equal parts of two complementary colors produces brown. Blue and predominantly blue colors are cool. Red, yellow, and predominantly red/yellow colors are warm. Colors identify objects, evoke moods, and influence emotions.

## Balance

Balance refers to how visual weight is distributed in a work of visual art. In two-dimensional art like paintings, balance is the visual equilibrium among the painting's elements, which makes the entire picture look balanced. Balance can be symmetrical (both sides are equal) or asymmetrical, with shapes and spaces that are unequal and/or unevenly distributed. This produces psychological rather than physical balance, creating tension and suggesting movement. Radial balance/symmetry uses images radiating from a center, such as wheel spokes or ripples around a pebble thrown into water. An example of balance is seen in the painting "Dressing for the Carnival" (1877) by Winslow Homer. The central figure of a carnival performer putting on his costume is the focal point. The performer is surrounded by two adult assistants and a group of fascinated children who are watching him. The shapes, values, and colors are balanced to produce overall visual equilibrium and unity (another organizing principle of art).

## Visual Movement

Artists create a visual sense of movement in paintings to direct the viewer's eyes. Direction is frequently toward a focal point or area within the painting. Artists can direct movement along lines, edges, shapes, and colors, but especially along parts with equal value (dark/light), which best facilitates the eyes' movement. For example, in "Liberation of the Peon" (1931), Diego Rivera depicts soldiers liberating a slave by cutting the ropes binding him while clothing his nakedness with a blanket or garment. Paths of movement in the painting all lead to the focal point of the knife cutting the ropes. (Emphasis, another art/design principle, is also seen in how the action of freeing the peon is made more important than the soldiers performing that action.) By painting all humans in the scene with their eyes focused on the slave, Rivera creates movement directing our view toward him. At the same time, he painted all horses with their eyes focused out at the viewer, drawing the viewer into the scene.

## Using Emphasis

Artists use the design principle of emphasis to call attention to particular elements in their works. Emphasis directs the viewer's focus to certain parts of a painting and makes certain components of a work dominant. Emphasis can be achieved in art by emphasizing various design elements like value (light/dark), color, shape, line, etc. Artists also use contrast (e.g., contrasting values, colors, shapes, etc.) to create emphasis. To emphasize a focal area, a center of interest that focuses on the most important part of a painting, an artist can create visual emphasis through extreme contrasts of light and dark values. Strongly contrasting shapes and/or marked contrasts in other design elements also create visual emphasis. As an example of visual emphasis, in the painting "At the Moulin Rouge" (1892/1895), Henri de Toulouse-Lautrec emphasizes the focal area of a group of friends conversing in a cabaret through contrasting colors and values, as well as through movement directing the eye toward the group. His use of color, light, and shape also help create the scene's atmosphere.

## Unity

One of the most important characteristics of a well-developed work of visual art is its visual unity. When we view a painting without unity, we may see a collection of disconnected parts that do not come together to form a whole. We may perceive it as fragmentary, disorganized, and incomplete. When an artist achieves visual unity, all of the elements in a painting appear to belong together. Unity affords paintings the quality of cohesion that makes them look and feel finished and complete. For example, in the painting "Starry Night" (1889), Vincent van Gogh used his characteristic large, visible brush strokes in a swirly pattern throughout the landscape, providing visual unity through the texture, rhythm, pattern, and movement of the lines and shapes. He used predominantly cool colors (blues and bluish browns), providing unity through color. (He also provided emphasis by adding contrasting yellow stars.) The result is a unified painting whose elements work together, strongly conveying the atmosphere, mood, emotion, and story that the artist wanted to express.

## Contrast

Contrast refers to significant differences in the values (lights and darks), colors, textures, shapes, lines, and other elements of visual artworks. Visual contrast creates interest and excitement and avoids monotony in art. For example, in the painting "Still Life with Apples and Peaches" (1905), Paul Cézanne combined all seven elements and all seven principles of design to create a unified composition. Among these, he used at least eight kinds of contrast:

- Unpatterned vs. intricately patterned surfaces (pattern contrast)
- Soft vs. hard/found edges (edge contrast)
- Dark vs. light vs. middle values (value contrast)
- Pure vs. muted/blended colors (intensity contrast)
- Cool vs. warm colors (temperature contrast)
- Textured vs. smooth surfaces (texture contrast)
- Organic vs. geometric shapes (shape contrast)
- Large vs. small objects/shapes (size contrast)

## Pattern

Pattern is the organized or random repetition of elements. Music is made up of sound patterns. Visual patterns often appear in nature. Artists frequently create works featuring repeated designs that produce patterns inspired by those seen in the natural world. Visual art is enhanced by pattern, which enriches surface interest to augment visual excitement. For example, in "Numbers in Color" (1958-59), the artist Jasper Johns created a regular pattern by assembling 11 rows of 11 stacked rectangles each. He painted various numerical digits from 0 to 9 within most of the rectangles. He made these numbers look irregular by irregularly distributing, varying, and applying the colors he used. Many patterned paintings do not include a focal point or area. This often makes them look more like designs—even when they include recognizable images—than portraits, landscapes, still-lifes, or other types of paintings that do not have such repetitive patterning.

## Involvement of Music in the Development of Infants and Young Children

Long before they can speak, and before they even comprehend much speech, infants respond to the sounds of voices and to music. These responses are not only to auditory stimulation but moreover to the emotional content in what they hear. Parents sing lullabies to babies; not only are these sounds pleasant and soothing but they also help children develop trust in their environment as secure. Parents communicate their love to children through singing and introduce them to experiences of pleasure and excitement through music. As children grow, music progresses to be not only a medium of communication but also one of self-expression as they learn to sing and play musical sounds. Music facilitates memory, as we see through commercial jingles and mnemonic devices. Experiments find music improves spatial reasoning. Children's learning of perceptual and logical concepts like beginning and ending, sequences, cause-and-effect, balance, harmony and dissonance, and mathematical number and timing concepts is reinforced by music. Music also promotes language development. Children learn about colors, counting, conceptual relationships, nature, and social skills through music.

### *Enhancing the Emotional, Social, Aesthetic, and School Readiness Skills with Music*

Young children who are just learning to use spoken language often cannot express their emotions very well verbally. Music is a great aid to emotional development in that younger children can express happiness, sadness, anger, and more through singing and/or playing music more easily than they can with words. Children of preschool ages not only listen to music and respond to what they hear, but they also learn to create music through singing and playing instruments together with other children. These activities help them learn crucial social skills for their lives, like cooperating with others, collaborating, and making group or team efforts to accomplish something. When children are given guided musical experiences, they learn to make their own judgments of what is good or bad music; this provides them with the foundations for developing an aesthetic sense. Music promotes preliteracy skills by enhancing phonemic awareness. As growing children develop musical appreciation and skills, these develop fundamental motor, cognitive, and social skills they need for language, school readiness, literacy, and life.

## Pitch, Tempo, and Rhythm in the Musical Arts

**Pitch** is the frequency of a sound, such as a musical note. We hear high-, middle-, and low-frequency sound waves as high-, middle-, and low-pitched sounds, respectively. Various pitches are combined in musical compositions to create variety. A series of connected notes of different pitches creates a melody. Sounding (playing/singing) several pitches simultaneously and combining them produces harmonies and chords. Connected series of harmonies/chords, in turn, create harmonic/chord progressions. **Tempo** is the speed of music. Fast tempo can evoke happiness, excitement, fear, anger, or urgency. Slow tempo can evoke serenity, grandeur, solemnity, sadness, or ominousness. Musical compositions commonly direct the tempo using terms like andante (walking speed), adagio (slow), allegro (happy/quick), lento (slow), and largo (expansively slow). **Rhythm** includes the overall beat/time signature (number of beats per measure) and the variations among note lengths that produce patterns (e.g., legato describes smoothly connected series of notes, while staccato describes sharply disconnected notes that are cut short and sounded separately). Composers combine pitch, tempo, and rhythm in music to create atmosphere and mood, and to evoke emotion in listeners. They also arrange these elements to construct/recall musical themes/motifs within compositions.

## Chapter Quiz

Ready to see how well you retained what you just read? Scan the QR code to go directly to the chapter quiz interface for this study guide. If you're using a computer, simply visit the online resources page at **mometrix.com/resources719/gacesegcelemed** and click the Chapter Quizzes link.

# Development and Characteristics of Learners

## Types of Disabilities

**Medical disabilities** include problems related to diseases, illnesses, trauma, and genetic conditions. **Physical disabilities** include problems related to fine and gross motor skills and can include sensory input or sensory perception disorders. Medical and physical disabilities often manifest with other disabilities, such as **learning disabilities**. Medical disabilities that affect educational performance usually fall under the "other health impairment" or "traumatic brain injury" categories of the Individuals with Disabilities Education Act (IDEA). Students with physical disabilities, such as cerebral palsy, can be eligible for special education under IDEA's "orthopedic impairment" category. However, for either medical or physical disabilities to qualify, they must **adversely affect educational performance**. For example, a student with cerebral palsy would not be eligible for special education or an **Individualized Education Program (IEP)** if the disability does not affect educational performance. The student would receive accommodations and modifications under a 504 Plan.

**Review Video: Medical Conditions in Education**
Visit mometrix.com/academy and enter code: 531058

### Low-Incidence Disabilities and High-Incidence Disabilities

Low-incidence disabilities account for up to 20 percent of all students' disabilities. Students with low-incidence disabilities have sometimes received assistance for their disabilities starting from an early age. **Low-incidence disabilities** include intellectual disabilities, multiple disabilities, hearing impairments, orthopedic impairments, other health impairments, visual impairments, certain autism spectrum conditions, deaf-blindness, traumatic brain injury, and significant developmental delays. **High-incidence disabilities** account for up to 80 percent of all students' disabilities. While students with high-incidence disabilities present with academic, social, communication, or behavioral problems, they can often be held to the same standards as their regular education peers. Children with high-incidence disabilities may perform at the same capacities as their similar-aged peers but have deficits in reading, math, writing, handwriting, or maintaining attention. High-incidence disabilities include speech and language impairments, learning disabilities, attention-deficit/hyperactivity disorder, emotional disorders, mild intellectual disabilities, certain autism spectrum conditions, and cognitive delays.

### Interventions for Students with Physical Disabilities

A physical disability refers to any disability that limits **gross mobility** and prevents **normal body movement**. For example, muscular dystrophy is a physical disability that weakens muscles over time. Students with physical disabilities require early interventions and should begin to receive them before grade school. When students with physical disabilities enter grade school, they may receive interventions and related services if they qualify for special education and receive IEPs or **504 Plans**. When physical disabilities do not affect the students' academic success, they may be put on 504 Plans to receive appropriate related services, accommodations, or modifications. When physical disabilities are present with other disabilities or the physical disabilities affect academic performance, students may be put on IEPs and receive appropriate related services, accommodations, and modifications. Teachers, intervention specialists, physiotherapists, occupational therapists, and speech language pathologists work as a team in implementing appropriate accommodations, modifications, and related services to assist students with physical disabilities.

### Working with Students with Physical Disabilities

Students with physical disabilities should be included in **general education classrooms** with accommodations if their disabilities do not coexist with other disabilities, such as learning disabilities. The

Individuals with Disabilities Education Act states that students must be assigned to a classroom that conforms with the student's least restrictive environment, which generally means the general education classroom, unless appropriate accommodations cannot be made. If sufficient accommodations or modifications are not able to be made within the general education classroom, a student may be placed in a more specialized environment that provides for his or her particular needs. In any of these settings, it is essential for educators to practice **instructional strategies** that facilitate the learning processes and accommodate the needs of students with physical disabilities. Classrooms should be arranged so they can be **navigated** easily by everyone. This includes giving students using wheelchairs adequate aisle space and workspace. **Partner work** is helpful for students with physical disabilities, who may struggle with handwriting or using keyboards. Partners can assist these students with skills like note-taking, which may be difficult for students with physical disabilities. Additionally, assignments can include **accommodations** or **modifications** to meet the specific needs of students with physical disabilities. For example, text-to-speech software can be provided for students who struggle with using regular keyboards.

## Accommodations and Modifications

Students with **speech, language, visual,** or **hearing impairments** (including **deafness**) that adversely affect their educational performance receive **accommodations**, modifications, and related services specific to their disabilities. Students with these impairments may be educated alongside peers and provided with related services outside of the general education classroom. Accommodations, modifications, and related services are provided based on the severity of the disability.

An **orthopedic impairment (OI)** severely hinders mobility or motor activity. Accommodations, modifications, and related services in the classroom environment may be appropriate for students with OI. Students with **intellectual disabilities**, such as Down syndrome, often need supports in place for communication, self-care, and social skills. The educational implications of a **traumatic brain injury** are unique to the individual and are therefore treated on a case-by-case basis. Students with **multiple disabilities** have needs that cannot be met in any one program. Sometimes their needs are so great that they must be educated in partial inclusion or self-contained settings.

## Disability Categories in IDEA

- **Specific Learning Disabilities (SLD)** is the umbrella term for children who struggle with issues in their abilities to read, write, speak, listen, reason, or do math.
- **Other Health Impairment (OHI)** is the umbrella term for a disability that limits a child's strength, energy, or alertness.
- **Autism Spectrum Disorder (ASD)** is a disability that mostly affects a child's social and communication skills, and sometimes behavior.
- **Emotional Disturbance (ED)** is a disability category for a number of mental disorders.
- **Speech or Language Impairment** covers children with language impairments.
- **Visual Impairment or Blindness** is a disability category for children with visual impairments that significantly impact their abilities to learn.
- **Deafness** is the category for students who cannot hear even with a hearing aid.
- **Hearing Impairment** describes hearing loss that is not as pervasive as deafness. This is distinguished from deafness categorically, as the types of interventions needed are very different.
- **Deaf-Blindness** covers children diagnosed with both deafness and blindness.
- Those with **Orthopedic Impairments** have impairments to their bodies that interfere with the performance of daily living skills.
- An **Intellectual Disability** is the diagnosis for children with below-average intellectual abilities or intelligence quotients (IQs).
- **Traumatic Brain Injury (TBI)** covers children who have suffered from TBIs.

- **Multiple Disabilities** as a category means a child has more than one disability defined by the Individuals with Disabilities Education Act and requires educational interventions that go beyond standard interventions for one category.

**Review Video: Understanding Learning Disability Needs of Students**
Visit mometrix.com/academy and enter code: 662775

## SPECIFIC LEARNING DISABILITY

### *EARLY INDICATIONS OF A SPECIFIC LEARNING DISABILITY*

Early indications of specific learning disabilities (SLDs) can include medical history, problems with speech acquisition, problems with socialization, academic delays, and behavioral delays. Delays in certain milestones may indicate learning disabilities, but these delays may also be due to other causes. Premature birth, serious childhood illnesses, frequent ear infections, and sleep disorders are **medical factors** that can influence the development of learning disabilities. Children that develop SLDs may demonstrate early delays in **speech**. Late speech development, pronunciation problems, and stuttering may indicate SLDs, but they may also be issues that are unrelated to SLDs and can be addressed by individualized speech instruction. Students with SLDs may also have problems adjusting **socially** and may demonstrate social skills that are not age appropriate. Depending on when the children enter academic settings, they may demonstrate academic delays compared to similar-aged peers. These delays are usually determined using formal and informal assessments in educational settings. **Behaviors** such as hyperactivity or difficulty following directions may also indicate a child has an SLD. However, these indicators do not definitely mean that a child has a learning disability, and some of the indicators overlap with characteristics of other disabilities.

### *INSTRUCTIONAL STRATEGIES FOR TEACHING STUDENTS WITH SPECIFIC LEARNING DISABILITIES*

While there is no one strategy that works effectively with all students with specific learning disabilities, there are some strategies that tend to produce **positive outcomes** for these students. Direct instruction, learning strategy instruction, and a multi-sensory approach are three large-scale interventions that can be used to promote student learning. **Direct instruction** is teacher-driven instruction that targets specific skills; this is sometimes delivered in resource rooms. **Learning strategy instruction** is a method for teaching students with disabilities different tools and techniques useful for learning new content or skills. This includes techniques like chunking the content, sequencing tasks, and small group instruction. A **multi-sensory approach** ensures that students are receiving and interacting with new information and skills using more than one sense at a time. This approach is helpful for students with learning disabilities because it targets many different ways of learning.

### *DYSLEXIA AND DYSGRAPHIA DISORDERS*

Students with dyslexia are eligible for special education under the specific learning disability category in the Individuals with Disabilities Education Act if their educational performance is significantly impacted by their disabilities. **Dyslexia** is a permanent condition that makes it difficult for people to read. This affects reading accuracy, fluency, and comprehension. Dyslexia also generalizes to difficulties in the content areas of writing, mathematics, and spelling. Children who have dyslexia often have difficulties with **phonemic awareness skills** and **decoding**. It is not a disability that affects vision or the way people see letters. Dyslexia may coexist with other conditions such as **dysgraphia**, which is a disorder that causes issues with written expression. With dysgraphia, children often struggle with holding pencils and writing letters accurately. It is difficult for students with dysgraphia to distinguish shapes, use correct letter spacing, read maps, copy text, understand spelling rules, and more.

**Review Video: Disorders That Impair Reading Comprehension**
Visit mometrix.com/academy and enter code: 306758

### *Sensory Processing Disorders*

A person with a deficit in the brain's ability to interpret sensory information has a sensory processing disorder (**SPD**). In people without SPD, brain receptors can interpret sensory input, and then the person demonstrates appropriate reactions. In people with SPD, sensory input is blocked from brain receptors, resulting in abnormal reactions. Previously known as a sensory integration disorder, SPD is not a disability specifically defined or eligible under IDEA. However, many students with disabilities defined by IDEA, like autism, also experience some sort of sensory processing disorder. Students with SPD may display **oversensitive or under-sensitive responses** to their environments, stimuli, and senses. They may not understand physical boundaries, such as where their bodies are in space, and may bump into things and demonstrate clumsiness. These students may get upset easily, throw tantrums, demonstrate high anxiety, and struggle with changes.

### *Importance of Reinforcing Word Recognition*

Many students with specific learning disabilities demonstrate **deficits in their reading abilities**. This includes **word recognition abilities**. Teaching **word identification** is important for these students because developing age-appropriate word recognition skills is one of the essential building blocks for creating efficient readers. Children who do not develop adequate reading skills in elementary school are generally below-average readers as they age in school. Most districts and teachers use **basal reading programs** that teach word recognition and phonics. Teachers often supplement basal reading programs with **instructional programs** that can be used at home and at school. These are especially useful for students with disabilities or students who are at risk and struggle with word recognition abilities. Elements of basal and supplementary reading programs include instruction for helping students make connections between letters and sounds, opportunities to become comfortable with reading, alphabetic knowledge, phonemic awareness, letter-sound correlations, word identification strategies, spelling, writing, and reading fluency.

## Other Health Impairments

### *Qualifications to Be Eligible for Special Education Under the Category of OHI*

The category of other health impairment (**OHI**) under IDEA indicates that a child has **limited strength, vitality, or alertness**. This includes hyper-alertness or hypo-alertness to environmental stimuli. In order to be eligible for special education under this category according to IDEA, the disability must **adversely affect educational performance**. It must also be due to **chronic or acute health problems**, such as attention-deficit/hyperactivity disorder, diabetes, epilepsy, heart conditions, hemophilia, lead poisoning, leukemia, nephritis, rheumatic fever, sickle cell anemia, or Tourette's syndrome. Since the OHI category encompasses a number of different disabilities, teachers and parents must rely on a student's Individualized Education Program to ensure that individual academic needs are met and appropriate accommodations and modifications are provided.

### *Educational Implications for Students with ADHD*

IDEA does **not** recognize attention-deficit/hyperactivity disorder (ADHD) in any of its 13 major disability categories. Students may be diagnosed with ADHD by a physician, but this diagnosis is not enough to qualify them for **special education services**. When ADHD is present alongside an IDEA-recognized disability, the student qualifies for special education services under that disability. A student whose ability to learn is affected by ADHD can receive services with a 504 Plan in place. **Section 504 of the Rehabilitation Act of 1973** requires that any child whose disability affects a major life activity receive appropriate **accommodations** and **modifications** in the learning environment. Parents who think a child's ADHD adversely affects educational functioning may request a formal evaluation to be performed by the school. If the child is found to qualify for special education services, they then receive services under IDEA's **other health impairment** category.

### *ADHD*

Children with **attention-deficit/hyperactivity disorder (ADHD)** may demonstrate inattention and/or hyperactivity and impulsivity. Students with ADHD may have difficulties with attention span, following instructions, and concentrating to the point that their educational performance is affected. Since ADHD symptoms are common among children, their presence does not necessarily indicate that a child has ADHD. ADHD is not caused by certain environmental factors, such as diet or watching too much television. Symptoms may be exacerbated by these factors, but the causes can be heredity, chemical imbalances, issues with brain functions, environmental toxins, or prenatal trauma, such as the mother smoking or drinking during pregnancy.

## Autism Spectrum Disorder

Autism is a **spectrum disorder**, which means the characteristics associated with the disability vary depending on the student. However, there are common repetitive and patterned behaviors associated with communication and social interactions for this population of students. Students with autism may demonstrate delayed or different speech patterns, the inability to understand body language or facial expressions, and the inability to exhibit appropriate speech patterns, body language, or facial expressions. In a classroom environment, students with autism may demonstrate **repetitive behaviors** that are distracting, such as hand flapping or making vocalizations. Some students with autism demonstrate **preoccupation** with doing activities, tasks, or routines in certain ways. This preoccupation can lead to difficulties when the students are asked to make changes to activities, tasks, or routines. Furthermore, some students with autism prefer to **participate** in a limited range of activities and may get upset when asked to participate in activities outside of their self-perceived ranges. This preference for a limited range of activities may even translate into repetitive behaviors or obsessive and fanatic focus on particular topics. Extreme interest in one topic can lead to disruptions when students with autism are asked to speak or write about different topics.

**Review Video: Autism Spectrum Disorder**
Visit mometrix.com/academy and enter code: 395410

### *Concurrent Autism Spectrum Disorder and Other Learning Disabilities*

Misinformation about autism spectrum disorder (ASD) and its relation to other learning disabilities runs rampant within school communication and needs clarification to prevent harmful stereotyping of students. As a spectrum disorder, the way ASD presents varies widely and does not always affect students in the same ways. Autism spectrum disorder is frequently confused with intellectual disabilities, which is when an individual has a low IQ; however, students with ASD can have IQs ranging from significantly delayed to above average or gifted. ASD is also distinctive in that it largely involves difficulties with social understanding and communication, as well as fixations on repetitive routines and behaviors. It is important for an educational professional to understand the difference between ASD and other types of disabilities that commonly co-occur or which have overlapping symptoms. For instance, students with learning disabilities and students with ASD may both have challenges with reading nonverbal cues, staying organized, and expressing themselves, but that does not mean that they have the same underlying conditions or needs. The professional educational community must be aware and cautious when describing various disabilities to prevent the spread of misinformation and harmful stereotyping.

### *Early Signs of a Child Having ASD*

Early signs of **autism spectrum disorder (ASD)** include impairments or delays in social interactions and communication, repetitive behaviors, limited interests, and abnormal eating habits. Students with ASD typically do not interact in conversations in the same ways as similar-aged peers without ASD. They may demonstrate inability to engage in pretend play and may pretend they don't hear when being spoken to. Hand flapping, vocal sounds, or compulsive interactions with objects are repetitive behaviors sometimes demonstrated by students with ASD. They may only demonstrate interest in talking about one topic or interacting with one object. They may also demonstrate self-injurious behavior or sleep problems, in addition to having a limited diet of preferred foods. **Early intervention** is key for these students in order to address and improve functioning. These students may also benefit from **applied behavior analysis** to target specific behaviors, and they may require speech and language therapy, occupational therapy, social skills instruction, or other services geared toward improving intellectual functioning.

### *Characteristics of Social Skill Delays in Students with ASD*

Autism spectrum disorder (ASD) is a disability that can affect a student's social, communication, and behavioral abilities. **Social skill delays and deficits** are common for students with ASD. Social skill delays go hand in hand with **communication limitations** for students with ASD. This includes conversational focus on one or two narrow topics or ideas, which makes it difficult for students with ASD to hold two-way conversations about things that do not interest them. Some students with ASD engage in repetitive language or echolalia or rely on standard phrases to communicate with others. Their **speech and language skills** may be delayed compared to their similar-aged peers. This may also impact their abilities to engage in effective conversations. The **nonverbal skills** of students with ASD may also be misinterpreted, such as when they avoid eye contact while speaking or being spoken to.

### *Early Communication and Social Skill Delays in Students with ASD*

Students with delays in communication development often need and receive some type of assistance or instruction with communication and social skills. Early intervention for these students is key, as communication difficulties may be a symptom of **autism spectrum disorder (ASD)**. For students with ASD, the need for communication and social skills instruction varies depending on the individual student. Key characteristics of **early communication difficulties** for a student with ASD include not responding to his or her name, not pointing at objects of interest, avoiding eye contact, not engaging in pretend play, delayed speech or language skills, or repeating words or phrases. Children with ASD may also exhibit overreaction or underreaction to environmental stimuli. Key characteristics of **early social skill difficulties** for a student with ASD may include preferring to play alone, trouble understanding personal feelings or the feelings of others, not sharing interests with others, and difficulty with personal space boundaries. Infants with ASD may not respond to their names and demonstrate reduced babbling and reduced interest in people. Toddlers with ASD may demonstrate decreased interest in social interactions, difficulty with pretend play, and a preference for playing alone.

### *Socratic Method for Students with ASD*

With the Socratic method of teaching, students are **guided** by their teachers in their own educational discovery learning processes. This involves students intrinsically seeking knowledge or answers to problems. This method can be helpful for facilitating and enhancing the **social and emotional abilities** of students with disabilities, particularly autism spectrum disorder (ASD). The Socratic method requires **dialogue** in order to successfully facilitate the teacher/student guided learning process. This is beneficial for students with ASD, who generally struggle with appropriate communication and social skills. This method emphasizes **information seeking and communication skills** by engaging students in class discussions, assignment sharing, and group work. Communication for information-seeking purposes is often a deficit of students with ASD. Sharing of ideas is a concept that develops naturally in guided learning and often requires flexibility in the thought process, another skill that students with ASD struggle with. These skills can be taught to and reinforced in students with and without disabilities in order to develop skills essential to lifelong learning processes.

### *Fostering the Communication Development of Students with ASD*

Students with **autism spectrum disorder (ASD)** vary in their need for communication and social skill assistance and instruction. Some students with ASD may demonstrate slight to extreme delays in language; difficulty sustaining conversations; and the inability to understand body language, tone of voice, and facial expressions. Since ASD is a **spectrum disorder**, there typically is no single instructional strategy or technique that works for all students with the disorder. Some **evidence-based strategies** are effective for teaching appropriate communication skills to students with ASD. **Applied behavior analysis (ABA)** is an evidence-based strategy that involves providing an intervention and analyzing its effectiveness for a student with ASD. **Discrete trial training (DTT)** is a teaching strategy that is more structured than ABA. It focuses on teaching and reinforcing skills in smaller increments. **Pivotal response treatment (PRT)** is an ABA-derived approach that focuses more on meaningful reinforcement when generally positive behaviors occur. Where ABA targets very specific tasks, PRT targets behaviors categorically or more generally. Furthermore, instead of using an unrelated, supplemented reward system, such as giving candy for completing a task, the rewards used should be related to the desired behavior. For instance, suppose a targeted goal is to have the individual work on politely asking for things generally. The PRT-based reward might be giving the individual the toy or desired object as a reward for asking for it.

## Emotional Disturbances

A diagnosis of an emotional disturbance (**ED**) can also be referred to as a **behavioral disorder** or **mental illness.** Causes of emotional disturbances are generally unclear. However, heredity, brain disorders, and diet are some factors that influence the development of emotional disturbances. The emotional disturbance category includes psychological disorders, such as anxiety disorders, bipolar disorder, eating disorders, and obsessive-compulsive disorder. Children who have emotional disturbances that affect their educational performance are eligible for **special education** under the Individuals with Disabilities Education Act. Indicators of emotional disturbances include hyperactivity, aggression, withdrawal, immaturity, and academic difficulties. While many children demonstrate these indicators throughout their development, an emotional disturbance is associated with **prolonged demonstration** of these behaviors.

### *Issues Students with Emotional Disturbances Experience in the Instructional Setting*

Students with the diagnosis of emotional disturbance (ED) as defined by the Individuals with Disabilities Education Act require **emotional and behavioral support** in the classroom. Students with ED may also require **specialized academic instruction** in addition to behavioral and emotional support. The amount of support given varies according to the needs of individual students. These students also need **scaffolded instruction** in social skills, self-awareness, self-esteem, and self-control. Students with ED often exhibit behaviors that impede their learning or the learning of others. **Positive behavioral interventions and supports (PBIS)** is a preventative instructional strategy that focuses on promoting positive behaviors in students. With PBIS, teachers or other professionals make changes to students' environments in order to decrease problem behaviors. PBIS involves collecting information on a problem behavior, identifying positive interventions to support the student before behaviors escalate, and implementing supports to decrease targeted negative behaviors. Supports can be implemented schoolwide or in the classroom. However, for students with ED, **classroom supports** are more effective because they can be individualized.

## Speech and Language Impairments

Speech and language impairments, sometimes referred to as **communication disorders**, are disabilities recognized by the Individuals with Disabilities Education Act. Students diagnosed with communication disorders are eligible for special education if they qualify for services. Early indicators of communication disorders include but are not limited to:

- Not smiling or interacting with others
- Lack of babbling or cooing in infants
- Lack of age-appropriate comprehension skills
- Speech that is not easily understood
- Issues with age-appropriate syntax development
- Issues with age-appropriate social skills
- Deficits in reading and writing skills
- Beginning or ending words with incorrect sounds
- Hearing loss
- Stuttering

These indicators may also be linked to other disabilities, such as hearing impairments or autism spectrum disorder. Although prolonged demonstration of these indicators may suggest communication disorders, some children demonstrate delays and then self-correct over time.

### *Facilitating Learning for Students with Speech or Language Impairments*

In order to teach students with speech or language impairments, also referred to as **communication disorders**, teachers and other professionals can use the **strategies** listed below:

- Use visuals and concrete examples to help students with communication disorders take in new information. Link the visuals with spoken words or phrases.
- Use visuals or photographs to introduce or reinforce vocabulary.
- Use repetition of spoken words to introduce or reinforce vocabulary.
- Model conversational and social skills, which helps students with communication disorders become familiar with word pronunciation.
- Speak at a slower rate when necessary, especially when presenting new information.
- Consistently check for understanding.
- Be aware that communication issues may sometimes result in other issues, such as behavioral or social skill issues.
- Pair actions and motions with words to emphasize meaning, especially for students with receptive language disorders.

### *Receptive Language Disorders*

Children with receptive language disorders often demonstrate appropriate expressive language skills and hear and read at age-appropriate levels. However, they may seem like they are not paying attention or engaging in activities, or they may appear to have difficulties following or understanding directions. They may refrain from asking questions or interrupt frequently during activities, especially during read-aloud activities. It may appear as if they are not listening, but children with receptive language disorders have difficulty perceiving **meaning** from what they hear. Children with this disorder may consistently leave tasks incomplete unless the tasks are broken down into smaller steps. This is due to issues with processing directions, especially **verbal directions**. Children with receptive language disorders may not respond appropriately or at all to questions from peers or adults. Answers to comprehension questions, especially when texts are read aloud, may be off topic or incorrect. Children with receptive language disorders have trouble gathering and connecting meaning to what they hear. A receptive language disorder is not exclusively a learning disability. However, children who have receptive disorders may have learning disabilities.

### *Expressive Language Disabilities*

Expressive language is the ability to express wants and needs. Children with **expressive language disabilities** may have trouble conversing with peers and adults and have trouble with self-expression. Answers to questions may be vague or repetitive. They may not demonstrate age-appropriate social skills with peers and adults. Children with expressive language disabilities have a limited vocabulary range and rely on familiar vocabulary words in their expressive language. They can be very quiet and seclude themselves from classroom activities because of difficulties expressing their thoughts and feelings. They may not be able to accurately express what they understand because children with expressive language difficulties have trouble speaking in sentences. Expressive language disabilities indicate issues with **language processing centers** in the brain. Children with these disabilities can sometimes understand language but have trouble **expressing** it. Children with traumatic brain injuries, dyslexia, autism, or learning disabilities demonstrate issues with expressive language.

### *Implications of Literacy Development for Children with Disabilities*

Children may not always meet the **literacy stage milestones** at specified ages. However, this does not always indicate a disability. Children who fall significantly behind in their literacy development, continually struggle with skill acquisition, or do not consistently retain skill instruction are more likely to be identified as having **disabilities**. Furthermore, children with **speech and language disorders** are more likely to experience problems learning to read and write. These issues are typically apparent before children enter grade school but can also become evident during their early grade school years. **Early warning signs** include disinterest in shared book reading, inability to recognize or remember names of letters, difficulty understanding directions, and persistent baby talk.

### *Effects of Deficits in Language Development on the Learning Processes*

Without interventions, children with deficits in language development will likely have issues with overall academic success. **Academic success** is inextricably linked with good language development. Good **language development skills** include the ability to understand spoken and written words, as well as literacy skills. When a core knowledge of language is developed in young children, it can be built upon as the children grow and develop during their grade school years. Reading and writing are language-based skills. **Phonological awareness** is an essential skill and key building block for language development. Phonological awareness is a term that refers to students' awareness of sounds, syllables, and words. Students that develop strong phonological skills typically develop good literacy skills. Students with deficits in reading, writing, or math may have difficulties with phonological awareness and miss some building blocks essential for academic success. These deficits generalize to core subject areas as students are required to demonstrate grade-level appropriate skills.

## Visual Impairment or Blindness

Visual impairments range from low vision to blindness. The Individuals with Disabilities Education Act defines a **visual impairment** as an impairment in vision that is great enough to affect a child's educational performance. **Blindness** is defined as a visual acuity of 20/200 or less in the dominant eye. Some people diagnosed with blindness still have minimal sight. Early indicators of a visual impairment or blindness in children include:

- Holding things close to the eyes or face
- Experiencing fatigue after looking at things closely
- Having misaligned eyes
- Squinting
- Tilting the head or covering one eye to see things up close or far away
- Demonstrating clumsiness
- Appearing to see better during the day

Students with visual impairments benefit the most from early interventions, especially when the impairments are present with other disabilities. Appropriate interventions vary based on students' needs and whether or not they have other disabilities. Modifications, such as magnified text, Braille, auditory support, and text-tracking software, can help improve access to learning for these students.

## Deafness, Hearing Impairment, and Deaf-Blindness

Deafness, hearing impairment, and deaf-blindness are each considered their own categories under the Individuals with Disabilities Education Act, as the types and levels of intervention vary widely between them. **Deafness** is defined as a complete or near-complete loss of hearing, to the degree that a hearing aid cannot help. Deaf students often need specialized interventions to help with safety and communication, such as communication aids, assistive devices, and sign language. **Hearing impairments** consist of all qualifying degrees of hearing loss that are not severe enough to qualify as deafness. Interventions may include communication aids and training, as well as hearing aids. **Deaf-blindness** is restricted to students who are both deaf and blind concurrently. Deaf-blind students usually require considerable help with communication and daily living skills.

### *Effect of Hearing Loss on Language Development*

Hearing language is part of learning language. Children with **hearing loss** miss out on sounds associated with language, and this can affect their listening, speaking, reading, social skills, and overall school success. Hearing loss can sometimes lead to delayed speech and language, learning disabilities in school, insecurities, and issues with socialization and making friends. Children with hearing loss may:

- Have trouble learning abstract vocabulary like *since* and *before*
- Omit article words in sentences like *a* and *an*
- Fall behind in core components of learning and development without early interventions
- Have difficulty speaking in and understanding sentences
- Speak in shorter sentences
- Have difficulty including word endings like *-ing* and *-s*
- Have issues speaking clearly because they cannot accurately hear sounds
- Omit quiet sounds like *p, sh,* or *f*
- Be unable to hear what their own voices sound like

Children with hearing loss are more likely to fall behind in school due to their hearing deficits. They can easily fall behind without support from interventions, teachers, and their families. Early **hearing testing** is essential to ensure that interventions, such as sign language, can be introduced to promote school and life success for children with hearing loss.

## Orthopedic Impairment

### *Qualifications to Receive Special Education for Orthopedic Impairment*

Students who qualify to receive special education under the Individuals with Disabilities Education Act orthopedic impairment category have an orthopedic impairment that adversely affects educational performance. This includes children with congenital anomalies, impairments caused by disease, or impairments from other causes, such as cerebral palsy or amputations. An orthopedic impairment alone does not qualify a student for special education and an IEP. Once a student's educational performance is proven to be affected by the orthopedic impairment, the student becomes eligible for special education and is placed on an IEP. The **IEP** determines the student's least restrictive environment, individualized goals for academic skills or adaptive behavior, and any appropriate accommodations or modifications. Students with orthopedic impairments whose educational performance is not affected may receive accommodations and modifications on **504 Plans**, if appropriate. Strategies for instruction should be determined and implemented on a case-by-case basis, as the orthopedic impairment category covers a broad range of disabilities.

## Intellectual Disabilities

### *Determining If a Child May Have an Intellectual Disability*

Intellectual disability (**ID**) is primarily diagnosed when a child displays impairments in adaptive functioning. Often, these children will score lower than 70 on an IQ test, but IQ scores are not diagnostic and are particularly inaccurate on the low end of the scale. Students diagnosed with intellectual disabilities demonstrate deficits in academic skills, abstract thinking, problem solving, language development, new skill acquisition, and retaining information. Students with ID often do not adequately meet developmental or social milestones. They demonstrate **deficits in functioning** with one or more basic living skills. Students with ID struggle conceptually and may have difficulties with time and money concepts, short-term memory, time management, pre-academic skills, planning, and strategizing. Students with ID demonstrate poor social judgment and decision-making skills because they have trouble understanding social cues and rules. They may grasp concrete social concepts before abstract ones and significantly later than their similar-aged, regular education peers. These students also tend to struggle with self-care skills, household tasks, and completing tasks that may be easy for similar-aged peers.

### *Determining Severity of Intellectual Disabilities*

There are four levels of intellectual disabilities: mild, moderate, severe, and profound. Specific factors are used to determine whether a disability is mild, moderate, severe, or profound. Intellectual levels are measured using cognitive- and research-based assessments. An **intellectual disability (ID)** is defined as significant cognitive deficits in intellectual functioning, such as reasoning, problem solving, abstract thinking, and comprehension. A

**mild intellectual disability** is the most common type of intellectual disability. People with mild to moderate ID can generally participate in independent living activities and learn practical life skills and adaptive behaviors. People diagnosed with **severe intellectual disabilities** demonstrate major developmental delays. They struggle with simple routines and self-care skills. Additionally, they often understand speech but have trouble with expressive communication. People with **profound ID** cannot live independently, and they depend heavily on care from other people and resources. They are likely to have concurrent congenital disorders that affect their intellectual functioning.

### *Educational Implications for Students with Intellectual Disabilities*

According to IDEA, students who are eligible for special education under the category of **intellectual disability** have significantly lower intellectual abilities, along with adaptive behavior deficits. Previously, intellectual disability was referred to as "mental retardation" in IDEA. In 2010, President Obama signed **Rosa's Law**, which changed the term to "intellectual disability." The definition of the disability category remained unchanged. Educational implications of a diagnosis of an intellectual disability differ depending on students' needs as determined by their IEPs. Students with intellectual disabilities often display **limitations to mental functioning** in areas like communication, self-care, and social skills (adaptive behavior). In many cases, these skills must be addressed in the educational environments in addition to any academic skill deficits. Learning adaptive behaviors and academic skills takes longer for students with intellectual disabilities. Their special education placements depend on what environments are least restrictive. This depends on the individual student and is determined in the IEP.

### *Promoting a Positive Performance for Students with Intellectual Disabilities*

Students with intellectual disabilities often present with skill levels that are far below those of similar-aged peers. Because of deficits in academic, behavioral, and social skills, these students require **specialized instruction**, which varies depending on the needs of each individual student. An effective strategy for promoting a positive educational performance is to collect observations and data on the academic, behavioral, and social skill levels of the individual student. Teachers usually work with professionals in related services, like speech language pathologists, to address needs and implement educational interventions that work for this population of students. These students can benefit from **communication interventions** focused on interactions they may have with adults and peers. Students may benefit from augmentative and alternative communication devices, visual activity schedules and other visual supports, and computer-based instruction when learning communication and social skills. Students with intellectual disabilities may also require **behavioral interventions** to teach appropriate behaviors or decrease negative behaviors. They may also benefit from increased **peer interactions** through structured social groups in order to promote appropriate communication skills.

## Multiple Disabilities

### *Components of the Multiple Disability Eligibility Category According to IDEA*

The multiple disabilities category according to IDEA applies to students who have two or more disabilities occurring simultaneously. The multiple disability category does not include deaf-blindness, which has its own category under IDEA. Students with **multiple disabilities** present with such **severe educational needs** that they cannot be accommodated in special education settings that address only one disability. Placement in special education programs is determined by students' **least restrictive environments** as defined in their **Individualized Education Programs**. Students with multiple disabilities often present with communication deficits, mobility challenges, and deficits in adaptive behavior and need one-on-one instruction or assistance when performing daily activities.

### *Intervention Strategies for the Instruction of Students with Multiple Disabilities*

Working with students with multiple disabilities can be challenging. However, strategies used in other special education settings can be implemented to promote the success of students with multiple disabilities. Effective strategies include the following:

- Setting **long-term goals**, which may last for a few years depending on how long students are in the same classrooms
- Working **collaboratively** with team members, like paraprofessionals and related service professionals, to ensure that they carry out students' educational objectives consistently
- Developing and maintaining **group goals** that the adults and students in the classrooms can strive to achieve together
- Working with students and paraprofessionals and consulting paraprofessionals frequently for **feedback**
- Demonstrating **patience** when waiting for students to respond or complete tasks
- Learning about how students **communicate**, which may involve gestures, a Picture Exchange Communication System, or other methods
- Driving instruction and education goals based on how students **learn best**
- Considering how students will **respond** when designing lessons, including accounting for response time during instruction

## Social and Functional Living Skills

### Targeting and Implementing Social Skills Instruction

Developing good social skills is essential for lifelong success, and people with disabilities often struggle with these skills. Addressing social skill behavior is most effective when specific **social skill needs** are identified, and **social skills instruction** is implemented as a collaborative effort between parents and teachers.

Evaluating **developmental milestones** is helpful in targeting social skills that need to be addressed and taught. If a child with a disability is not demonstrating a milestone, such as back-and-forth communication, the skill can be evaluated to determine if it should be taught. However, meeting milestones is not a reliable way to measure a student's social skill ability, as some children naturally progress more slowly. **Social skill deficits** may be acquisition deficits, performance deficits, or fluency deficits. A student with an **acquisition deficit** demonstrates an absence of a skill or behavior. A student with a **performance deficit** does not implement a social skill consistently. A student with a **fluency deficit** needs assistance with demonstrating a social skill effectively or fluently. Once a student's social skill need is identified, teachers, parents, and other professionals can collaborate to address it by establishing a routine or a behavior contract or implementing applied behavior analysis.

### Using Instructional Methods to Address Independent Living Skills

When applicable, goals for independent living skills are included in the **transition section** of students' Individualized Education Programs (IEPs). However, **independent living skills education** should begin well before students reach high school, regardless of whether these skills are addressed in their IEP goals. **Functional skills instruction** is necessary to teach students skills needed to gain independence. Instructional methods used to address independent living skills for students with disabilities include making life skills instruction part of the daily curriculum. An appropriate **task analysis** can be used to determine what skills need to be taught. **Functional academic skills**, especially in the areas of math and language arts, should also be included in the curriculum. Telling time, balancing a checkbook, and recognizing signs and symbols are just some examples of basic skills that students can generalize outside of the classroom environment. The goal of **community-based instruction** is to help students develop skills needed to succeed in the community, such as skills needed when riding a bus or shopping. This type of instruction may be harder to implement than basic social skills training, which should be part of the daily curriculum.

## Purposes and Benefits of Social Skills Groups

Social skills groups are useful for helping students with social skill deficits learn and practice appropriate skills with their peers. Social skills groups are primarily composed of similarly aged peers with and without disabilities. An adult leads these groups and teaches students skills needed for making friends, succeeding in school and life, and sometimes obtaining and maintaining a job. Other professionals, such as school psychologists or speech language pathologists, may also lead social skills groups. Social skills groups work by facilitating **conversation** and focusing on **skill deficits**. These groups can help students learn to read facial cues, appropriately greet others, begin conversations, respond appropriately, maintain conversations, engage in turn-taking, and request help when needed.

## Evidence-Based Methods for Promoting Self-Determination

Students with disabilities often need to be taught **self-determination** and **self-advocacy** skills. These skills may not come easily to students with specific disorders, like Autism Spectrum Disorder. Self-determination involves a comprehensive understanding of one's own **strengths and limitations**. Self-determined people are **goal-oriented** and intrinsically motivated to **improve themselves**. Teachers can facilitate the development of these skills in a number of ways, starting in early elementary school. In early elementary school, teachers can promote self-determination by teaching choice-making skills and providing clear consequences for choices. Teachers can also promote problem-solving and self-management skills, like having students evaluate their own work. At the middle school and junior high school level, students can be taught to evaluate and analyze their choices. They can also learn academic and personal goal-setting skills and decision-making skills. At the high school level, teachers can promote decision-making skills, involvement in educational planning (e.g., students attending their Individualized Education Program meetings), and strategies like self-instruction, self-monitoring, and self-evaluation. Throughout the education process, teachers should establish and maintain high standards for learning, focus on students' strengths, and create positive learning environments that promote choice and problem-solving skills.

## Teaching Self-Awareness Skills

Students engage in private self-awareness and public self-awareness. Some students with disabilities have the additional challenge of needing instruction in **self-awareness skills**. Special educators and other professionals can facilitate the instruction of self-awareness skills by teaching students to be **aware** of their thoughts, feelings, and actions; to recognize that other people have needs and feelings; and to recognize how their behaviors **affect other people**. Students can be taught self-awareness by identifying their own strengths and weaknesses and learning to self-monitor errors in assignments. They can also be taught to identify what materials or steps are needed to complete tasks and to advocate for accommodations or strategies that work for them. Special educators or other professionals should frequently talk with students about their performance and encourage them to discuss their mistakes without criticism.

## Importance of Learning Self-Advocacy Skills

Self-advocacy is an important skill to learn for people entering adulthood. For students with disabilities, **self-advocacy skills** are especially important for success in **postsecondary environments**. Teaching and learning self-advocacy skills should begin when students enter grade school and be reinforced in the upper grade levels. Students with disabilities who have the potential to enter postsecondary education or employment fields need to learn self-advocacy skills in order to **communicate** how their disabilities may affect their education or job performance and their need for supports and possible accommodations. Students with disabilities who graduate or age out of their Individualized Education Programs do not receive the **educational supports** they received at the grade school level. It is essential for students to advocate for themselves in the absence of teachers or caregivers advocating for them, especially when students independently enter postsecondary employment, training, or educational environments. Many colleges, universities, communities, and workplaces offer services to students with disabilities, but it is up to the students to advocate for themselves and seek them out.

## Teaching Functional Living Skills

Also known as life skills, functional living skills are skills that students need to live independently. Ideally, students leave high school having gained functional skills. For students with special needs, **functional living skills instruction** may be needed to gain independent living skills. Students with developmental or cognitive disabilities sometimes need to acquire basic living skills, such as self-feeding or toileting. **Applied behavior analysis** is a process by which these skills can be identified, modeled, and taught. Students must also learn functional math and language arts skills, such as managing money and reading bus schedules. Students may also participate in **community-based instruction** to learn skills while completing independent living tasks in the community. These skills include grocery shopping, reading restaurant menus, and riding public transportation. **Social skills instruction** is also important for these students, as learning appropriate social interactions is necessary to function with community members.

## Adaptive Behavior Skills Instruction

Adaptive behavior skills refer to age-appropriate behaviors that people need in order to live independently and function in daily life. **Adaptive behavior skills** include self-care, following rules, managing money, making friends, and more. For students with disabilities, especially severely limiting disabilities, adaptive behavior skills may need to be included in daily instruction. Adaptive behavior skills can be separated into conceptual skills, social skills, and practical life skills. **Conceptual skills** include academic concepts, such as reading, math, money, time, and communication skills. **Social skills** instruction focuses on teaching students to get along with others, communicate appropriately, and maintain appropriate behavior inside and outside the school environment. **Practical life skills** are skills needed to perform the daily living tasks, such as bathing, eating, sitting and standing, and using the bathroom. Adaptive behavior assessments are useful in assessing what adaptive behavior skills need to be addressed for each student. These assessments are usually conducted using observations and questionnaires completed by parents, teachers, or students.

## Social Skill Deficits

Social skills generally develop alongside language development and emotional development, as they are a major component of communication and awareness. Social skills need to be taught to some students with disabilities, such as students with autism. **Social skills instruction** involves the teaching of basic communication skills, empathy and rapport skills, interpersonal skills, problem-solving skills, and accountability. These are skills that do not come naturally to students with social skill deficits.

- **Basic communication skills** include listening, following directions, and taking turns in conversations.
- **Emotional communication skills** include demonstrating empathy and building rapport with others.
- **Interpersonal skills** include sharing, joining activities, and participating in turn-taking.
- **Problem-solving skills** include asking for help, apologizing to others, making decisions, and accepting consequences.
- **Accountability** includes following through on promises and accepting criticism appropriately.

## Instructional Methods for Teaching Students with Social Skill Deficits

Students with social skill deficits may or may not require explicit social skills instruction. These deficits can be addressed in inclusive settings. **Social skills instruction** can be delivered to entire classes or individual students, depending on the needs of the students. Also, **one-on-one** or **small group social skills instruction** can be delivered by professionals like speech-language pathologists. In both settings, it is important to model appropriate manners, hold students responsible for their actions, and have clear and concise rules and consequences. This creates educational environments that are both predictable and safe. Social situations that produce undesired outcomes can be remediated by **role-playing** the situations and teaching students positive responses. **Social stories** are another way to foster social skills growth. Often, these social stories demonstrate appropriate responses to specific social situations. The goal is for the students to generalize learned concepts to their school and home environments.

# Language Development

## Stages of Language Development

The first stage of language development and acquisition, the **pre-linguistic stage**, occurs during an infant's first year of life. It is characterized by the development of gestures, making eye contact, and sounds like cooing and crying. The **holophrase** or **one-word sentence stage** develops in infants between 10 and 13 months of age. In this stage, young children use one-word sentences to communicate meaning in language. The **two-word sentence stage** typically develops by the time a child is 18 months old. Each two-word sentence usually contains a noun or a verb and a modifier, such as "big balloon" or "green grass." Children in this stage use their two-word sentences to communicate wants and needs. **Multiple-word sentences** form by the time a child is two to two and a half years old. In this stage, children begin forming sentences with subjects and predicates, such as "tree is tall" or "rope is long." Grammatical errors are present, but children in this stage begin demonstrating how to use words in appropriate context. Children ages two and a half to three years typically begin using more **complex grammatical structures**. They begin to include grammatical structures that were not present before, such as conjunctions and prepositions. By the age of five or six, children reach a stage of **adult-like language development**. They begin to use words in appropriate context and can move words around in sentences while maintaining appropriate sentence structure. Language development and acquisition has a wide range of what is considered normal development. Some children do not attempt to speak for up to two years and then may experience an explosion of language development at a later time. In these cases, children often emerge from their silent stage with equivalent language development to babies who were more expressive early on. A child who does not speak after two years, however, may be exhibiting signs of a developmental delay.

## Oral Language Development

Oral language development begins well before students enter educational environments. It is learned first without formal instruction, with **environmental factors** being a heavy influence. Children tend to develop their own linguistic rules as a result of genetic disposition, their environments, and how their individual thinking processes develop. Oral language refers to both speaking and listening. Components of oral language development include phonology, syntax, semantics, morphology, and pragmatics. **Phonology** refers to the production and recognition of sounds. **Morphology** refers to how words are formed from smaller pieces, called morphemes. **Semantics** refers to the meaning of words and phrases and has overlap with morphology and syntax, as morphemes and word order can both change the meaning of words. Semantic studies generally focus on learning and understanding vocabulary. **Syntax** refers to how words and morphemes are combined to make up meaningful phrases. In English, word order is the primary way that many components of grammar are communicated. Finally, **pragmatics** refers to the practical application of language based on various social situations. For instance, a college student is likely to use different vocabulary, complexity, and formality of language when speaking with a professor than when speaking with his or her peer group. Each of these five components of language are applied in oral language. Awareness and application of these components develops over time as students gain experience and education in language use. **Oral language development** can be nurtured by caregivers and teachers well before children enter educational environments. Caregivers and teachers can promote oral language development by providing environments full of language development opportunities. Additionally, teaching children how conversation works, encouraging interaction among children, and demonstrating good listening and speaking skills are good strategies for nurturing oral language development.

**Review Video: Components of Oral Language Development**
Visit mometrix.com/academy and enter code: 480589

### *Helping Students Develop Oral Language Abilities*

Children pick up oral language skills in their home environments and build upon these skills as they grow. Early language development is influenced by a combination of genetic disposition, environment, and individual thinking processes. Children with **oral language acquisition difficulties** often experience difficulties in their

**literacy skills**, so activities that promote good oral language skills also improve literacy skills. **Strategies** that help students develop oral language abilities include developing appropriate speaking and listening skills; providing instruction that emphasizes vocabulary development; providing students with opportunities to communicate wants, needs, ideas, and information; creating language learning environments; and promoting auditory memory. Developing appropriate speaking and listening skills includes teaching turn-taking, awareness of social norms, and basic rules for speaking and listening. Emphasizing **vocabulary development** is a strategy that familiarizes early learners with word meanings. Providing students with opportunities to **communicate** is beneficial for developing early social skills. Teachers can create **language learning environments** by promoting literacy in their classrooms with word walls, reading circles, or other strategies that introduce language skills to students. Promoting **auditory memory** means teaching students to listen to, process, and recall information.

**Review Video: Types of Vocabulary Learning (Broad and Specific)**
Visit mometrix.com/academy and enter code: 258753

## HELPING STUDENTS MONITOR ERRORS IN ORAL LANGUAGE

Oral language is the primary way people communicate and express their knowledge, ideas, and feelings. As oral language generally develops, their **speaking and listening skills** become more refined. This refinement of a person's language is called fluency, which can be broken down into the subdisciplines of language, reading, writing, speaking, and listening. **Speaking fluency** usually describes the components of rate, accuracy, and prosody. **Rate** describes how fast a person can speak, and **prosody** describes the inflection and expressions that a person puts into speech. **Accuracy** describes how often a person makes an error in language production. In early stages of language development, individuals generally do not have enough language knowledge to be able to monitor their own speech production for errors and require input from others to notice and correct their mistakes. As an individual becomes more proficient, he or she will be able to monitor his or her own language usage and make corrections to help improve fluency. In the classroom, the teacher needs to be an active component of language monitoring to help facilitate growth. Teachers can monitor **oral language errors** with progress-monitoring strategies. Teachers can also help students monitor their own **oral language development** as they progress through the reading curriculum. Students can monitor their oral language by listening to spoken words in their school and home environments, learning and practicing self-correction skills, and participating in reading comprehension and writing activities. Students can also monitor oral language errors by learning oral language rules for phonics, semantics, syntax, and pragmatics. These rules typically generalize to developing appropriate oral language skills.

## EXPRESSIVE AND RECEPTIVE LANGUAGE

**Expressive language** refers to the aspects of language that an individual produces, generally referring to writing and speaking. **Receptive language** refers to the aspects of language that an individual encounters or receives and generally refers to reading and listening. Both expressive and receptive language are needed for communication from one person to another.

| | Expressive | Receptive |
|---|---|---|
| **Written** | Writing | Reading |
| **Oral** | Speaking | Listening |

### *Expressive Language Skills*

Expressive language skills include the ability to use vocabulary, sentences, gestures, and writing. People with good **expressive language skills** can label objects in their environments, put words in sentences, use appropriate grammar, demonstrate comprehension verbally by retelling stories, and more. This type of language is important because it allows people to express feelings, wants, needs, thoughts, ideas, and individual points of view. Strong expressive language skills include pragmatic knowledge, such as using gestures and facial expressions or using appropriate vocabulary for the listener or reader and soft skills, such as checks for comprehension, use of analogies, and grouping of ideas to help with clarity. Well-expressed language should be relatively easy for someone else to comprehend.

### *Receptive Language Skills*

Receptive language refers to a person's ability to perceive and understand language. Good receptive language skills involve gathering information from the environment and processing it into meaning. People with good **receptive language skills** perceive gestures, sounds, words, and written information well. Receptive language is important for developing appropriate communication skills. Instruction that targets receptive language skills can include tasks that require sustained attention and focus, recognizing emotions and gestures, and listening and reading comprehension. Games that challenge the players to communicate carefully, such as charades or catchphrase, can be a great way to target receptive language skills. As one student tries to accurately express an idea with words or gestures, the rest of the class must exercise their receptive language skills. Lastly, focusing on **social skills and play skills instruction** encourages opportunities for children to interact with their peers or adults. This fosters receptive language skills and targets deficits in these skills.

## Stages of Literacy Development

The development of literacy in young children is separated into five stages. Names and ranges of these stages sometimes vary slightly, but the stage milestones are similar. Stage 1 is the **Emergent Reader stage**. In this stage, children ages 6 months to 6 years demonstrate skills like pretend reading, recognizing letters of the alphabet, retelling stories, and printing their names. Stage 2 is the **Novice/Early Reader stage** (ages 6–7 years). Children begin to understand the relationships between letters and sounds and written and spoken words, and they read texts containing high-frequency words. Children in this stage should develop orthographic conventions and semantic knowledge. In Stage 3, the **Decoding Reader stage**, children ages 7–9 develop decoding skills in order to read simple stories. They also demonstrate increased fluency. Stage 4 (ages 8–15 years) is called the **Fluent, Comprehending/Transitional Reader stage**. In this stage, fourth to eighth graders read to learn new ideas and information. In Stage 5, the **Expert/Fluent Reader stage**, children ages

16 years and older read more complex information. They also read expository and narrative texts with multiple viewpoints.

**Review Video: Stages of Reading Development**
Visit mometrix.com/academy and enter code: 121184

### *Relationship between Language Development and Early Literacy Skills*

Language development and early literacy skills are interconnected. **Language concepts** begin and develop shortly after birth with infant/parent interactions, cooing, and then babbling. These are the earliest attempts at language acquisition for infants. Young children begin interacting with written and spoken words before they enter their grade school years. Before they enter formal classrooms, children begin to make **connections** between speaking and listening and reading and writing. Children with strong speaking and listening skills demonstrate strong literacy skills in early grade school. The development of **phonological awareness** is connected to early literacy skills. Children with good phonological awareness recognize that words are made up of different speech sounds. For example, children with appropriate phonological awareness can break words (e.g., "bat" into separate speech sounds, "b-a-t"). Examples of phonological awareness include rhyming (when the ending parts of words have the same or similar sounds) and alliteration (when words all have the same beginning sound). Success with phonological awareness (oral language) activities depends on adequate development of speech and language skills.

### *Promoting Literacy During the Early Stages of Literacy Development*

Teachers and parents can implement strategies at different stages of literacy development in order to build **good reading skills** in children with and without disabilities. During the **Emergent Reader stage**, teachers and parents can introduce children to the conventions of reading with picture books. They can model turning the pages, reading from left to right, and other reading conventions. Book reading at this stage helps children begin to identify letters, letter sounds, and simple words. Repetitive reading of familiar texts also helps children begin to make predictions about what they are reading. During the **Novice/Early Reader** and **Decoding Reader stages**, parents and teachers can help children form the building blocks of decoding and fluency skills by reading for meaning and emphasizing letter-sound relationships, visual cues, and language patterns. In these stages, increasing familiarity with sight words is essential. In the **Fluent, Comprehending/Transitional Reader stage**, children should be encouraged to read book series, as the shared characters, settings, and plots help develop their comprehension skills. At this stage, a good reading rate (fluency) is an indicator of comprehension skills. **Expert/Fluent readers** can independently read multiple texts and comprehend their meanings. Teachers and parents can begin exposing children to a variety of fiction and non-fiction texts before this stage in order to promote good fluency skills.

**Review Video: Phonics (Encoding and Decoding)**
Visit mometrix.com/academy and enter code: 821361

**Review Video: Fluency**
Visit mometrix.com/academy and enter code: 531179

## Chapter Quiz

Ready to see how well you retained what you just read? Scan the QR code to go directly to the chapter quiz interface for this study guide. If you're using a computer, simply visit the online resources page at **mometrix.com/resources719/gacesegcelemed** and click the Chapter Quizzes link.

# Planning the Learning Environment and Social Interactions

## Learning Environments for Students with Disabilities

### Determining the Special Education Setting Placement

Special education setting placement is determined in a student's Individualized Education Program (IEP), as specified by the Individuals with Disabilities Education Act (IDEA). IDEA requires that students be placed in **general education classrooms** to the maximum extent possible. Students should be placed in environments that are most appropriate for them, known as the **least restrictive environment**. If students can be educated in general education classrooms (**inclusion**) when provided with appropriate accommodations, they can be placed in general education classrooms. When students with disabilities need modifications to curriculum that are significantly below grade level or different than their peers, the students may be placed in **resource rooms** for remedial instruction. However, the students may also participate in the general education curriculum with modified work that meets their current abilities. For example, a student who struggles in math can use a calculator accommodation in the inclusion setting. A student whose math skills are two grade levels below the skills of same-aged peers may be placed in an inclusion setting with modifications or receive instruction in a resource room.

### Full or Partial Inclusion Settings vs. Self-Contained Classrooms

Students with mild to moderate disabilities are often placed in **inclusion** or **partial inclusion classrooms**. The responsibilities of the special educator include assisting and collaborating with the general education teacher to create a curriculum with **modifications** that meets the learning styles and needs of the students with disabilities. The special educator may circulate during lessons or classwork to help students when needed and provide modifications to the general education curriculum to best meet the individual needs of each student.

The role of a special educator in a **self-contained classroom** is much different. Students in a self-contained classroom typically have disabilities that significantly limit their ability to receive quality education in inclusion or partial inclusion settings. Students with moderate disabilities in self-contained classrooms receive **modified instruction** with accommodations. The special educator is usually assisted by teaching assistants or paraprofessionals who help the educator meet the needs of individual students.

Special educators in inclusion, partial inclusion, and self-contained classrooms share some similar **responsibilities**. These responsibilities include monitoring IEP data on annual goals for each student, giving standardized pre-tests and post-tests, facilitating parent-teacher conferences, completing annual IEP reviews, and developing curriculum.

### Structured Learning Environments

A structured learning environment is an important component of good **classroom management**. Teachers that create environments that are conducive for teaching and learning create environments where students feel safe. In **effective structured learning environments**, teachers create solid relationships with students by getting to know them and their interests. Often, this information can be used to implement learning activities based on students' interests. Another way to promote effective structured learning environments is to consistently follow implemented rules and maintain **consistency** in procedures in order to communicate what to expect to students. Transitioning students appropriately between activities increases time spent learning. Additionally, teachers create solid environments for their students by spending time designing effective lesson plans that anticipate student behaviors. Teachers can also establish good learning environments by promoting target behaviors. This means promoting standards of behavior and clear consequences for breaking rules. Students that have clear expectations learn in effective structured learning environments.

### Non-Traditional Classroom Seating Arrangements

Seating arrangements are part of good classroom management strategies, especially for students with disabilities. Special education settings and inclusion settings often require flexibility with instruction and versatility with **seating arrangements**. The traditional setting includes rows of desks facing the area where the teacher conducts instruction. More **student-centered arrangements** include a horseshoe seating arrangement, a group pod arrangement, or a paired arrangement. A **horseshoe seating arrangement** is conducive to student-centered instruction because it allows the students to face each other and the instructor to move around the classroom easily. This setup facilitates classroom discussions and encourages interactions between instructors and students and among peers. The **group pod** or **paired-pod arrangement** is useful for student-centered instruction like small group work. This arrangement is also helpful when students need to rotate through lesson stages or work in small groups on projects. Effective teachers do not use one seating arrangement for the entire year. Best practices indicate that seating arrangements should change and be tied to the intent of lesson objectives.

### Inclusive Learning Environments That Meet Unique Needs

Effective inclusive environments abide by the **universal design for learning (UDL) framework**. Special educators and general educators can work together to create learning environments that are accessible to students with unique language or physical needs. This can be done by providing **multiple ways** for students to access lesson concepts, express learned concepts, and engage in the learning process. For students with language barriers, signs, symbols, pictures, and learning concepts may have different meanings than they do for students without language barriers. Keeping this in mind, teachers can address UDL guidelines for students with **language barriers** by providing diverse ways to activate prior knowledge, emphasizing key learning elements, and using visuals to guide the learning process. For students with **physical barriers**, teachers can level the learning process by making their physical classroom environments accessible and providing different ways for students to express what they have learned. In general, teachers abiding by the UDL framework would have these supports in place in order to ensure that the needs of diverse learners are met.

### Positive and Inclusive Learning Environments

Whether in the general education classroom or special education classroom, the UDL model should foster **positive and inclusive learning environments**. General education and special education teachers can take measures to ensure the UDL concept is implemented to address the unique needs of students with **cognitive or behavioral needs**. Since each student presents different needs, a one-size-fits-all approach to learning is not suitable or UDL compliant for these students. Special educators and general educators should openly communicate about students' unique learning or cognitive needs. General strategies include receiving regular **input from special educators** on how to best meet the needs of the students in the classroom. This includes sharing information with any **paraprofessionals and aides** regarding how to assist the students in the general education classroom. UDL-based strategies include the general educators providing multiple means by which students can complete the assignments. Students with cognitive disabilities may also benefit from the use of concrete examples and instruction, especially when addressing abstract concepts.

### Learning Environments that Support Students with Behavioral Needs

The **UDL concepts** can be implemented to reduce challenging behavior in the classroom. They can also be used to help students with behavioral needs find success in the general education classroom. **Lack of student engagement** is compatible with the presentation of **challenging behaviors**. When UDL concepts are demonstrated appropriately, engagement can improve. Providing **multiple means of representation** is one UDL strategy for improving engagement and challenging behavior. This means the classroom teacher provides multiple ways of presenting the teaching material in order to engage as many students as possible. Teachers that provide multiple means of representation look to activate prior knowledge and help students make sense of the current content. UDL-compliant strategies also include providing **multiple means of expression**.

Teachers applying UDL principles recognize that differentiating activities and assignments addresses a variety of abilities and learning styles. UDL-compliant teachers should also provide **multiple means of engagement**. Successful engagement in learning can often offset challenging behaviors by helping students focus on lesson material. Offering both challenging and simplistic work options and making engaging, solid connections to past and/or future lesson content can minimize the possibility of problems arising in the classroom.

## Classroom Strategies Promoting Social-Emotional Development and Growth

Classroom environments should emanate **positivity** and **growth**. Classrooms that promote **social-emotional development and growth** provide security for students and create environments where learning takes place. Teachers can promote social-emotional development and growth by creating predictable classroom routines with visual reminders, keeping classrooms free of dangerous objects and materials, and arranging for learning to take place in large and small groups. They can also rotate activities and materials to keep students engaged, provide appropriate materials for learning centers, and create opportunities for children to engage socially. Teachers can act as nurturing adults by encouraging social interactions and problem solving, modeling appropriate language and social skills, encouraging and validating children's thoughts and feelings, and using clear signals to indicate transitions between activities. Teachers should build community environments in their classrooms, build appropriate relationships with students by getting to know their strengths and weaknesses, and demonstrate good conflict resolution and problem-solving abilities.

### *Effect of Emotional and Psychological Needs of Students with Disabilities*

When a child is diagnosed with a disability, educators often primarily focus on the educational implications. However, students with disabilities also have **emotional needs** associated with their disabilities. These needs vary by student and disability. Generally, students with disabilities struggle emotionally. Symptoms may include low self-esteem, anxiety, acting out, reduced intrinsic motivation, and physical effects, like headaches. Educators, parents, and other professionals can manage the emotional needs of students with disabilities by talking with them about the disability diagnoses and educational implications. Educators can increase their **awareness** of how students might be feeling about the diagnoses and identify situations that may cause anxiety or acting out. Educators can also help by praising students consistently, even for small actions, which can help with confidence. Parents, educators, and other professionals can also work together to ensure that the students receive instruction in the most appropriate educational environments for their disabilities.

## Lifting Guidelines for Students Who Require Physical Lifting

Teachers and paraprofessionals may encounter students with physical disabilities who require **assisted transfers**. In some circumstances, students must be **lift-assisted** from their wheelchairs in order to participate in physical therapy or floor activities. While this practice is more common in low-incidence classrooms and not always a job requirement, it is important to know school guidelines for **lifting techniques** to keep staff and students safe. Knowing school guidelines for lifting can also help prevent back injuries from occurring. Physical therapists working with the students should be consulted before attempting student lifts. They are trained professionals who know specific procedures for lifting students in order to keep the students and staff members safe. Every school district has policies for lift-assisted student transfers. Each student should be evaluated to determine if a one-person lift or two-person lift is needed. Two-person lifts are for heavier students, and some school districts do not allow two-person lifts for safety reasons.

## Managing Distractions That May Affect Learning and Development

Managing distractions is a part of good teaching practices. Special educators demonstrate good **classroom management strategies** when they do the following:

- Create positive learning environments by getting to know students' individual emotional, intellectual, social, and physical needs.
- Remove or accommodate environmental triggers specific to students.
- Remove or accommodate behavioral triggers.
- Encourage students to help with classroom jobs and small tasks.

- Create lesson plans with anticipated behaviors in mind.
- Attempt verbal de-escalation first when behavioral issues arise.
- Set clear, consistent rules.
- Set and follow through with consequences for breaking the rules.
- Take time to get to know students and their triggers.
- Create seating arrangements that minimize distractions, such as placing distractible students closer to the teacher.
- Teach social, thinking, test-taking, problem-solving, and self-regulation skills alongside academic content.
- Use visual aids in lessons.
- Utilize peer-instruction opportunities.
- Provide opportunities for breaks.
- Incorporate computer-based programs, which can hold the attention of students with disabilities like autism.

### Effect of Home Life Factors on Learning and Development

Students' home lives are interconnected with their school lives. **Home life factors**, especially negative ones, are difficult for students to avoid generalizing to the school environment. **Home stressors** can often develop into dysfunction at school. Factors that affect the learning and development of students with disabilities include academic, environmental, intellectual, language, medical, perceptual, and psychological factors. **Academic factors** include developmental delays in core content areas, lack of basic skills, and apparent inconsistency of learning in certain stages of development. **Environmental factors** occur when children are exposed to home life trauma, such as divorce, drug abuse, alcoholism, parental fighting, or family illness. **Intellectual factors** include limited intellectual abilities or unnoticed gifted abilities. **Language factors** include issues with language barriers or language acquisition, such as aphasia, bilingualism, expressive language disorder, and pragmatic language disorder. **Medical factors** include attention-deficit/hyperactivity disorder, muscular problems, and hearing problems. **Perceptual factors** include any factors that affect or slow down students' processing of information. **Psychological factors** include depression, anxiety, and conduct disorders.

## Team Teaching Models

### Components of a Successful Team-Teaching Model

A successful team-teaching model is one where the teachers involved set clear, effective, specific **goals** for performance. These goals must demonstrate clarity. All team-teaching members must be clear on the components of the goals and their potential outcomes. Clear goals allow team members and students to know what they are working towards as a classroom. Goals should be specific and measurable. **Goal criteria** should be qualified in percentages or quantities. This provides hard evidence for how effectively the team-teaching classroom is meeting the goals. Challenging goals set high expectations for what the team needs to work towards. Challenging goals ensure that team members and classroom students are working to achieve goals right outside their ability levels. Goals that are too challenging can be frustrating for all team members and students. A successful team-teaching model also reflects **commitment** from team members and any other professionals involved in the classroom.

### Function of a Multidisciplinary Team-Teaching Model

The three disciplinary team models include a multidisciplinary team, an interdisciplinary team, and a transdisciplinary team. The **multidisciplinary team** is usually composed of the special educator, general education teacher, parents, paraprofessionals, principal, and school psychologist. As a whole, this team presents a comprehensive group of expertise, qualifications, and skills. In the multidisciplinary team model, these professionals do not collaborate but instead work alongside each other to pursue a **common goal** for the individual student with special needs. The multidisciplinary team model is effective for evaluating a student for referral for special education, completing pre-referral testing, and completing an Individualized Education Program or Evaluation Team Report. Sometimes this team is referred to as the child study team or student support team. In this model, professionals usually pull out students to work with them individually. Parents and legal guardians are a part of this process. Professionals working with the student should openly communicate their processes and the results of any evaluations or informal observations.

### Interdisciplinary Team Model

An interdisciplinary team model features the **general education teacher** providing all curriculum and accommodations for a student with an Individualized Education Program (IEP). In this model, the special educator and other professionals relevant to the education of the student collaborate to ensure that the curriculum meets the needs of the student and the accommodations are appropriate. This model is not a team-teaching model. Advantages of this model include the collaboration of all IEP team members towards a common goal and the student's needs being addressed by one teacher instead of several different teachers or professionals. The disadvantages of this model include difficulties with collaboration between professionals and issues with delivering related services to students who need them. Related service provision sometimes includes one-on-one instruction, which requires the student to be pulled out for a certain amount of time during general education instruction. This model may also not be appropriate for students with intense needs, as they often require **individualized education** in order to meet IEP goals. They may also require specific accommodations and modifications not suitable for the general education classroom.

### Transdisciplinary Team-Teaching Model

In this model, professionals working with the student work together collaboratively to ensure the individual needs of the student are met. The **special educator** may teach in the general education classroom, delivering instruction to both students with and without disabilities. This model features a team-teaching experience for classroom students, where the special educator and general educator may take turns teaching. The presence of the special educator in the general education setting means the special educator can offer advice for **accommodating** the students with special needs in the classroom. Additionally, this model provides opportunities for teachers and other professionals to communicate consistently about students' progress, share ideas, and work collaboratively to solve any issues that arise. The effectiveness of this model relies heavily on the collaboration of the special educator and the general educator in addressing the major features of this team-teaching model.

### Advantages and Disadvantages of Team-Teaching Models

Students with and without disabilities present a variety of **learning abilities** in the general education classroom. One advantage of team-teaching models in this setting is being able to target the unique abilities, learning methods, and skills that each student brings to the classroom. Another advantage is effective classroom management. In an **effective team-teaching model**, one teacher provides the instruction, while the other practices classroom management skills to minimize disruptions and promote a safe learning environment. This model encourages class participation, facilitates group activities, and provides multiple means of engagement for learning content. One disadvantage is there may be an offset between the teachers sharing a class. When one teacher is not open to multiple methods of delivering instruction, the team-teaching approach is ineffective. Planning and making group decisions regarding curriculum can be time consuming and stressful in a team-teaching environment.

## Behavioral Issues for Students with Disabilities

### Behavioral Issues and Intervention Strategies

Behavior issues occur with students with and without disabilities. However, they may occur more frequently or to a higher degree for some students with disabilities. Behavior issues are often a **manifestation** of a child's disability. For example, students with attention-deficit/hyperactivity disorder may present with attention and focus issues and impulsivity. **Common behavior issues** include the following:

- Emotional outbursts
- Inattention and inability to focus
- Impulsivity
- Aggression
- Abusive language
- Oppositional defiance
- Lying or stealing
- Threatening adults or peers

Other behavior issues may include inappropriate sexual behavior, inability to control sexual behavior, self-harm, or self-harm attempts. Behavior issues can be **avoided** or **remediated** with classroom management skills like setting clear and consistent classroom goals, setting time limits, and providing visuals to assist with transitions or concepts. When a student is in an aggressive state, it is important for the teacher to remain calm, provide choices for the student, and restate the consequences of any aggressive outbursts.

> **Review Video: Student Behavior Management Approaches**
> Visit mometrix.com/academy and enter code: 843846
>
> **Review Video: Promoting Appropriate Behavior**
> Visit mometrix.com/academy and enter code: 321015

## Managing Students with Emotional Disorders

Managing a classroom of students with emotional disorders can be challenging and unpredictable. Students with emotional disorders have Individualized Education Program (IEP) goals that focus on **controlling** or **monitoring** their daily behavior choices. However, this does not always mean they will engage in meeting these goals. It is important for educators to know how to **manage** issues that students with emotional disorders may bring to the classroom. When creating resources and lesson plans, an educator should do the following:

- Establish a **safety plan**, which includes knowing how to implement a **crisis prevention plan**.
- Maintain an environment that reduces **stimulation** and provides **visual cues** for expected behavior.
- Implement **intervention-based strategies** for managing student behavior.
- Collect and use **data** to identify triggers, track behaviors, and recognize strategies that produce positive outcomes.
- Practice open **communication** about classroom expectations to students, parents, and other teachers.

Special education teachers can be helpful in implementing these guidelines, especially when students with emotional disorders are in inclusive settings.

## Supporting Students with Mental Health Issues

Students with disabilities may also have mental health issues. These students may not necessarily be diagnosed with emotional disturbances, as mental health issues can occur concurrently with other disabilities. Students' mental health symptoms may fluctuate on an hourly, daily, or weekly basis. Intervention techniques and supports must be determined by the individual needs of each student. General and special educators across all special education settings can **support** these students by learning how to **recognize mental health issues** in schools. Teachers can use observations and research-based strategies for identifying issues. Training in working with students who have certain mental health disorders may also be useful. Occasionally, training in crisis prevention plans is required of teachers working with students who may become aggressive due to their disorders.

# Behavior Assessment and Intervention

## Cognitive Behavioral Theory

The cognitive behavioral theory states that people form their own negative or positive concepts that affect their behaviors. The cognitive behavioral theory involves a **cognitive triad** of thoughts and behaviors. This triad refers to thoughts about the **self**, the **world and environment**, and the **future**. In times of stress, people's thoughts can become distressed or dysfunctional. Sometimes cognitive behavioral therapy, based on the cognitive behavioral theory model, is used to help people address and manage their thoughts. This process involves people examining their thoughts more closely in order to bring them back to more realistic, grounded ways of thinking. People's thoughts and perceptions can often affect their lives negatively and lead to unhealthy emotions and behaviors. **Cognitive behavioral therapy** helps people to adjust their thinking, learn ways to access healthy thoughts, and learn healthier or safer behaviors.

## Antecedents, Behavior, and Consequences as Stimuli Used in Behavior Analysis

Antecedents and consequences play a role in behavioral analysis, which is important for evaluating the behaviors of students. The purpose of behavior analysis is to gather information about a specific behavior demonstrated by a student. **Antecedents** are the actions or events that occur before the behavior occurs. It is important to recognize antecedents for behaviors to better understand under what circumstances the behavior is occurring. The **behavior** is the undesirable action that occurs as a result of the antecedent. **Consequences** are what happens immediately after the behavior occurs. These can be natural or enforced. A student might desire a certain consequence when engaging in the behavior. Understanding the relationships between antecedents, behavior, and consequences allows a professional to determine how to minimize or eliminate the behavior. In some circumstances, antecedents and consequences can be manipulated, changed, or removed in order to avoid reinforcing the undesired behavior.

## Behavior Rating Scale Assessments

Behavior rating scales address the needs of students with emotional disorders who are referred to special education. Problems with behavior are often the reason a student has been referred for special education. These scales are used in determining a student's **eligibility** for special education, and in addressing **undesirable behaviors** demonstrated by students already in special education for reasons other than behavior problems. They are similar to adaptive behavior scales in that teachers or other professionals can administer the scales with little training as long as they are familiar with the students. Behavior rating scales help measure the frequency and intensity of the behaviors for a particular student often by assigning numbered ratings. They serve as a starting point for learning more about a student's behavior so that behavior interventions and management can take place. These scales are **norm-referenced**, so the outcomes of the behavior rating scales are compared to the behaviors of others.

## Negative and Positive Reinforcement Related to Applied Behavior Analysis

Part of applied behavior analysis (**ABA**) is applying negative and positive reinforcement strategies, which are forms of conditioning strategies. In behavioral conditioning, the term **reinforcement** refers to trying to increase the frequency of a desired behavior, whereas the term **punishment** refers to trying to decrease the frequency of an undesired behavior. Similarly, when discussing behavioral conditioning methods, the word **positive** refers to the *addition* of a stimulus, whereas the word **negative** refers to the *removal* of a stimulus. These four terms tend to be confused but are very specifically used to denote particular types of behavioral conditioning.

**Positive reinforcement** works by providing a desired **reward** for a desired behavior. For example, parents may give a child an allowance (the positive reinforcement) for doing chores (the behavior). In contrast, **negative reinforcement** removes an aversive stimulus to encourage a desired behavior. An example of this might be that a parent rewards a child's behavior by taking away some of his chores. Negative reinforcement is different from a punishment because the goal of punishment is to *discourage* an unwanted behavior while the goal of negative reinforcement is to *encourage* a desirable behavior. Although it is not commonly discussed, positive and negative stimuli may be used at the same time in conditioning to effect a greater change.

| Term: | Example: |
|---|---|
| Positive Reinforcement | A teacher *gives* the high-scorers on a test a sticker. |
| Negative Reinforcement | A teacher *takes away* an assignment if the class performs well on a test. |
| Positive Punishment | A police officer *gives* a driver a speeding ticket. |
| Negative Punishment | A parent grounds a student, *taking away* video games for two weeks. |
| Combination Reinforcement | A physical education teacher *replaces* a workout (negative) with a game (positive) because the class was well-behaved. |
| Combination Punishment | A student gets low grades and is required to complete extra schoolwork (positive) and is not allowed to participate in sports for a week (negative). |

## Developing Positive Behavioral Interventions and Supports

Positive behavioral intervention and support (**PBIS**) plans can be implemented in classrooms or schoolwide to encourage specific, positive outcomes in groups of students with and without disabilities. A PBIS plan, such as an anti-bullying campaign, is put in place to encourage **good behavior** and **school safety** and to remove **environmental triggers** of undesirable behavior. The goal of a PBIS plan is for students to learn appropriate behavior just as they would learn an academic subject. Effective PBIS plans are based on research and analysis of data collected on targeted, large-scale behaviors. As with any behavioral plan, the success of PBIS plans is determined by monitoring student progress. PBIS plans should change if they do not work or if they stop working.

## Developing a Functional Behavior Assessment

A functional behavior assessment (**FBA**) is a formal process used to examine student behavior. The goal of an FBA is to identify what is causing a specific behavior and evaluate how the behavior is affecting the student's educational performance. Once these factors are determined, the FBA is useful in implementing **interventions** for the behavior. When an FBA is developed, a student's behavior must be specifically defined; then the teacher or other professional devises a plan for collecting data on the behavior. These points of data are helpful in determining possible causes of the behavior, such as environmental triggers. The teacher or other professional can then implement the most appropriate plan for addressing the student's behavior. Often, this means implementing a **behavior intervention plan**, which includes introducing the student to actions or processes that are incompatible with the problem behavior. It is important to monitor the plan to ensure its effectiveness or remediate certain steps.

**Review Video: Functional Behavior Assessments**
Visit mometrix.com/academy and enter code: 783262

## Developing Behavior Intervention Plans

A behavior intervention plan (**BIP**) is based on a functional behavior assessment. The purpose of the BIP is to teach the student actions, behaviors, or processes that are incompatible with the problem behavior. The BIP may be included in an Individualized Education Program (IEP) or 504 Plan, or components of the BIP may be written out as IEP goals. Once an FBA is conducted, a BIP is put in place that describes the target behavior, lists factors that trigger the behavior, and lists any interventions that help the student avoid the behavior. The interventions include problem-solving skills for the student to use instead of demonstrating the target behavior. If the interventions fail to target the problem behavior or are no longer effective for targeting the behavior, then the FBA must be revisited and a new BIP developed.

### POSITIVE CLASSROOM DISCIPLINE STRATEGIES

A core element of effective classroom management, positive classroom discipline is a means of holding students accountable for their actions, and it starts with establishing clear and consistent **consequences** for poor choices. Students learn to predict consequences and self-correct their behaviors. It is helpful to give students **reminders** about behavior and rules instead of immediately resorting to consequences. **Pre-reminders** about expectations can be given before starting a lesson. **Nonverbal reminders** such as looks, touches, silence, or removal are possible ways to discourage students from engaging in poor choices. Removal as a consequence involves sending the student out of the classroom either to protect the other students from harm or to prevent a student from impeding the course of instruction. Removal laws vary between states and local districts, but removal is generally mandatory whenever a student is being violent. **Spoken reminders** can be used to further encourage self-management skills and should be used as precursors for reminding students about expectations instead of delivering immediate consequences.

### PROMOTING APPROPRIATE BEHAVIOR IN INCLUSIVE LEARNING ENVIRONMENTS

Effective classrooms have good management strategies in place that promote good learning environments and minimize disruptions. Teachers with effective classroom management strategies demonstrate good leadership and organization skills. They also promote positive classroom experiences, establish clear expectations for behavior, and reinforce positive behaviors. In **inclusive learning environments**, it is important for teachers to keep all students on track with their learning. When it comes to students with disabilities, planning classroom management strategies presents different challenges. Effective teachers understand how students' special needs come into play with expected classroom behaviors. General and special educators can demonstrate effective classroom management strategies by figuring out what is causing students to act out or misbehave. They should collaborate with other professionals and students' parents to ensure the success of students with special needs in their classrooms. Lastly, effective classroom management includes setting goals for inclusive classrooms to achieve. Clear goals help establish good rapport with students with special needs because they know what is expected of them.

## Crisis Prevention and Management

### CRISES AND CRISIS PREVENTION AND MANAGEMENT PLANS

#### *CRISES*

A **crisis** is generally defined as a situation that is so emotionally impactful that an individual is not able to cope with the situation by normal means and is at risk of harming themselves or others. Crises can arise from either developmental changes that happen throughout life, such as going through puberty or graduating from school, or they can be situational and arise at any time. Examples of situational crises include sickness, losses, family deaths, and any other kind of unpredictable situation that comes up throughout life. Students with disabilities often have particular difficulty coping with stressful life situations and may need the help of a **crisis prevention plan** as a result. Crisis prevention and management goals generally focus on coping mechanisms and healthy anticipation of unavoidable situations to help the individual understand and safely navigate their way through a crisis.

#### *CRISIS PREVENTION PLANS*

Crisis prevention plans essentially serve to help with early identification of a crisis and to provide the necessary support to help the individual through a crisis to an effective resolution. These plans are often put together with the help of various members of an individual's support team, taking into account past behaviors, health, and other factors of his or her life. Some organizations, such as the Crisis Prevention Institute, specialize in crisis prevention and intervention training for professionals. Crisis prevention plans should take into account principles of least restrictive environment to support individuals in their normal environments, while also removing or being aware of any known **behavioral triggers** that may be problematic. In the event that the individual in crisis becomes physically violent or harmful to themselves, stronger emergent response may be warranted. The ultimate goal is to keep the individual and others safe until his or her emotional state has been normalized. There is no specific duration of time for a crisis, but any intervention should be treated as short-term to prevent restricting the individual's rights through unnecessary intervention. It is important to provide the individual with clear structures and expectations to help understand direct consequences for undesired choices prior to entering a crisis. Crisis prevention plans should also provide clear processes that professionals and family members can use when students do enter a crisis in order to de-escalate the situations.

**Review Video: Crisis Management and Prevention**
Visit mometrix.com/academy and enter code: 351872

# Special Education Settings

## Least Restrictive Environment

The Individuals with Disabilities Education Act (IDEA) requires a free and appropriate public education to be provided in a student's **least restrictive environment (LRE)**. This means that a student with a disability who qualifies for special education should be educated in a free, appropriate, and public setting and be placed in an instructional setting that meets the LRE principle. IDEA states that LRE means students with disabilities should participate in the general education classroom "to the maximum extent appropriate." **Mainstreaming** and **inclusion** are ways for students with disabilities to participate in general education classrooms while receiving appropriate accommodations, modifications, interventions, and related services. The amount of time students spend in an LRE suitable for their individual needs is stated in their Individualized Education Program (IEP). The accommodations, modifications, interventions, and related services the student should receive are also outlined in the IEP. Students who need special education services for more than 50% of the day may be placed in other instructional settings that meet their LRE needs, such as resource rooms or self-contained classrooms.

**Review Video: Least Restrictive Environment**
Visit mometrix.com/academy and enter code: 100354

## Continuum of Special Education Services

IDEA mandates that school systems educate students with disabilities with students who do not have disabilities to the maximum extent that is appropriate. IDEA also mandates that schools not take students out of regular education classes unless the classes are not benefiting the students. Supplementary aids and support services must be in place before students can be considered for removal. Schools must offer a **continuum of special education services** that range from restrictive to least restrictive. In a typical continuum of services, regular education classrooms offer the **least restrictive access** to students with disabilities. Next on the continuum are resource rooms, followed by special classes that target specific deficits. Special schools, homebound services, hospitals, and institutions are the most restrictive education environments. The number of students at each stage of the continuum decreases as restriction increases. Fewer students benefit more from being educated in hospitals or institutions than in resource rooms.

## Inclusion Classroom Setting

The principle of least restrictive environment (LRE) is a right guaranteed under IDEA to protect a student from unnecessary restriction or seclusion from the general population. IDEA does not expressly define an LRE for each specific disability, so it is the responsibility of the IEP team of professionals, including the student's parent or legal guardian, to determine the best **LRE setting** possible for an individual student. **Mainstreaming** or **inclusion** is the practice of keeping students with disabilities in the general education setting for the entire school day. The students may receive supports and services like aides, assistive technology, accommodations, and modifications that are appropriate for their individual needs. These supports and services are intended to help students with disabilities gain access to the general education curriculum with the fewest possible barriers. The principle of LRE also sits on a spectrum and allows for variable inclusion or separation throughout parts of the day depending on a student's particular needs. As this is a student right, any more restrictive setting must be **justified by necessity** in students' IEPs and cannot be determined by convenience or financial considerations of the school or staff.

### *Collaborative Teaching in an Inclusion Classroom*

If determined by an IEP, a student with a disability may participate in an **inclusive setting**. In some classrooms, students participate in **co-taught settings**. In this **collaborative teaching environment**, the general educator and special educator work together to meet the goals of the students with disabilities in the regular education classroom. Students in this setting are all taught to the same educational standards. However, accommodations and modifications may be implemented for students with disabilities. In a successful collaborative teaching model, the special educator and general educator may cooperatively implement the accommodations and modifications for these students. A two-teacher setting also gives students more opportunities to receive individualized instruction, work in small groups, or receive one-on-one attention. Collaborative teaching in the co-taught setting can facilitate differentiated instruction, help teachers follow the universal design for learning framework, and provide individualized learning opportunities.

### *Implementing Modifications and Accommodations in an Inclusion Classroom*

General educators can work with special educators to create an effective **co-teaching model**. In an effective co-teaching model, both general educators and special educators are guided by the **universal design for learning framework**. This helps ensure that the needs of the diverse group of learners are being met. Students' IEPs expressly document any required modifications, such as reduced work. In a co-teaching model, student modifications are communicated to the **general educator**. The **special educator** can work with the general educator to provide the modifications in an inclusive classroom setting. Students' IEPs also expressly document any required **accommodations**. These accommodations may or may not be used in an inclusive setting, depending on the relevancy of the accommodation. For example, the accommodation of using a calculator would be utilized in a math class but not a social studies class. In addition to expressly written accommodations, special educators and general educators can work together in an inclusive setting to provide appropriate accommodations during the learning process. These accommodations may be part of informal assessments used to adjust instruction.

### *Role of Paraeducators*

Paraeducators, sometimes referred to as aides or paraprofessionals, are part of students' education teams. **Paraeducators** work under the supervision of special educators or principals and are key contributors to the learning process for certain students. Their primary role, especially if their positions are funded by the Individuals with Disabilities Education Act, is to provide **educational support** for students. The use of paraeducators is noted in students' IEPs. Paraeducators can facilitate the learning process for students by removing learning barriers, keeping track of goal progress, and organizing goal-tracking activities. Paraeducators cannot introduce new concepts or take over the role of teachers. Paraeducators cannot make changes to what students are learning unless specific modifications are listed in students' IEPs. They cannot provide accommodations unless the accommodations are appropriate for what is written in students' IEPs. Paraeducators may also be instructed by supervising teachers or principals to facilitate and monitor accommodations or modifications for students and reinforce learned concepts.

## Self-Contained Classroom Setting

According to the Individuals with Disabilities Education Act, LRE standards require students to spend as much time as possible with their nondisabled peers in the **general education setting**. This means students should receive general education "to the maximum extent appropriate," and special classes, special schools, or removal from the general education classroom should only be considered when students' needs are greater than what can be provided by supplementary aids and services. A **self-contained classroom setting** can be a separate class within a school or a separate school for students with disabilities whose needs are greater than what can be offered in the general education classroom even with educational supports. These settings may provide specialized instruction and support for students with similar needs. Placement in self-contained classrooms must be justified in students' IEPs.

### Partial Mainstream/Inclusion Classroom Setting

It is generally up to the IEP team of professionals and the parent or legal guardian to determine the LRE that best suits the needs of a student. In a partial mainstream/inclusion classroom setting, a student spends part of the day in the general education classroom and part of the day in a separate, special education classroom. This type of LRE is appropriate when a student's needs are greater than what can be provided in the general education classroom even with educational supports or services in place. For example, a student with severe deficits in mathematical skills may receive math instruction in a separate classroom or receive one-on-one or small group instruction. Placement in partial mainstream/inclusion classrooms must be justified in students' IEPs.

### Specialized Education Settings

School districts sometimes offer specialized education settings for students with disabilities, such as **special preschools**. Preschools for children with disabilities typically focus on children aged 3–5 years. They are important resources for teaching early learning, communication, and social skills that are essential for children with disabilities. In **life skills settings**, students with disabilities can receive specialized instruction in academic, social, behavioral, and daily-living skills. **Social behavior skills settings** are sometimes called "applied behavior skills settings" or "behavior skills settings." In this setting, the primary focus is on social and decision-making skills. **Transition settings** are available for students making the transition from high school to life after high school. Students with IEPs can stay in high school until the age of 21 or 22, depending on the calendar month they turn 22. Transition settings assist students with work experiences, postsecondary education experiences, and independent living skills.

## Chapter Quiz

Ready to see how well you retained what you just read? Scan the QR code to go directly to the chapter quiz interface for this study guide. If you're using a computer, simply visit the online resources page at **mometrix.com/resources719/gacesegcelemed** and click the Chapter Quizzes link.

# Instruction and Assessment

## Instructional Planning

### Designing Lesson Plans and Units to Align with Instructional Goals

The effective sequencing of units and lesson plans is key to developing coherent, comprehensible instruction that aligns with instructional goals and fosters success in learning. Teachers must first determine the instructional goals that students will be expected to achieve based on state academic standards as a framework and students' individual needs, knowledge, and abilities. Teachers must then logically arrange specific units of instruction aimed toward achieving the determined instructional goals. Each unit should build upon knowledge from the prior unit. Within each unit, teachers must determine what students must achieve as they work toward instructional goals and determine objectives that facilitate success based on individual need and ability. Once objectives are defined, teachers must design lesson plans in a logical sequence that will facilitate students in reaching these objectives and increasingly build upon knowledge as students work toward achieving the learning goal. When planning lessons, teachers must decide which activities, procedures, and materials are necessary for successfully completing lesson objectives while ensuring that individual learning needs are met. The teacher must also decide what will be assessed at the end of each lesson and unit to determine student success in achieving instructional goals.

**Review Video:** Creating Effective Lesson Plans
Visit mometrix.com/academy and enter code: 100377

### Creating Developmentally Appropriate Learning Experiences and Assessments

Multiple factors must be considered when designing developmentally appropriate learning experiences and assessments that effectively facilitate student growth and achievement. Teachers must consider the general cognitive, physical, social, and emotional developmental levels of students as well as individual differences in background, skill, knowledge, and learning needs. With this understanding, teachers must then evaluate whether learning experiences are simultaneously appropriate to students' developmental levels and individual needs. This includes ensuring that learning activities and teaching strategies are varied in approach, are tailored to students' interests, and that they incorporate student choice in learning. Learning experiences must build upon students' background knowledge and experiences and provide challenging yet attainable learning opportunities based on individual skills and abilities. Additionally, teachers must consider whether learning experiences promote student participation and engagement as well as cooperative learning to ensure development across domains. Just as with learning experiences, the developmental appropriateness of assessments must also be evaluated. The teacher must consider whether assessments allow for choice in how students demonstrate their learning so as to address individual learning needs. Furthermore, it is important that teachers consider the purpose of each assessment regarding the feedback they are seeking and how it can help determine further instruction.

### Role of Learning Theory in Instructional Process and Student Learning

Multiple learning theories exist to explain how people acquire knowledge, abilities, and skills. Each theory proposes its own approach for best practices in teaching and learning, and their effectiveness varies depending on the context of learning and individual student needs. These theories serve as frameworks for the instructional process and facilitating student learning. Teachers must understand the principles of various learning philosophies as well as their students' unique learning needs to effectively design and implement instruction from the perspective of the most applicable theory. Upon identifying desired learning outcomes, teachers can draw on applicable learning theories to make informed decisions about designing instruction, activities, and assessments that are most effective based on their students' learning styles, skills, and abilities.

The following are examples of some common learning theories that can be used as a framework in the instructional process:

- **Constructivism (Jean Piaget):** This theory proposes that students learn by interacting with the learning environment and connecting new information to their background knowledge to build understanding. This active process allows students to personalize their learning and construct their own perceptions of the world through the lens of their previous experiences.
- **Humanism (Abraham Maslow, Carl Rogers):** This theory proposes that learning should take a person-centered approach, with a focus on the individual's innate capacity for personal growth and self-actualization. It operates axiomatically from the principle that all humans have a natural desire to learn; therefore, a failure to learn is due to the learning situation or environment rather than a person's inability to learn. Teachers should act as facilitators and strive to create a safe, accepting learning environment, celebrate students' differences, and praise academic and personal achievement.
- **Connectivism (George Siemens, Stephen Downes):** This theory proposes that learning occurs by making a series of connections across pieces of information, ideas, concepts, and perspectives. Connectivism is rooted in the notion that learning occurs externally, and technology facilitates connections by giving learners access to several outlets for acquiring and processing new information.
- **Experiential Learning (David Kolb):** This theory proposes that students learn and retain information best through physical exploration and interaction with the learning environment. In the classroom, teachers can facilitate this student-led approach by providing students with varying relevant experiences and opportunities for hands-on learning, such as projects or learning centers.
- **Multiple Intelligences (Howard Gardner):** Gardner's theory proposes there are several versions of intelligence, and as such, the process of learning differs among individuals. Some learners may have a stronger intelligence in one domain but have difficulty in another and, therefore, learn best when instruction is presented through the lens of their dominant intelligence. Intelligences are categorized as logical-mathematical, verbal-linguistic, visual-spatial, bodily-kinesthetic, interpersonal, intrapersonal, musical, and naturalistic.

## Connecting New Information and Ideas to Prior Knowledge

When students connect new information to prior knowledge, learning becomes relevant and engaging. Effective instruction encourages students to connect learning to background knowledge and experiences, which increases retainment, deepens understanding, and enhances the effectiveness of the overall learning experience. Fostering personal connections to learning is achieved through incorporating an array of strategies and technologies into instruction. Activities including KWL charts, anticipatory guides, graphic organizers, and brainstorming encourage students to consider what they know before learning new concepts, thus allowing them to build upon their prior knowledge and ability to make connections that strengthen learning. Cooperative learning strategies promote sharing and building prior knowledge with other students, thus increasing students' connections to new information. Numerous technologies exist to enhance the learning experience by fostering connections between prior knowledge and new information. Teachers can incorporate a wide range of apps and games across subject areas that build upon prior knowledge by providing activities with increasing levels of difficulty. Online polls, surveys, and word association websites allow students to demonstrate prior understanding of a topic to begin making connections. Self-reflection and closure opportunities at the end of instruction further strengthen learning by encouraging students to connect new material to prior knowledge and experiences.

## Making Learning Meaningful and Relevant

Effective instruction occurs when learning is meaningful and relevant. When the purpose of learning is clear, students are engaged, motivated, and retain new information. Instruction must be student-centered, foster personal connections, and be applicable to real-life situations to create meaningful and relevant instruction. Teachers achieve this through an array of methods and technologies that are tailored to students' learning needs. Through forging positive relationships with students, teachers learn their unique interests, preferences, and experiences. Activities such as interest inventories, surveys, and community building develop a positive rapport between teachers and students. This allows teachers to make learning meaningful by creating learner-centered instruction that facilitates personal connections and builds upon prior knowledge. Field trips and community outreach programs are effective in enhancing relevancy through demonstrating the real-world applications of instruction. Additionally, technologies including virtual field trips and tours, videos, and documentaries assist in increasing students' understanding the purpose of learning by illustrating the real-world applications of instruction. Self-assessments make learning meaningful and relevant through encouraging student ownership and responsibility over learning as students seek areas for improvement. Moreover, closure activities serve to demonstrate overall purpose for learning through encouraging students to connect learning to the lesson's objective and their prior knowledge.

## INTRADISCIPLINARY AND INTERDISCIPLINARY INSTRUCTION

Intradisciplinary and interdisciplinary instruction are both valuable strategies for teaching and learning. In **intradisciplinary** instruction, several elements of a single broad subject area are incorporated into the lesson. For example, in a science lesson, the teacher could incorporate elements of chemistry, biology, and physics into instruction. This method of instruction is beneficial in deepening students' understanding of the nuances of a particular subject area through demonstrating the various components that comprise the overarching discipline. **Interdisciplinary** instruction refers to the simultaneous integration of ideas, knowledge, and skills from several subject areas when approaching an idea, problem, or theme and applying principles of one subject area to another. For example, in an interdisciplinary unit on food, the teacher could incorporate elements of math by teaching students to measure ingredients, language arts by teaching them to read or write a recipe, science through examining chemical reactions of the cooking process, and social studies through having students explore the impact of food agriculture on economy and society. Interdisciplinary instruction is beneficial in deepening students' understanding across subject areas and developing real-world critical thinking skills by encouraging them to make connections between disciplines and teaching them to consider an idea or problem from multiple perspectives.

### *EXAMPLES OF INTRADISCIPLINARY INSTRUCTION*

- **Language arts:** A single language arts lesson can incorporate components of reading, writing, grammar, and listening skills. For example, a lesson on a particular poem can include a close reading of the poet's use of grammar, symbolism, imagery, and other literary techniques as well as an audio recording of the poet reading aloud. At the end of the unit, students can be assigned to use what they learned to compose their own original poems.
- **Social studies:** Social studies units can incorporate elements of history, anthropology, archaeology, sociology, psychology, or any other field that involves the study of humans, civilizations, cultures, and historical events. For example, a unit on the Aztec people may include an examination of their religious beliefs, customs, architecture, and agricultural practices.
- **Science:** Intradisciplinary units in science can include several branches within the field, such as chemistry, biology, physics, earth science, botany, or geology. For example, a unit on volcanoes may incorporate lessons on plate tectonics, the Earth's layers, chemicals released during a volcanic eruption, islands formed from cooled volcanic rock, as well as plants that grow best near volcanoes.
- **Mathematics:** An intradisciplinary math lesson may simultaneously include several branches within the field, such as arithmetic, algebra, or geometry. For example, in a geometry lesson on the Pythagorean theorem, students must utilize algebraic equations and arithmetic to determine the length of the sides of a right triangle.

### *EXAMPLES OF INTERDISCIPLINARY INSTRUCTION*

- **Language arts:** A unit based in language arts may also incorporate several other disciplines, such as social studies, art, or music. For example, a unit on William Shakespeare's *Romeo and Juliet* may include a reading of the play, an analysis of the use of literary techniques within it, and study of William Shakespeare's life and the society in which he lived, thereby incorporating social studies into the language arts lesson. Students can also act out the play to incorporate the arts and participate in a rhythmic study on iambic pentameter to incorporate music.

- **Social studies:** Units based in social studies can include lessons focused on multiple disciplines, including language arts, music, science, and math. For example, an interdisciplinary unit on Ancient Egypt may include a historical study of the culture, religion, architecture, and practices of the Ancient Egyptians while integrating other subject areas, such as a study of hieroglyphics to incorporate language arts and creating Egyptian masks to incorporate art. Students can also study the scientific advancements of the Ancient Egyptians and incorporate math to study how the ancient pyramids were constructed.
- **Science:** Scientific units can also incorporate elements of art, math, social studies, and language arts in order to become interdisciplinary. For example, a unit on Punnett squares focuses on biology and genetics but can also include several other subject areas. Math can be incorporated by integrating lessons on probability or students can be assigned to research their genetics, create a family tree, and write a report on their findings to incorporate language arts and social studies. Art can also be incorporated by having students create portraits of the potential outcomes from Punnett squares.
- **Mathematics:** Interdisciplinary units in mathematics can also include lessons focused on art, social studies, science, and music. For example, a geometry unit on measuring triangles may also incorporate songs to memorize equations, lessons on the pyramids of Ancient Egypt to incorporate social studies, as well as an art project in which students use only triangles to create an original piece.

### Incorporating Cooperative Learning and Consideration from Multiple Viewpoints

In any classroom, teachers will encounter a wide range of diversities among students' backgrounds, cultures, interests, skills, and abilities. Thus, providing students with several opportunities for cooperative learning gives them access to others' perspectives and is highly valuable in teaching students to consider ideas from multiple viewpoints. As each student has different experiences and background knowledge, collaborative learning allows them to share their views on ideas with others. Additionally, in working together, students have the opportunity to work with others from different backgrounds that they may have otherwise never encountered and gain exposure to approaching ideas from multiple viewpoints. Cooperative learning opportunities allow students to understand and appreciate others' perspectives and teach them that there are multiple approaches to problem solving and ideas.

### Learning Experiences That Develop Real-World Life Skills

The ultimate goal of education is to develop the whole child into a productive, contributing member of society; therefore, it is imperative to provide learning experiences that will develop life skills that are applicable and beneficial in the real world. In an increasingly fast-paced global society, students must be prepared to enter the professional and societal world as confident, independent, responsible, and adaptive individuals. They must have the leadership skills necessary to compete in the professional arena. Students must be able to work cooperatively with others, respect and value multiple perspectives, and be effective problem solvers and critical thinkers in order to be successful outside of the classroom. Teachers must also aim to help students develop the skills necessary to become lifelong learners to ensure continuous growth and development as they enter society; therefore, learning experiences that promote the development of real-world life skills in addition to academic skills are necessary in adequately preparing students for success.

### Cross-Curricular Instruction for Exploring Content from Varied Perspectives

Cross-curricular instruction allows teachers to demonstrate that elements from one subject area can be applied to ideas or problems in another. Thus, this instructional strategy is highly valuable in developing students' abilities to explore content from varied perspectives. As this method incorporates several disciplines in approaching a topic, it deepens students' understanding that there are several perspectives that one can take when solving a problem and that elements of one subject area are relevant in another. In addition, cross-curricular instruction prepares students for the real world through developing critical thinking skills and allowing them to make connections between disciplines, thus allowing them to understand how to successfully approach ideas from varied perspectives.

### Benefits of Multicultural Learning Experiences

Multicultural learning experiences demonstrate to students the array of diversities that exist both inside and outside of the classroom. Just as each culture has its own values, norms, and traditions, each has its own perspectives and approaches to ideas and problem solving. Incorporating multicultural experiences in the classroom exposes students to cultures and groups that they may have otherwise never encountered and teaches them to respect and value perspectives outside of their own. As students learn other cultures' beliefs, customs, and attitudes, they develop the understanding that each culture solves problems and considers ideas from multiple viewpoints and that each approach is valuable. As students learn other perspectives, they can apply this knowledge and build problem solving and critical thinking skills that will be beneficial in developing successful lifelong learning habits.

### Incorporating Multiple Disciplines into a Thematic Unit

In **cross-curricular** (or **interdisciplinary**) instruction, multiple disciplines are incorporated into a thematic unit in order to deepen students' understanding through fostering connections and demonstrating multiple perspectives and methods of problem solving. Effective interdisciplinary instruction requires careful planning to ensure that all activities are relevant to the overall lesson theme and effectively support students in achieving desired learning outcomes. Teachers must first select a thematic unit based on state academic standards and then determine desired learning outcomes. Then, teachers must design lessons and activities for students to reach learning goals and objectives. When integrating multiple disciplines into a thematic unit, teachers must seek out materials, resources, and activities from various subject areas that are applicable to the main topic and reinforce lesson objectives. Teachers can then integrate these elements into lesson planning to create multifaceted instruction. Additionally, teachers can create activities that approach the overarching lesson theme from the perspective of different subject areas. The activities and materials should be coordinated and relate to one another in order to deepen students' understanding of the overall concept.

### Effectively Allocating Time When Creating Lessons and Units

Effective time management is vital for successful teaching and learning. To ensure that all academic standards are covered within a school year, teachers must consider how to best allocate specific amounts of time for units and lessons that allow for review, enrichment, and reteaching. A unit plan for the school year is an effective strategy in allowing the teacher to visualize and plan the amount of content that must be covered. A unit plan can also be utilized on a smaller scale, as a framework for designing and allotting time for instructional goals, objectives, and lessons within each unit. By setting learning goals and daily objectives within individual units, teachers can determine the amount of time available for completing each unit. This ensures more effective lesson planning by allowing teachers to develop daily schedules with dedicated time for teaching and learning. When planning lessons, teachers must consider how much instructional time is necessary to cover each topic and the time students will need to complete lesson activities. Additionally, teachers must ensure that they allow time at the end of each lesson for reteaching if students have misconceptions, as extra time can be utilized for enrichment if reteaching is unnecessary.

#### *Opportunities for Reflection*

Opportunities for reflection within lesson plans enhance learning experiences through strengthening student understanding and influencing further instruction. When students are given the opportunity to reflect, they are able to connect their learning back to the original objective and better understand the overall purpose for learning, thus fostering engagement. Reflection deepens students' understanding by allowing them to connect new concepts to their own personal experiences, which ultimately helps in comprehension and retainment by making learning relevant. Reflecting on performance empowers students to become self-motivated lifelong learners by allowing them to analyze what they understood and did well. Reflection also encourages students to identify areas for improvement. Teachers can utilize students' reflections to influence and drive further instruction. Students' reflections allow teachers to identify areas in which students excelled and areas in which they need improvement. They can also aid teachers in tailoring future lesson plans to adapt to students' needs and interests.

### *OPPORTUNITIES FOR SELF-ASSESSMENT*

Including self-assessments within lessons is a valuable formative assessment strategy that enriches student learning and provides insight to the teacher. Providing students with the opportunity to monitor their progress and assess their learning supports them in developing a wide range of skills that are beneficial both inside and outside of the classroom. Self-assessments create a sense of ownership and responsibility over learning, which foster self-motivation and engagement. They also serve to create a sense of independence and objectivity within students to effectively review their own work and identify areas of improvement, which is a vital skill needed to become a lifelong learner. When students evaluate their own performance, teachers are able to effectively assess student understanding, thus allowing them to identify areas of weakness or misconception for reteaching.

### *OPPORTUNITIES FOR CLOSURE ACTIVITIES*

Closure activities at the end of each lesson or topic are short activities that allow teachers to formatively assess student understanding of content covered within a lesson and identify areas of misconception for reteaching. Additionally, closure activities are valuable in measuring whether the intended lesson objective was achieved before moving to the next topic. For students, closures at the end of a lesson provide structure and organization to learning as well as emphasize the purpose for instruction by allowing them to connect what they learned back to the original objective. Moreover, in having students restate what they have learned in a closure activity, learning is strengthened by giving students the opportunity to internalize new information. In demonstrating their understanding, they can better make personal connections between their own learning, background knowledge, and experiences.

# Instructional Techniques

## IMPLEMENTING MULTIPLE INSTRUCTIONAL TECHNIQUES TO MAXIMIZE STUDENT LEARNING

Incorporating multiple instructional techniques into the classroom maximizes student learning by enhancing intellectual involvement and overall engagement. When instructional material is presented through a variety of means, it facilitates an **active learning** environment in which students' interest is captured and they are motivated to participate in learning. Varying teaching strategies stimulates engagement and fosters achievement by encouraging students to actively participate in their own learning and implement critical thinking skills to consider information more deeply. Students' understanding is strengthened when content is presented in different ways through various instructional techniques by providing them with multiple frames of reference for making connections and internalizing new concepts. In addition, utilizing multiple instructional techniques allows the teacher to effectively **differentiate instruction** to access multiple learning styles and address individual student needs to ensure understanding and enhance the overall learning process.

## INSTRUCTIONAL STRATEGIES TO DIFFERENTIATE INSTRUCTION

Implementing a variety of strategies for differentiation helps to ensure that instruction appeals to students' varying learning styles and needs. By incorporating **multiple modalities** into direct instruction, such as visual representations, written directions, video or audio clips, songs, graphs, or mnemonic devices, teachers can differentiate the presentation of new concepts and information. Using strategies to differentiate instructional activities is also beneficial in diversifying the learning experience. By providing opportunities for **independent, collaborative**, and **hands-on** learning, teachers can ensure that learning is accessible and engaging to all students. In addition, learning activities should allow for a degree of flexibility in order to appeal to students' varying needs and preferences. Activities such as task cards, educational technology resources, and learning stations provide this **flexibility** and allow for a student-directed experience in which students can choose to learn in the way that best suits their needs. Similarly, assigning open-ended projects as summative assessments allows for a degree of **student-choice**, thus differentiating the method in which students demonstrate their understanding.

## Varying the Teacher and Student Roles in the Instructional Process

Varying the roles of the teacher and students as an instructional technique is beneficial in creating an engaging, dynamic classroom environment that maximizes learning. When different roles are implemented, instruction is diversified, thus stimulating student interest and engagement. In addition, certain teacher and student roles are most applicable and effective in specific learning situations. When teachers acknowledge this and understand when to adopt and assign particular roles, they can effectively deliver instruction in a way that deepens student understanding and fosters success in learning. In presenting new content, directions, or modeling new skills, for example, the roles of **lecturer** and student **observer** are effective. In hands-on learning situations, students can take on the role of **active participant** while the teacher acts as a **facilitator** to create a student-centered and engaging learning environment in which students are given ownership over their own learning. Such variation enhances intellectual involvement by promoting critical thinking and problem-solving skills through self-directed learning. Skillfully assigning different roles throughout the learning process also allows the teacher to effectively address students' individual learning needs and preferences to promote engagement and enhance the learning experience.

## Fostering Intellectual Involvement and Engagement

Effective instruction includes a variety of strategies for fostering intellectual involvement and engagement to promote academic success. Presenting instruction using various approaches provides multiple avenues for learning new content, thus ensuring and strengthening student understanding to facilitate achievement. In addition, diversifying instructional strategies creates variety in the classroom that effectively stimulates students' interest and motivation to engage in learning. Strategies such as **cooperative learning**, **discussion**, and **self-directed opportunities** encourage active student participation that enhances intellectual involvement by allowing students to build on background knowledge, deepen understanding by exploring others' perspectives, and take ownership over their own learning. This ultimately increases student engagement and motivation for success in learning. Similarly, incorporating **inquiry**, **problem-solving**, and **project-based** strategies promotes curiosity in learning, creativity, and the development of critical thinking skills that stimulate intellectual participation and engagement to create a productive learning environment. Implementing **digital resources** and media throughout instruction is integral in enhancing academic success by making learning relevant, interesting, and differentiated to accommodate various learning needs. At the end of a lesson or activity, allowing students the opportunity to reflect is a valuable strategy in increasing intellectual involvement, retainment, and academic success by facilitating personal connections with learning to build understanding.

## Actively Engaging Students by Incorporating Discussion into Instruction

Classroom discussion is a valuable instructional technique in engaging students throughout the learning process. When teachers skillfully pose higher-level questions in discussions, they establish an active learning environment in which students are encouraged and motivated to participate, thus enhancing overall engagement. Effective discussions prompt students to become **intellectually invested** in instruction by promoting the use of **critical** and **higher-order thinking** skills to consider information more deeply and devise creative solutions to problems. In addition, discussions stimulate engagement by providing students the opportunity to express their own thoughts and reasoning regarding a given topic to establish a sense of ownership over their learning. Furthermore, discussions foster a collaborative learning environment that actively engages students by prompting them to understand others' perspectives, consider alternative approaches, and build on one another's experiences to make deeper connections to learning.

## Promoting Student Inquiry

The promotion of inquiry is a valuable instructional technique in enhancing student engagement and intellectual involvement. In an **inquiry-based** learning environment, students are encouraged to explore instructional material and devise their own conclusions or solutions to problems. This increases the effectiveness of the learning process by providing students with a sense of agency over their own learning. In addition, implementing this strategy fosters curiosity, self-motivation, and active participation, as it allows for hands-on, **student-led** learning that increases overall engagement. Incorporating inquiry into the classroom stimulates critical and higher-order thinking skills as students construct their own understanding by interacting with learning materials, analyzing their findings, and synthesizing their learning to create new conclusions, results, and responses. To effectively incorporate inquiry into the learning process, the teacher must provide several opportunities for self-directed learning, project-based learning, and student choice to stimulate curiosity. Questions must be open-ended, and students must be encouraged to hypothesize, predict, and experiment in their learning. The teacher must be flexible in instruction to allow space and opportunity for exploration and allow time for reflection and extended learning opportunities to facilitate further inquiry.

## Incorporating Problem-Solving into Instruction

Providing opportunities for creative problem solving within instruction effectively creates an engaging and successful learning experience. Students become more **intellectually involved** when encouraged to actively participate in learning and utilize **critical thinking skills** to test hypotheses, analyze results, and devise creative solutions to problems. This hands-on, **student-directed** approach promotes success in learning by allowing students to interact with learning materials as they seek answers to complex ideas and problems in an engaging environment. Problem-solving enables students to make deeper connections to their learning to enhance understanding, as this strategy prompts them to employ and develop background knowledge. In addition, problem-solving activities allow for collaborative learning in which students can actively engage with peers to build on one another's knowledge and experience, thus enhancing successful learning.

## Intellectual Involvement, Active Student Engagement, and Success in Learning

A productive learning environment is composed intellectually involved students that are actively engaged in successful learning. A strong correlation exists between **intellectual involvement**, **active student engagement**, and **success in learning**, and each component is necessary for effective instruction. Effective instruction consists of challenging students based on their abilities and teaching them to think deeply about new ideas and concepts. This ultimately encourages students' intellectual involvement, as it prompts them to utilize their critical thinking skills to build on their background knowledge, consider alternative perspectives, and synthesize their learning to devise creative solutions. When students are intellectually involved in instruction, they become more personally invested and engaged, as learning becomes relevant, interesting, and challenging. Engaged students are active participants in their learning, thus enhancing their overall productivity and academic success.

## Effectively Structuring Lessons

When developing instruction, it is imperative that the teacher is knowledgeable on how to effectively structure lessons to maximize student engagement and success. Each lesson must include a clear **objective** and explicitly state the process for achieving it. To initiate engagement, effective lessons begin with an **opening**, or "warm-up," activity to introduce a new topic, diagnose student understanding, and activate prior knowledge. Instruction of new material must be delivered through a variety of teaching strategies that are consciously tailored to students' individual learning needs to enhance participation and ensure comprehension. Direct instruction should be followed by **active learning** activities with clear directions and procedures to allow students to practice new concepts and skills. Throughout a successful lesson, the teacher checks frequently for understanding and comprehension by conducting a variety of **formative assessments** and adjusts instruction as necessary. Including **closure** activities is essential to successful learning, as it gives students the opportunity to reflect, process information, make connections, and demonstrate comprehension. In structuring lessons effectively according to students' learning needs, the teacher establishes a focused and engaging learning environment that promotes academic success.

**Example of a Daily Lesson Plan Structure**

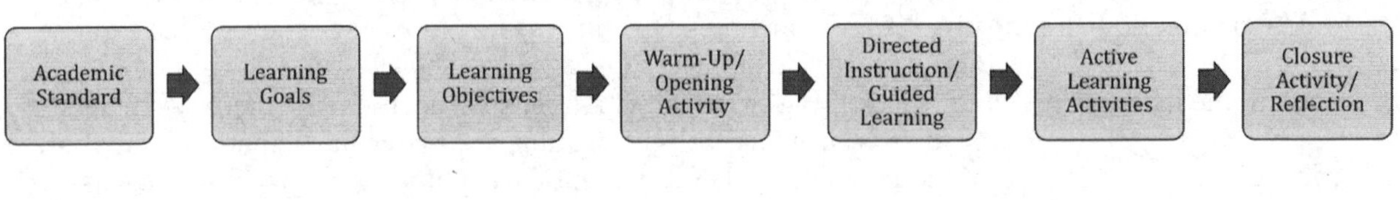

## Flexible Instructional Groupings

**Flexible instructional groupings** provide the teacher and students with a versatile, engaging environment for successful learning. Skillfully grouping students allows for productive, cooperative learning opportunities in which individual strengths are enhanced and necessary support is provided, thus enhancing motivation and engagement. When working in groups, students' understanding of instruction is strengthened, as they are able to learn and build upon one another's background knowledge, perspectives, and abilities. Instructional groups can include students of the **same** or **varied abilities** depending on the learning objective and task to increase productivity and provide scaffolding as necessary for support. This strategy is effective in enabling the teacher to **differentiate** instruction and adjust groups as needed to accommodate varying learning styles, abilities, and interests to maximize engagement and success in learning.

## Effective Pacing of Lessons and Importance of Flexibility to Students' Needs

Effective pacing is imperative to focused and engaging instruction. Teachers must be conscientious of the pace of their instruction and ensure that it is reflective of their students' learning needs and sustains their attention. Instruction that is delivered too quickly results in confusion and discouragement, whereas if instruction is too slow, students will lose interest and become disengaged. A well-paced lesson states clear learning goals and objectives while clearly outlining the means to achieve them to elicit student motivation. The teacher must consider the most **efficient** and **engaging** instructional strategies for presenting new material to establish a steady pace and maintain it by incorporating smooth **transitions** from one activity to the next. It is important that teachers are conscious of the rate of instruction throughout all stages of learning while maintaining **flexibility** in pacing in order to be responsive to their students. As individual students have different learning needs and processing times, they may require a faster or slower rate of instruction to understand new concepts and remain engaged in learning. Frequent checks for understanding and reflection activities are essential strategies in determining if the pace of instruction must be adjusted to accommodate students' needs.

## Connecting Content to Students' Prior Knowledge and Experiences

Implementing effective instructional strategies for connecting content to students' prior knowledge and experiences enhances the relevancy of learning and fosters deeper connections that strengthen understanding. To achieve this, teachers must educate themselves on students' backgrounds, experiences, communities, and interests to determine what is important and interesting to them. With this knowledge in mind, teachers can successfully locate and implement **authentic materials** into instruction to enhance relevancy. Additionally, encouraging students to bring materials to class that reflect their backgrounds and including these materials in instruction makes learning relevant by allowing students to make **personal connections** to content. Instructional strategies such as brainstorming, KWL charts, prereading, and anticipation guides allow the teacher to determine what students know prior to learning a new concept, thus enabling them to connect content to students' background knowledge in a relevant way. Incorporating digital resources further enhances relevancy in learning. Teachers can locate videos or audio clips that relate to instruction and reflect students' background experiences and interests. Using digital resources to introduce a new concept is a valuable strategy in developing students' **schema** on a topic to build prior knowledge and make learning meaningful by fostering connections.

### *Making Learning Relevant and Meaningful*

For learning to be relevant and meaningful, it is essential that teachers present content in a way that connects with students' **prior knowledge** and experiences. When students are able to apply new ideas and information to what they already know through effective instructional techniques, it facilitates strong **personal connections** that make learning relevant and meaningful. In addition, personal connections and **relevancy** are strengthened when teachers consciously incorporate materials to reflect students' individual backgrounds and experiences in instruction. Linking content to students' background experiences enables them to relate instruction to real-world situations, thus establishing a sense of purpose for learning by making it applicable to their lives. Intentionally connecting content with students' prior knowledge and experiences enhances the effectiveness of the instructional process and fosters positive attitudes toward learning.

### *Enhancing Student Engagement and Success in Learning*

Engaging instruction employs a variety of instructional strategies and materials to create a relevant, meaningful, and successful learning experience. Effective content establishes a clear and applicable purpose for instruction that increases student participation in the learning process. Presenting relevant and meaningful content enhances understanding and engagement by enabling students to create real-world, **personal connections** to learning based upon their own backgrounds and experiences. In addition, when instruction is tailored to reflect students' unique interests and preferences, content becomes more appealing and students' willingness to learn is enhanced. When students can perceive content through their own frames of reference with instructional materials that reflect their unique differences, they are able to effectively internalize and relate information to their lives, thus increasing engagement. Engaged learning ultimately facilitates academic success in that when students are motivated to learn, they demonstrate positive attitudes toward learning and are more likely to actively participate.

# Adapting Instruction to Individual Needs

## Evaluating Activities and Materials to Meet Learning Needs

The careful selection of instructional activities and materials is integral to accommodating students' varying characteristics and needs. When evaluating the appropriateness of activities and materials, several considerations must be made. Teachers must consider whether activities and materials align with state and district **academic standards**. Teachers must also evaluate the quality and effectiveness of the activities and materials in supporting students' unique differences as they achieve learning goals and objectives. All materials and activities must be **developmentally appropriate** across domains yet adaptable to individual students' learning needs. In addition, they must be challenging yet feasible for student achievement relative to students' grade levels and abilities to promote engagement and the development of critical and **higher-order thinking** skills. Teachers must evaluate activities and materials for versatility to allow for student choice and differentiation in order to address varying characteristics and needs. Teachers must also ensure that activities and materials are accurate, **culturally sensitive**, and reflective of students' diversities to foster an inclusive learning environment that promotes engagement.

### *Instructional Resources and Technologies*

The implementation of varied instructional resources and technologies is highly valuable in supporting student engagement and achievement. Effective use of resources and technologies requires teachers to evaluate their appropriateness in addressing students' individual characteristics and learning needs for academic success. Teachers must be attuned to students' unique differences in order to seek high quality technologies and resources that address their students' needs and support the achievement of learning goals and objectives. Technologies and resources must be **accurate**, **comprehensible**, easily **accessible** to students, and **relevant** to the curriculum and the development of particular skills. Teachers must also consider the grade-level and **developmental appropriateness** of technologies and resources as well as their adaptability to allow for differentiation. Effective technologies and resources are interactive, engaging, and multifaceted to allow for varying levels of complexity based on students' abilities. This allows teachers to provide appropriate challenges while diversifying instruction to appeal to varied characteristics and learning needs, thus fostering an engaging environment that supports success in learning for all students.

## Adapting Activities and Materials to Meet Individual Characteristics and Needs

In effective instruction, activities and materials are adapted to accommodate students' individual characteristics and needs. Teachers must be attuned to students' unique differences and understand how to adjust activities and materials accordingly to facilitate academic success and growth. To achieve this, teachers must incorporate a **variety** of activities and materials that appeal to all styles of learners. Activities and materials should provide **student choice** for engagement in learning and demonstration of understanding. By differentiating instruction, teachers can effectively scaffold activities and materials to provide supports as necessary as well as include extensions or alternate activities for enrichment. **Chunking** instruction, allowing extra time as necessary, and accompanying activities and materials with aids such as graphic organizers, visual representations, and anticipation guides further differentiates learning to accommodate students' learning characteristics and needs. Conducting **formative assessments** provides teachers with valuable feedback regarding student understanding and engagement, thus allowing them to modify and adjust the complexity of activities and materials as necessary to adapt to varied characteristics and learning differences.

### *Instructional Resources and Technologies*

When teachers understand students' individual characteristics and needs, they can adapt instructional resources and technologies accordingly to maximize learning. To do so effectively, the teacher must incorporate a diverse array of **multifaceted** resources and technologies that support and enhance learning through a variety of methods. This ensures that varying learning needs are met, as students of all learning styles are provided with several avenues for building and strengthening understanding. Additionally, the teacher can adapt resources and technologies to accommodate individual students by **varying the complexity** to provide challenges, support, and opportunities for enrichment based on ability level. Supplementing technologies and resources with **scaffolds**, such as extra time, visual representations, or opportunities for collaborative learning, further enables the teacher to adapt to individual learning needs. When effectively implemented and adapted to students' characteristics and needs, instructional technologies and resources serve as valuable tools for differentiating curriculum to enhance the learning experience.

## Modifications, Accommodations, and Adaptations

### Accommodations and Modifications

Accommodations and modifications are different types of educational supports put in place to help a student participate effectively in school. An **accommodation** changes *how* a student is taught or assessed by providing more time or other supports that remove barriers to the material. Students who receive accommodations are taught and assessed to the same standards as students without accommodations. A **modification** changes *what* is taught or assessed by changing or omitting parts of the materials. Students with modifications may receive fewer problems to solve or lower-rigor versions of the materials compared to other students.

### Modifications

**Modifications** are changes to *what* students are taught or expected to learn. Students with disabilities can receive modifications as determined by their specific needs and as written out in their Individualized Education Programs.

- **Curriculum modifications** allow students to learn material that is different from what their general education peers learn. For example, students with classroom modifications may receive assignments with fewer math problems or with reading samples appropriate for their reading levels. Students with curriculum modifications may receive different grading tiers than their peers. The ways teachers grade their assignments may be different from how the teachers grade their peers' assignments. Students may also be excused from particular projects or given project guidelines that are different and better suited to their individual needs.
- **Assignment modifications** include completing fewer or different homework problems than peers, writing shorter papers, answering fewer questions on classwork and tests, and creating alternate projects or assignments.

### Environmental Modifications

Students with disabilities may need environmental modifications in order to be successful in their classrooms, homes, and communities. **Environmental modifications** are adaptations that allow people with disabilities to maneuver through their environments with as little resistance as possible. They allow for more **independent living experiences**, especially for those with limited mobility. Environmental modifications ensure the health, safety, and welfare of the people who need them. Examples of environmental modifications in the home, community, or school include ramps, hydraulic lifts, widened doorways and hallways, automatic doors, handrails, and grab bars. Roll-in showers, water faucet controls, worktable or work surface adaptations, and cabinet and shelving adaptations are also environmental modifications that can be provided if necessary. Other adaptations include heating and cooling adaptations and electrical adaptations to accommodate devices or equipment. Environmental modifications in the home are typically provided by qualified agencies or providers. The Americans with Disabilities Act ensures that environmental modifications are provided in the **community** to help avoid discrimination against people with disabilities.

## ACCOMMODATIONS

Accommodations are flexible classroom tools because they can be used to provide **interventions** without time or location boundaries. They remove **barriers** to learning for students with disabilities, and they change how students learn. Accommodations do not change what students are learning or expected to know. Classroom accommodations may be outlined in students' Individualized Education Programs (IEPs) and 504 Plans or simply provided as needed by special educators or general educators. Accommodations are put into place to ensure that students with disabilities are accessing the learning process with the fewest barriers, putting them on the same levels as their peers without disabilities. **Presentation accommodations** include allowing students to listen to oral instructions, providing written lists of instructions, and allowing students to use readers to assist with comprehension. **Response accommodations** include allowing students to provide oral responses, capture responses via audio recording, and use spelling dictionaries or spell-checkers when writing. **Accommodations to setting** include special seating (wherever the students learn best), use of sensory tools, and special lighting.

### *TYPES OF ACCOMMODATIONS*

Timing, schedule, and organizational accommodations change the ways students with disabilities have access to classrooms with the fewest barriers to learning. Students who need these accommodations receive them as written statements in their IEPs, 504 Plans, or as teachers see fit during classroom time.

- **Timing accommodations** allow students more time to complete tasks or tests and/or process instructions. They also allow students to access frequent breaks during assignments or tests.
- **Schedule accommodations** include taking tests in chunks over periods of time or several days, taking test sections in different orders, and/or taking tests during specific times of day.
- **Organizational skill accommodations** include assistance with time management, marking texts with highlighters, maintaining daily assignment or work schedules, and/or receiving study skills instruction.

When accommodations are written in a student's IEP, the student has access to them for state standardized tests. When and how accommodations are put into place is left to the discretion of the teacher unless specifically written in the student's IEP or 504 Plan.

### *OBTAINING ACCOMMODATIONS*

When parents or legal guardians of children with disabilities believe that **accommodations** may help their children, they can arrange to speak with teachers about informal supports. **Informal supports** are strategies teachers can put into place to assist students with their learning processes. These changes do not require paperwork and can be implemented during classroom instruction. Teachers can experiment with informal supports to determine what will be most helpful for removing the barriers to learning students might be experiencing. If it is determined that students need bigger changes to how they learn, **formal evaluations** can take place. Students who do not already have IEPs or 504 Plans may be evaluated to collect data on their needs. For students with IEPs or 504 Plans, accommodations can be included the next time these plans are updated. The IEPs or 504 Plans can also be **amended** if the need for the accommodations is immediate, such as when they need to be put in place before standardized testing time. **Data** supporting the need for the accommodations must be provided and listed in the comprehensive initial evaluations and all versions of IEPs and 504 Plans.

## Parents and Legal Guardians Ensuring Accommodations Are Being Provided

Accommodations are changes to the ways children with disabilities learn, not changes to what the children are learning. While parents and legal guardians may only receive **formal updates** on how accommodations are being provided or helping the students during specified reporting times (unless students' IEPs or 504 Plans specifically state otherwise), they can ask for **reports** on goal progress or accommodations for their students at any time. Parents and legal guardians can ensure that accommodations are successfully implemented by using the progress reports and asking the right questions. Parents and legal guardians can ensure that accommodations are being provided in a number of ways. They can **advocate** for their students by making sure the accommodations are being implemented on a regular basis. Parents and legal guardians also have the right to ask if their students are using the accommodations on a **regular basis**. If they are being used on a regular basis, parents and legal guardians can explore additional options that might help their students. Parents and legal guardians can work with special education teachers and the IEP teams to ensure that their students' accommodations are being received and are effective.

## Informal Supports vs. Formal Accommodations

Informal supports are generally easier to implement in the classroom setting. They do not necessarily have to be implemented only for students with Individualized Education Programs or students with disabilities. Students who have not been evaluated for special education services can receive **informal supports** to ensure classroom success. Teachers may use informal supports to help students who are struggling with the ways they are learning. They may demonstrate that the students are able to learn with the accommodations in place. Informal supports are often the first step to indicating that students are in need of **special education services**.

**Formal accommodations** are put in place when students become eligible for IEPs or 504 Plans. Formal supports are written into the IEPs or 504 Plans and then required by law to be provided. Examples of informal supports include frequent breaks, special seating, quiet areas for test taking or studying, teacher cues, and help with basic organizational skills. These informal supports may eventually turn into formal supports if students become eligible for special education services.

### *Reasonable Accommodations According to ADA*

According to the Americans with Disabilities Act (ADA), a **reasonable accommodation** is a change to workplace conditions, equipment, or environment that allows an individual to effectively perform a job. Title I under the ADA requires businesses with more than 15 employees to abide by certain regulations, ensuring that their needs are reasonably met. Any change to the work environment or the way a job is performed that gives a person with a disability access to **equal employment** is considered a reasonable accommodation. Reasonable accommodations fall into **three categories**: changes to a job application process, changes to the work environment or to the way a job is usually done, and changes that enable employee access to equal benefits and privileges that employees without disabilities receive. These effectively level the playing field for people with disabilities to receive the same benefits as their peers. It also allows for the fewest barriers to success in the workplace. Many communities have resources available to help people with disabilities find jobs. They also have resources that help employers make their workplaces accessible for people with disabilities.

## Types of Assistive Technology

Assistive technology (AT) tools can be physical objects and devices or online resources that assist students with disabilities in their learning. The purpose of AT tools is to provide students with disabilities **equal access to the curriculum** by accommodating their individual needs to promote positive outcomes. **Personal listening devices (PLDs)**, sometimes called FM systems, are devices that clarify teachers' words. With a PLD, a teacher speaks into a small microphone and the words transmit clearly into a student's headphone or earpiece. **Sound field systems** amplify teachers' voices to eliminate sound issues in classroom environments. **Noise-cancelling headphones** are useful for students who need to work independently and limit distractions or behavioral triggers. **Audio recorders** allow students to record lectures or lessons and refer to the recordings later at their own pace. Some note-taking applications will transcribe audio into written words. Captioning is available to pair visual words with spoken words. **Text-to-speech (TTS) software** lets students see and hear words at the same time. TTS and audiobook technology can help students with fluency, decoding, and comprehension skills.

### *VOICE RECOGNITION SOFTWARE*

Voice recognition software and communication software can assist students who struggle with speaking or communicating. **Voice recognition software** allows people to speak commands into microphones to interact with the computer instead of using a keyboard. This feature helps create a **least restrictive environment** for a student with a disability because it removes the sometimes challenging aspect of using a keyboard while working on a computer. Voice recognition software allows users to carry out actions such as opening documents, saving documents, and moving the cursor. It also allows users to "write" sentences and paragraphs by speaking into the microphones in word processing programs. In order for voice recognition software to be effective, the user must learn to dictate words distinctly into a microphone. This ensures that the correct word is heard and dictated by the voice-to-text software. Some programs collect information and familiarize themselves with people's particular voice qualities. Over time, the systems adapt to people's voices and become more efficient.

### *EFFECTIVELY INSTRUCTING STUDENTS USING ASSISTIVE TECHNOLOGY*

Assistive technology (**AT**) refers to tools that are effective for teaching students with learning disabilities, as they address a number of potential special needs. The purpose of AT is to level the playing field for students with **learning disabilities**, particularly when they are participating in general education classrooms. AT can address learning difficulties in math, listening, organization, memory, reading, and writing. **AT for listening** can assist students who have difficulties processing language. For example, a personal listening device can help a student hear a teacher's voice more clearly. **AT for organization and memory** can help students with self-management tasks, such as keeping assignment calendars or retrieving information using handheld devices. **AT for reading** often includes text-to-speech devices that assist with students' reading fluency, decoding, comprehension, and other skill deficits. **AT for writing** assists students who struggle with handwriting or writing development. Some AT writing devices help with actual handwriting, while others assist with spelling, punctuation, grammar, word usage, or text organization.

### *AUGMENTATIVE AND ALTERNATIVE COMMUNICATION SYSTEMS*

Students with communication disorders may require the use of augmentative or alternative communication systems. Communication systems are used to help the students effectively demonstrate **expressive and receptive language** and engage in **social skills**. Teaching appropriate communication skills is a collaborative effort between the students' caretakers, teachers, and other professionals. Typically, **speech services** are written into students' IEPs, and the services are delivered by **speech language pathologists (SLPs)**. Depending on the requirements in the IEPs, the SLPs may work one-on-one with students or work with the teachers to incorporate speech and language skills throughout students' school days. In order for communication systems to work for nonverbal students, measures must be taken to ensure that the particular systems are appropriate for what the students need. It is important for the caretakers, teachers, other professionals, and even classmates to model using the devices so the students can learn how to "talk" appropriately. Students must also have constant access to the systems and receive consistent opportunities to communicate using the systems at home and at school.

### *USE OF VISUAL REPRESENTATION SYSTEMS WITH STUDENTS WITH AUTISM*

**Assistive technology (AT)** helps increase learning opportunities for students with autism by eliminating barriers to learning. AT can help improve students' expressive communication skills, attention skills, motivation skills, academic skills, and more. **Visual representation systems** in the form of objects, photographs, drawings, or written words provide concrete representations of words for students with autism. Visual representations, such as simple pictures paired with words, can be used to create visual schedules for students with autism. Photographs can be used to help students learn vocabulary words and the names of people and places. Written words should be paired with the visual representations in order to create links between the concrete objects and the actual words. The goal is for students to eventually recognize the words without the pictures. Visual representation systems can also help facilitate easier transitions between activities or places, which can be difficult for students with autism.

### COMMUNICATION SYSTEMS

Students who are nonverbal may have access to **communication systems** implemented by trained professionals. Teachers, caretakers, and other professionals work with the students to use the communication systems effectively. The goal of a communication system is to teach a nonverbal student how to "talk" and engage in **age-appropriate social skills**. In order for nonverbal students to learn appropriate social interactions, they must spend time learning communication skills, just as they learn academic content. Communication skills can be taught in isolation or as part of students' daily activities. Giving nonverbal students opportunities to foster communication skills in **familiar environments** makes it easier for them to learn appropriate social interactions. Teachers, caregivers, and other professionals must demonstrate how to use communication systems to engage in conversations, make requests, and answer questions. Most importantly, nonverbal students must be instructed to **access** their "words" (communication systems) at all times throughout the school and home environments.

### ACCESSIBILITY COMPONENTS OF A PICTURE EXCHANGE COMMUNICATION SYSTEM

A Picture Exchange Communication System (**PECS**) is a communication system for people with little or no **communicative abilities**. This system is a way for the students to access their environments using **picture symbols** to communicate meaning, wants, and needs. For example, a child may point to a picture symbol to request a book. A PECS provides a way for students with communication disorders to develop their **verbal communication** without actually speaking. It reduces frustration and problem behaviors by providing students with an avenue to express what they want to say. It is commonly used for students with autism spectrum disorder in the form of augmentative communication devices. It can also be used for students with other impairments whose communicative abilities are affected. A PECS focuses on **functional communication skills** and can be practiced in home, school, and community environments.

## SUPPORTING NONVERBAL STUDENTS

Nonverbal students have extra challenges in addition to learning content. These students may need extra instruction in academic areas as well as specialized instruction in the area of communication skills. Students with **nonverbal disabilities** may also need social skills instruction, struggle with abstract concepts, and dislike changes to their routines. Teachers can **facilitate learning** for nonverbal students by making changes to their classroom environments, by teaching strategies for comprehending concepts, and by providing materials to accommodate their needs. Teachers can also provide accommodations or modifications to classwork and tests to make the content accessible to nonverbal students. Using visuals to represent actions, words, or concepts is a helpful instructional strategy for teaching nonverbal students, especially when teaching new material. Additionally, teachers can assist nonverbal students by taking measures to prevent undesirable behaviors from occurring.

## STRATEGIES AND ACCOMMODATIONS FOR STUDENTS WITH WORKING MEMORY DEFICITS

Working memory is critical for remembering letters and numbers, listening to short instructions, reading and understanding content, completing homework independently, and understanding social cues. When **working memory skills** are absent or slow to develop, learning may be difficult. This may get worse for children over time. As they fail to develop or retain working memory capabilities, their overall **cognitive abilities** begin to suffer. Working memory deficits vary among people with disabilities, but accommodations can make up for missing or underdeveloped skills. Educators can implement **strategies** like reducing the children's workload; being aware of when children might be reaching memory overload; and providing visual cues, positive feedback, testing alternatives, and extra time. **Accommodations** in an Individualized Education Program for a student with working memory deficits might include frequent breaks, small group instruction, and extended time for tests and assignments.

# Life Stage Transitions

## Supporting Students Through Transitions

Transitioning to life after high school can be a difficult process, particularly for students with disabilities. It is important for teachers to facilitate and support these **transitions** before students exit their special education programs. **Structured learning environments** that include independent workstations and learning centers provide opportunities for independent learning to occur. **Independent workstations** give students chances to practice previously introduced concepts or perform previously introduced tasks. **Learning centers** provide small group settings where new skills can be taught. Students can also rotate through different learning centers that offer art lessons, focus on academic skills, or provide breaks or leisure activities. **Classroom layout** also plays an important role. Teachers should plan their classroom layouts based on individual student needs in order to create comfortable, predictable environments for students with disabilities. **Visual schedules** help students transition between centers by providing them with concrete schedule references.

## Benefits of Vocational Education

Students with disabilities often participate in vocational education in order to gain **independent living skills.** Often, schools and communities offer services that provide vocational training for people with disabilities. These programs offer students **job-specific skills training** and opportunities to earn certifications, diplomas, or certificates. They often involve **hands-on learning experiences** focused on building skills specific to certain occupations. These programs are beneficial to students with disabilities who may struggle with grasping abstract concepts learned in typical classroom environments. Hands-on training in vocational programs can be a meaningful way for students with disabilities to learn academic concepts and gain living skills needed to function in postgraduate life. Vocational education opportunities offer alternatives for students with disabilities who might otherwise drop out of high school. These programs also serve as a viable option for younger students to work towards, as most vocational education programs are offered to students in upper grade levels.

## Vocational Skills Needed to Be Successful in Work Environments

**Informal vocational training** often begins before students even get to high school. Teachers include informal vocational training skills in their classrooms by teaching academic and communication skills. **Academic skills** can both spark and strengthen students' career interests and provide learning platforms to build upon. **Communication skills**, like giving and following instructions and processing information, generalize to work environments. **Social and interpersonal skills**, like problem-solving abilities and participating in phone conversations, are important for performance in workplaces. Students need to learn important **vocational and occupational skills** required by most jobs, such as interacting appropriately with coworkers and keeping track of worked hours. Students also need formal or informal training in completing resumes, cover letters, and tax forms. Training may also include interview practice and job search guidance.

## Resources to Promote Successful Transitions to Life after High School

In some states, **statements of transition** should be included in Individualized Education Programs (IEPs) at age 14 for students with disabilities. In most states, the Individuals with Disabilities Education Act mandates that transition plans be put in place for students with IEPs at age 16 and every year thereafter. Some schools and communities have programs and resources available to facilitate students' successful transitions to life after high school. Throughout the transition process, it is important that students and their caregivers participate in any decision-making processes. **Vocational education courses**, sometimes called career and technical education courses, offer academic course alternatives. The courses usually specialize in specific trades or occupations. They can serve to spark or maintain students' interests in vocational fields. Some schools offer **postsecondary enrollment options**, where students can participate in college courses, earning both high school and college credits. **Career assessments**, including interest inventories and formal and informal vocational assessments, serve to gauge students' career interests. These can be worked into students' transitional goals in their IEPs and should be conducted frequently, as students' interests change.

## Components of a Transition Plan

**Transition plans** are flexible but formal plans that help a student identify his or her goals for after school and act as a roadmap to help the support team advocate for the student's future. They generally include postsecondary goals and expected transition services. The four goal areas are vocational training, postsecondary education, employment, and independent living. **Transition goals** must be results oriented and measurable. Goals can be general, but the transition activities need to be quantified to reflect what the student can complete in the IEP year. It is common for interests to change from year to year; therefore, goals and plans may change as well. **Transition services** are determined once the goals are established. Transition services include types of instruction the student will receive in school, related services, community experiences, career or college counseling, and help with adaptive behavior skills. Goals and transition services must be reviewed and updated each year. Academic goals in the IEP can also support transition goals. For example, math goals can focus on money management skills as part of a transition plan.

## Factors That Influence Successful Transitions to Postsecondary Life

Parents or legal guardians, teachers, school professionals, community members, and students themselves can all contribute to successful transitions to postsecondary life. Key **factors** that help students successfully transition include the following:

- Participation in standards-based education
- Work preparation and career-based learning experiences
- Leadership skills
- Access to and experience with community services, such as mental health and transportation services
- Family involvement and support

Standards-based education ensures that students receive consistent and clear expectations with a curriculum that is aligned to the universal design for learning standards. Exposure to work preparation and career-based learning experiences ensures that students receive opportunities to discover potential career interests or hobbies. Connections and experiences with community activities provide students with essential postsecondary independent living skills. Family involvement and support ensure that students have advocates for their needs and interests. Families can also help students connect with school and community-based supports that facilitate their career interests.

# Instructional Design for Students with Disabilities

## Developmentally Appropriate Curriculum

Choosing a developmentally appropriate curriculum is challenging for educators. Special educators have the additional challenge of finding a curriculum that meets the needs of the **individual students with disabilities**. The end result is not usually a one-size-fits-all curriculum because that goes against the intentions of Individualized Education Programs (IEPs) designed to meet the needs of students with special needs. Instead, special educators often pick and choose curriculum components that best meet the needs of differing abilities in the classroom. When selecting an appropriate curriculum, special educators should consider the following:

- Standards and goals that are appropriate to the needs of the students
- Best practices that have been found effective for students
- Curricula that are engaging and challenging
- Instruction and activities that are multimodal
- IEP goals
- Real-world experiences
- Different ways of learning that help teachers understand students' learning processes
- Collaboration with co-teachers to deliver appropriate instruction

In some special education settings, the curriculum is already chosen. In these settings, teachers can collaborate with co-teachers to find ways to provide instruction that meets standards and the individual needs of the students.

## Components of Differentiated Instruction

Differentiated instruction is different from individualized instruction. It targets the strengths of students and can work well in both special education and general education settings. **Differentiated instruction** is also useful for targeting the needs of students with **learning and attention deficits**. With differentiated instruction, teachers adjust their instructional processes to meet the needs of the individual students. Teaching strategies and classroom management skills are based largely on each particular class of students instead of on methods that may have been successful in the past. Teachers can differentiate content, classroom activities, student projects, and learning environments. For example, students may be encouraged to choose topics of personal interest to focus on for projects. Students are held to the same standards but have many choices in terms of project topics. **Differentiated content** provides access to a variety of resources to encourage student choice over what and how they learn. **Differentiated learning environments** are flexible to meet the ever-changing needs of the students.

**Review Video: Differentiated Instruction**
Visit mometrix.com/academy and enter code: 100342

### *Effectiveness of Differentiated Instruction*

Differentiated instruction is effective in general education settings, team-teaching settings, and special education settings because it targets the **strengths** of students. Differentiated instruction is used to target the different ways that students learn instead of taking a one-size-fits-all approach. Differentiated instruction is used in lieu of individualized instruction because it uses a variety of instructional approaches and allows students to use a variety of materials to help them access the curriculum. **Effective differentiated instruction** includes small group work, reciprocal learning, and continual assessment.

**Small group work** allows for the individual learning styles and needs of students to be addressed. In small groups, students receive instruction by rotating through groups. Group work should be used sparingly or be well-regulated to ensure that all of the students in the group are learning for themselves and contributing to group work sufficiently. Groups may be shuffled or have assigned roles within the group to ensure a good division of labor. In **reciprocal learning**, students play the role of the teacher, instructing the class by sharing what they know and asking content questions of their peers. Teachers who practice **continual assessment** can determine if their differentiated instructional methods are effective or if they need to be changed. Assessments can determine what needs to be changed in order for students to participate in effective classroom environments.

## Different Educational Levels and Learning Styles

**Learning styles** of students differ, regardless of whether or not the students have disabilities. When addressing groups of students in inclusion settings, it is important for teachers to organize and implement teaching strategies that address learning at **different educational levels**. Students generally fall into one or more learning modes. Some are visual learners, some are auditory learners, some are kinesthetic or tactile learners, and some learn best using a combination of these approaches. Teachers can address students' educational levels by creating lessons that allow learning to take place visually, auditorily, and kinesthetically. **Visual learners** prefer information that has been visually organized, such as in graphic organizers or diagrams. **Auditory learners** prefer information presented in spoken words. Lessons that target auditory learners provide opportunities for students to engage in conversations and question material. **Kinesthetic learners** prefer a hands-on approach to learning. These learners prefer to try out new tasks and learn as they go. Lessons that include opportunities for these three types of learning to occur can successfully target different educational levels.

### *Multiple Modality Instruction and Activities*

The purpose of multiple modality instruction is to engage students by offering different ways to learn the same material. **Multiple modality teaching** also addresses students' unique learning styles. Learning modalities are generally separated into four categories: **visual** (seeing), **auditory** (hearing), **kinesthetic** (moving), and **tactile** (touch) modalities. This way of teaching targets students who may have deficits in one or more modalities. It is also helpful for students who struggle in one or more of the learning categories. If a student struggles with understanding content that is presented visually, a lesson that includes auditory, kinesthetic, and tactile components may engage learning. Additionally, presenting lesson material and activities in a multimodal approach helps improve student memory and retention by solidifying concepts through multiple means of engagement. This approach is also useful for students with **attention disorders** who may struggle in environments where one mode of teaching is used. The multiple modality approach ensures that activities, such as kinesthetic or tactile activities, keep more than one sense involved with the learning process.

**Review Video: Teaching Through Multiple Modalities**
Visit mometrix.com/academy and enter code: 100371

### *Using Visual Supports to Facilitate Instruction and Self-Monitoring Strategies*

Many students learn best when provided with instruction and activities that appeal to multiple senses. A **multimodal approach** is especially important for students with developmental disabilities, who may need supports that match their individual ways of learning. **Visual supports** are concrete representations of information used to convey meaning. Teachers can use visual supports to help students with developmental disabilities understand what is being taught and communicated to them. Visual supports can help students with understanding classroom rules, making decisions, communicating with others, staying organized, and reducing frustrations. **Visual schedules** show students visual representations of their daily schedules. This assists with transitions between activities, which can sometimes be difficult for students with disabilities. Visuals can be used to help students share information about themselves or their school days with their peers and parents. Visual supports can also be used with checklists to help facilitate independence. For example, behavior checklists can be used to help students monitor their own behaviors.

## Universal Design for Learning

Universal design for learning (UDL) is a flexible approach to learning that keeps students' individual needs in mind. Teachers that utilize **UDL** offer different ways for students to access material and engage in content. This approach is helpful for many students but particularly those with learning and attention issues. The **principles**

**of UDL** all center on varying instruction and assessment to appeal to the needs of students who think in various ways.

| Principles of the Universal Design for Learning | |
|---|---|
| Multiple means of *representation* | *Instructional content* should be demonstrated in various ways so that students may learn in a mode that is effective for them. |
| Multiple means of *expression* | *Assessment* should be administered in a variety of ways to adequately allow students to demonstrate their knowledge. This includes quizzes, homework, presentations, classwork, etc. |
| Multiple means of *engagement* | Instruction should include a variety of *motivational factors* that help to interest and challenge students in exciting ways. |

**Review Video: Universal Design for Learning**
Visit mometrix.com/academy and enter code: 523916

### *Evaluating, Modifying, and Adapting the Classroom Setting Using the UDL*

The **universal design for learning (UDL)** is a framework that encourages teachers to design their instruction and assessment in ways that allow **multiple means** for the student to learn and express their knowledge. The UDL model is most successful when the teacher prepares a classroom setting that encourages the success of students with and without disabilities. Knowledge of the **characteristics** of students with different disabilities, as well as the unique **learning needs** of these students, enables the teacher to address these needs in the classroom setting. Setting clear short- and long-term goals for students is one way to meet the UDL standards. A traditional classroom may offer one assignment for all students to complete, but a UDL-compliant classroom may offer **different assignments** or **different ways** for students to complete assignments. UDL-compliant classrooms often offer **flexible workspaces** for students to complete their classwork and may offer quiet spaces for individual work or group tables for group work. UDL-compliant teachers recognize that students access information differently and provide different ways for students to gain **access** to the information, such as through audio text or physical models to work with. The universal design for learning assumes students learn in a variety of ways, even if those ways have not been clearly identified; it follows that all instruction and assessment can be improved by making it more varied and accessible.

### *Modifying Classroom Curriculum and Materials for UDL*

In order for a **universal design for learning (UDL) model classroom** to be successful, the teacher must evaluate, modify, and adapt the **curriculum** and **materials** to best suit the needs of the individual students. UDL contrasts with a one-size-fits-all concept of curriculum planning, where lesson plans are developed and implemented strictly based on how teachers expect students to learn. Instead, a successful UDL model addresses the many **specific needs** of the students. These needs vary depending on the unique abilities each classroom of students presents. UDL-compliant teachers can evaluate the success of lessons by checking for comprehension throughout lessons instead of only upon lesson completion. Evaluation methods used informally can provide a lot of information about whether students are grasping the concepts. Teachers use the results of the evaluations to modify and adapt classroom instruction to meet the needs of the students. Other means for diversifying the materials include using multiple assignment completion options and varied means of accessing the materials, such as both written, digital, and audio forms of a text. These means of instruction can take place simultaneously. For instance, a UDL-compliant teacher may choose to pair audio output and text for all students during a reading assignment in order to target students with listening or comprehension difficulties.

### *Principles of the Universal Design for Learning Model*

The universal design for learning (UDL) model contains three principles that aim to level the playing field for all learners. **Principle I** of the UDL model primarily focuses on what **representation or version** of information is being taught. This principle aims to target an audience of diverse learners. By providing multiple ways for students to approach content, teachers can ensure that the unique needs of all learners in their classrooms are met. **Principle II** examines how people learn. This principle focuses on the concept that students learn best when provided with **multiple ways** to demonstrate what they have learned. In classrooms compliant with Principle II, students are given more than one option for expressing themselves. **Principle III** focuses on providing multiple ways for students to engage in the learning process. Teachers compliant with Principle III provide options for keeping content **interesting and relevant** to all types of learners. Effective UDL-model classrooms provide multiple ways to present content, engage in learning, and express what was learned.

## Specially Designed Instruction

Specially designed instruction (**SDI**) in special education refers to specialized teaching given to students in a co-taught inclusion classroom. While a teacher teaches the class, the special education teacher provides specialized instruction in parallel to a student to help clarify the information. This is distinctive from adaptation and modification, as the content and its medium do not change for SDI. While the general education class engages in instruction, a special education teacher provides SDI to meet the specific needs of learners who may not be successful learning in the same ways as their similar-aged peers. The main purpose of SDI is to provide a student with access to the general education setting without substantially changing the content as it is aligned with state standards.

### *Diagnostic Prescriptive Method*

The diagnostic prescriptive approach to teaching is based on the fact that all students are unique learners. The **diagnostic prescriptive approach** examines factors that impede student learning and how to remedy specific issues. A successful approach begins with a **diagnosis** of what students are bringing to the classroom. This can be completed through careful observations and assessments. Once the skill deficits are clear, **prescriptive teaching** can be put into effect. In this process, teachers examine what will help students the most. It may be switching materials, changing to group settings, or recognizing the need for specialized interventions due to disabilities. In order to address multiple needs in the classroom, lesson plans should be **multimodal**. Developing strategies in advance to address students' needs is also a highlight of this method. Another important part of this method is evaluating results to determine what was effective or ineffective for entire classes and individual students.

## Guided Learning

Guided learning is practice or instruction completed by the teacher and students together. The goal of **guided learning** is to help students engage in the learning process in order to learn more about how they think and acquire new information. **Guided practice** occurs when the teacher and students complete practice activities together. The advantage of guided practice is that students can learn ways to approach concepts they have just learned. It allows students to understand and ask questions about lesson-related activities before working independently. Guided practice is useful in classrooms for students with and without disabilities because it helps teachers gauge how students learn and what instructional methods work best for them. Additionally, guided practice allows teachers to understand how students are learning the material. It also allows teachers to revisit concepts that are unclear or fine tune any missed lesson objectives.

## How Cooperative Learning Works

Cooperative learning is an interpersonal group learning process where students learn concepts by working together in **small groups**. Cooperative learning involves collaboration among small groups to achieve common goals. With **formal cooperative learning**, an instructor oversees the learning of lesson material or completion of assignments for students in these small groups. With **informal cooperative learning**, the instructor supervises group activities by keeping students cognitively active but does not guide instruction or assignments. For example, a teacher might use a class period to show a movie but provide a list of questions for students to complete during the movie. In the special education classroom, cooperative learning is helpful when students need specific skills targeted or remediated. It is also helpful for separating students who are learning different content at different levels. For example, a cooperative learning activity may involve multiple groups of students with differing levels of mathematic abilities. Group work also promotes development of interpersonal skills as students interact with one another.

### Intrinsic Motivation

Intrinsic motivation is a person's inner drive to engage in an activity or behavior. Students with special needs often struggle with intrinsic motivation as a skill. This requires special educators and other professionals to promote and teach intrinsic motivation to students. Teachers can **promote intrinsic motivation** by giving students opportunities to demonstrate **achievement**. This can be done by challenging students with intellectual risks and helping them focus on difficult classwork or tasks. Teachers can build upon students' strengths by providing daily opportunities in the classroom for students to demonstrate their **strengths** instead of focusing on their weaknesses. Offering choices throughout the day provides students with ownership of their decision-making and communicates that they have choices in the classroom environment. Teachers should allow students to **fail without criticism** and should promote self-reflection in order to build students' confidence. Teachers should promote self-management and organizational skills like instructing students on how to **break down tasks**.

### Promoting Critical Thinking Skills

Critical thinking is a self-directed thinking process that helps people make logical, reasonable judgments. This is an especially challenging skill for students with **developmental disabilities**, who often demonstrate deficits in logical thinking and reasoning abilities. In order to teach these students **critical thinking skills**, the focus should be on encouraging critical thinking across **home and school environments** and providing opportunities for students to practice this type of thinking. Teachers and parents can encourage critical thinking by implementing teaching strategies focused on fostering **creativity** in students. Instead of providing outlines or templates for lesson concepts, students can use their prior knowledge to figure out the boundaries of the lessons independently and explore new concepts. Parents and teachers should not always be quick to jump in and help students who are struggling. Sometimes the best way to help is by facilitating ways for students to solve problems without doing things for them. Opportunities for brainstorming, classifying and categorizing information, comparing and contrasting information, and making connections between topics are teaching strategies that also facilitate critical thinking skills.

### Career-Based Education

During their schooling years, students with disabilities have the additional challenge of determining possible **career options** for life after high school. Fortunately, instruction can be provided during the school day or within after-school programs that address career-based skills. Effective **career-based programs** for students with disabilities should work collaboratively with community and school resources. Students should receive information on career options, be exposed to a range of experiences, and learn how to self-advocate. Information regarding career options can be gathered via **career assessments** that explore students' possible career interests. Students should receive exposure to **postsecondary education** to determine if it is an option that aligns with their career interests. They should also learn about basic job requirements, such as entry requirements for different types of jobs and what it means to earn a living wage. Students should be given opportunities for job training, job shadowing, and community service. It is helpful to provide students with opportunities to learn and practice **work and occupational skills** that pertain to specific job interests. Students need to learn **self-advocacy skills**, such as communicating the implications of their disabilities to employers, in order to maintain success in postsecondary work environments.

# Individualized Education Programs

## Developing and Writing Measurable IEP Goals

According to the Individuals with Disabilities Education Act, students eligible for special education receive Individualized Education Program (IEP) goals, which must contain specific **components**. Components of a **measurable IEP goal** include condition, performance, criteria, assessment, and standard. Measurable goals also include how skill mastery will be **assessed**, such as through observations or work samples. In the provided example below, the criterion is clearly measurable, as Jacob will either succeed or fail at multiple trials, and the ratio of successes to numbers of attempts should be recorded and dated throughout the IEP year to show his progress. Goals should also be **standards-based** whenever possible and may be required.

For example, an IEP goal may state, "By the end of this IEP, Jacob will use appropriate skills to communicate his needs in four out of five trials."

- **Condition** refers to when, where, and how the disability will be addressed. "By the end of this IEP" is the condition of the goal.
- **Performance** is what the student is expected to accomplish during the condition of the goal. In this case, that is "Jacob will use appropriate skills to communicate his needs."
- The last part of the goal stating "in four out of five trials" is the **criterion** that outlines how well the goal will be performed.

**Review Video: IEPs**
Visit mometrix.com/academy and enter code: 153484

## Role of Local Education Agency Representatives in IEP Meetings

A **local education agency** (LEA) representative is a required member of the IEP team who must meet the following criteria:

- LEA representatives must be qualified to provide or supervise specially designed instruction.
- LEA representatives must be knowledgeable about the general education curriculum.
- LEA representatives must be knowledgeable about the availability of the school district's resources.

In many cases, a school building leader or principal may fulfill the role of LEA representative. An LEA representative must be qualified and familiar with the IEP process. The role of the LEA representative in IEP meetings is to help ensure that the services and supports discussed can be provided by the district in a manner consistent with the Individuals with Disabilities Education Act (IDEA). LEA representatives also help the school district meet IDEA's procedural requirements and ensure that eligible students are provided a free appropriate public education (FAPE). This role is necessary on the IEP team because the LEA representative brings knowledge of district resources and IDEA requirements to the team's decisions and helps support effective implementation of the IEP.

## Involvement of Students with IEPs in the Transition Process in High School

Most states require **transition statements** to be made when students reach age 14 during the IEP year. Federal law requires students 16 years of age or older to have transition statements; postsecondary goals for independent living, employment, and education; and summaries of performance that include the results of the most recent transition assessments. Per federal law, students of transition age must be invited to their **IEP meetings**. It is important for students on IEPs to **participate** in the transition process because it helps them figure out what they want to do after they graduate from high school. Participation in the process gets them thinking about living independently, postsecondary education options, and employment options. Students usually have opportunities to participate in formal and informal assessments like interest inventories that help them define their interests. Transition goals for independent living, employment, and education should be based on the results of these assessments and any other interests the students have expressed. The students participate in the **implementation** of the transition goals by completing activities associated with their indicated interests.

## Student Support Teams

A **student support team (SST)** is a team made up of parents and educational professionals who work to support students in the general education classroom who are struggling with academics, discipline, health problems, or any other anticipated or actual problem that does not qualify the student for special education or supports from an Individualized Education Program. In this support team model, a group of educators works to identify and provide early intervention services for any student exhibiting academic or behavioral problems. The purpose of this kind of SST is to offer different supports, such as monitoring student progress, developing intervention plans, and referring students for intervention services. While the primary goal of this kind of SST is to provide support for students **struggling with school**, it can also shift focus to supporting students at risk of **dropping out of school**. Another primary objective of an SST is to identify students who are likely to have disabilities or who may need 504 Plans to succeed in school and to recommend them for referrals so they are not left without necessary supports.

## Amendments to an Individualized Education Program

A student's IEP is in effect for one year. Academic goals, objectives, benchmarks, transition goals, and any accommodations and modifications are to be in place for the student for the duration of the IEP. An **amendment** to the IEP can be made when a change is needed before the year is over. An amendment is an agreement between the student, parents or legal guardians, and the IEP team. IEP meetings for amendments can be requested at any time. IEP amendments can be requested if a student is not making adequate progress toward the goals, if the goals become inappropriate in some way for the student, or when the student has met all IEP goals and requires new ones. If new information about the student becomes available, the IEP can be amended. Students, parents, and other team members may also request amendment meetings if they think that other accommodations and modifications are needed or should be removed.

## How the Needs of Students with IEPs Are Met in the School Environment

IEPs communicate what **services** are to be provided for children with disabilities in the school setting, the children's **present levels of performance**, and how their disabilities affect **academic performance**. IEPs also specify **annual goals** appropriate to the students' specific needs and any accommodations or modifications that need to be provided. Schools and teachers have the responsibility to implement these IEP components when working with students with disabilities. Additionally, schools and teachers working with students with disabilities must ensure that students' individualized annual goals are met within a year of the students' IEP effective dates. It is up to the IEP teams to determine what classroom settings would most benefit the students while also appropriately meeting their IEP goals with the fewest barriers. Special educators must determine how data is collected and then obtain and record data on how the students are meeting their IEP goals. Special educators are responsible for providing intervention services based on the data results. They must also ensure that any accommodations or modifications listed on the IEPs are implemented in both general education and self-contained classrooms.

## Accommodation vs. Modification in IEPs

Formal accommodations, adaptations, and modifications for a student with a disability are listed on the Individualized Education Program. **Accommodations** change *how* a student learns the material, while an **adaptation** or **modification** changes *what* a student is taught or expected to learn.

- **Accommodations** are changes to the instruction or assessment that do *not* alter the curricular requirements. For instance, a student with accommodations may be allowed to answer a test orally instead of writing the answers or might be given pre-structured notes to help organize thoughts during instruction. These types of changes do not fundamentally change the information taught or the requirements for passing.

- **Adaptations** or **modifications** are changes to the instruction or assessment that fundamentally change the curricular requirements, but which enable a student with a disability to participate. Examples of adaptations include substitution of activities for related materials, exemption from answering particular types of questions on assessments, and removing or reducing time limits when taking tests.

For state standardized tests, accommodations like extra time and frequent breaks can be provided. Students that need modifications to state tests may complete alternate assessments that may not cover the same material as the standard exams.

**Review Video: Adapting and Modifying Lessons or Activities**
Visit mometrix.com/academy and enter code: 834946

### Determining the Placement of a Student with a Disability

With every student, the ideal goal is placement in the **general education classroom** as much as possible while still meeting the student's educational needs and ensuring a successful educational experience. The Individuals with Disabilities Education Act does not require that students be placed in the regular education classroom, but it does require that students be placed in their **least restrictive environment** as defined by the student's IEP team. Ultimately, the IEP team determines what **environment** best suits the student based on the student's specific needs. The IEP team is responsible for determining what educational environment would provide the student with the maximum appropriate educational benefit. While justification for removing a student from the regular education classroom is common and appropriate, as occurs when a student is placed in a resource room, the IEP team must explain the reasoning in the student's IEP. **Justification** must specifically state why the student cannot be educated with accommodations and services in the regular education classroom during any part of the school day. Justification for removal cannot be the perceived instructional limitations of the regular education teacher or concerns over extra instructional time needed to educate a student with a disability.

### Creating a SMART Annual Goal in an IEP

A good IEP goal describes how far the student is expected to **progress** toward the goal by the next IEP. Since IEPs should be revised once a year, a good annual IEP goal should describe what the student is capable of doing in a one-year time frame. Creating **SMART** IEP goals can help the student determine realistic expectations of what can be achieved in a year. SMART IEP goals are specific, measurable, attainable, relevant, and time-bound. Goals are **specific** when they list the targeted result in the skill or subject area. Goals should also be specific to the student's needs. Goals that are **measurable** state the way a student's progress will be measured. Measurable goals list how accurately a student should meet the goal. **Attainable** goals are realistic for the student to achieve in one year. **Relevant** goals outline what a student needs to do to accomplish the goal. For example, a SMART goal may state, "During the school week, Robert will use his device to communicate greetings 80 percent of the time in four out of five trials." **Time-bound** goals include a time frame for the student to achieve the goal. They also list when and how often progress will be measured.

**Review Video: SMART Goals**
Visit mometrix.com/academy and enter code: 100378

### Role of an Initial Evaluation Assessment in Qualifying for Special Education

When a student is determined to need special education, it means the student has a disability or disabilities adversely affecting educational performance. It may also mean the student's needs cannot be addressed in the general education classroom with or without accommodations and that **specially designed instruction** is required. An **initial evaluation** of the student is required for special education eligibility. The evaluation is comprehensive and includes existing data collected on the student and additional assessments needed to determine eligibility. Individual school districts decide what assessments should be completed for the student's initial evaluation. Each district is responsible for and should provide assessments that measure functional, developmental, and academic information. The student's parents or legal guardians are responsible for providing outside information relevant to the student's education, such as medical needs assessed outside of the school district by qualified providers.

### Purpose of an IEP

The purpose of an IEP is to guide the learning of a student with a **disability** in the educational environment. An IEP is a written statement for a student eligible for **special education**. An initial IEP is **implemented** once the child has been evaluated and determined to be in need of special education. After the initial IEP, **IEP meetings** are conducted annually (or more often) in order to update the plan to meet the needs of the student. IEPs are created, reviewed, and revised according to individual state and federal laws. These plans include the amount of time the student will spend in the special education classroom based on the level of need. They also include any related services the student might need (such as speech-language therapy) as well as academic and behavioral goals for the year. As the student learns and changes, performance levels and goals change as well. A student's present levels of performance are included and updated yearly, as are the academic and behavioral goals.

### Members of an Individualized Education Program Team

IEPs are updated **annually** following the initial IEP. IEP team members meet at least once a year to discuss a student's progress and make changes to the IEP. The required members of a student's IEP team include the student's parents or legal guardians, one of the student's general education teachers, the special education teacher, a school representative, an individual who can interpret the instructional implications of evaluation results, and if appropriate, the student. Anyone else who has knowledge or expertise about the student may also attend. **Parents and legal guardians** contribute unique expertise about the student, typically having the benefit of knowing the child well. **General education teachers** can speak to how the student is performing in the general education classroom. The **special education teacher** can report on progress made toward academic and behavioral goals and present levels of performance. A **school representative** must be qualified to provide or supervise specially designed instruction, be knowledgeable of the general education curriculum, and be knowledgeable about school resources. The **individual who can interpret evaluation results** can be an existing team member or someone else who is qualified to report on evaluation results. **Advocates**, such as counselors or therapists who see the student outside the school day, can also attend the meeting to speak on the student's behalf.

### Legal Rights of Parents or Legal Guardians

IEP meetings occur annually for each student. However, it is a **parent or legal guardian's right** to request a meeting at any point during the school year. The student's school is responsible for identifying and evaluating the child; developing, reviewing, or revising the IEP; and determining what placement setting best suits the needs of the student. It is within the parent or legal guardian's rights to have **input** in all processes related to the student. Under the Individuals with Disabilities Education Act, parents have the right to participate in IEP meetings, have an independent evaluation in addition to the one the school provides, give or deny consent for the IEP, contest a school's decision, and obtain private education paid for by the public school. In specific circumstances, if the student is determined to need services that the public school cannot provide, the public school district may need to pay for the student's tuition at a private school where the student's needs can be met.

### Collaborative Consultation between Educational Professionals

Collaborative consultation refers to the special educator or other professional providing advice to the general education teacher about a student on an IEP. Special educators and other IEP team members, such as school psychologists and related service professionals, serve as the **experts** and have knowledge about how individual students learn and behave. This is especially important when students with IEPs are included in the general education classroom. Special educators and general education teachers must work collaboratively to ensure that students are reaching their potential in the general education setting. Examples of **collaborative consultation** include the special educator serving as a consultant to the general education teacher by providing advice on a student's IEP, accommodations, modifications, and IEP goal tracking. Another way the special educator or other professional can assist the general educator is by providing skill and strategy instruction to students on IEPs outside the general education classroom. The idea behind this method is for students to generalize these skills and strategies to the general education classroom.

> **Review Video: Collaborating with Other Professionals**
> Visit mometrix.com/academy and enter code: 100351

### PUBLIC SCHOOL RESPONSIBILITIES TO PARENTS OF STUDENTS ON IEPS

The school must invite the parents or legal guardians to any **IEP meetings** and provide advance notice of the meetings. Each meeting notice is required to include the purpose of the meeting, its time and location, and who will attend. The location of the meeting is likely the student's school, but legally it must be held at a mutually agreed-upon place and time. If the parent or legal guardian cannot attend the IEP meeting, the school must ensure participation in another way, such as video or telephone conference. The meeting can be conducted without the parent or legal guardian if the school district cannot get the parent or legal guardian to attend. A parent or legal guardian can request a meeting, and the school can refuse or deny the request. If denied, the school must provide a **prior written notice** explaining their refusal. A prior written notice is a document outlining important school district decisions about a student on an IEP.

## Chapter Quiz

Ready to see how well you retained what you just read? Scan the QR code to go directly to the chapter quiz interface for this study guide. If you're using a computer, simply visit the online resources page at **mometrix.com/resources719/gacesegcelemed** and click the Chapter Quizzes link.

# Evaluation and Assessment

## Assessment Methodology

### Assessment Methods

Effective teaching requires multiple methods of assessment to evaluate student comprehension and instructional effectiveness. Assessments are typically categorized as diagnostic, formative, summative, and benchmark and are applicable at varying stages of instruction. **Diagnostic** assessments are administered before instruction and indicate students' prior knowledge and areas of misunderstanding to determine the path of instruction. **Formative** assessments occur continuously to measure student engagement, comprehension, and instructional effectiveness. These assessments indicate instructional strategies that require adjustment to meet students' needs in facilitating successful learning and include strategies like checking for understanding, observations, total participation activities, and exit tickets. **Summative** assessments are given at the end of a lesson or unit to evaluate student progress in reaching learning targets and identify areas of misconception for reteaching. Such assessments can be given in the form of exams and quizzes or be project-based activities in which students demonstrate their learning through hands-on, personalized methods. Additionally, portfolios serve as valuable summative assessments in allowing students to demonstrate their progress over time and provide insight regarding individual achievement. **Benchmark** assessments occur less frequently and encompass large portions of curriculum. These assessments are intended to evaluate the progress of groups of students in achieving state and district academic standards.

#### *Assessment Types*

- **Diagnostic:** These assessments can either be formal or informal and are intended to provide teachers with information regarding students' level of understanding prior to beginning a unit of instruction. Examples include pretests, KWL charts, anticipation guides, and brainstorming activities. Digital resources, such as online polls, surveys, and quizzes are also valuable resources for gathering diagnostic feedback.
- **Formative:** These assessments occur throughout instruction to provide the teacher with feedback regarding student understanding. Examples include warm-up and closure activities, checking frequently for understanding, student reflection activities, and providing students with color-coded cards to indicate their level of understanding. Short quizzes and total participation activities, such as four corners, are also valuable formative assessments. Numerous digital resources, including polls, surveys, and review games, are also beneficial in providing teachers with formative feedback to indicate instructional effectiveness.
- **Summative:** Summative assessments are intended to indicate students' levels of mastery and progress toward reaching academic learning standards. These assessments may take the form of written or digital exams and include multiple choice, short answer, or long answer questions. Examples also include projects, final essays, presentations, or portfolios to demonstrate student progress over time.
- **Benchmark:** Benchmark assessments measure students' progress in achieving academic standards. These assessments are typically standardized to ensure uniformity, objectivity, and accuracy. Benchmark assessments are typically given as a written multiple choice or short answer exam, or as a digital exam in which students answer questions on the computer.

**Review Video: Formative and Summative Assessments**
Visit mometrix.com/academy and enter code: 804991

### Determining Appropriate Assessment Strategies

As varying assessment methods provide different information regarding student performance and achievement, the teacher must consider the most applicable and effective assessment strategy in each stage of instruction. This includes determining the **desired outcomes** of assessment as well as the information the teacher intends to ascertain and how they will apply the results to further instruction. **Age-** and **grade-level-** appropriateness must be considered when selecting which assessment strategies will enable students to successfully demonstrate their learning. Additionally, the teacher must be cognizant of students' individual differences and learning needs to determine which assessment model is most **accommodating** and reflective of their progress. It is also important that teachers consider the practicality of assessment strategies and methods they will use to implement the assessment for maximized feedback regarding individual and whole-class progress in achieving learning goals.

## Assessments That Reflect Real-World Applications

Assessments that reflect **real-world applications** enhance relevancy and students' ability to establish personal connections to learning that deepen understanding. Implementing such assessments provides authenticity and enhances engagement by defining a clear and practical purpose for learning. These assessments often allow for hands-on opportunities for demonstrating learning and can be adjusted to accommodate students' varying learning styles and needs while measuring individual progress; however, assessments that focus on real-world applications can be subjective, thus making it difficult to extract concrete data and quantify student progress to guide future instructional decisions. In addition, teachers may have difficulty analyzing assessment results on a large scale and comparing student performance with other schools and districts, as individual assessments may vary.

## Diagnostic Tests

**Diagnostic tests** are integral to planning and delivering effective instruction. These tests are typically administered prior to beginning a unit or lesson and provide valuable feedback for guiding and planning instruction. Diagnostic tests provide **preliminary information** regarding students' levels of understanding and prior knowledge. This serves as a baseline for instructional planning that connects and builds upon students' background knowledge and experiences to enhance success in learning. Diagnostic tests allow the teacher to identify and clarify areas of student misconception prior to engaging in instruction to ensure continued comprehension and avoid the need for remediation. They indicate areas of student strength and need as well as individual instructional aids that may need to be incorporated into lessons to support student achievement. In addition, these tests enable the teacher to determine which instructional strategies, activities, groupings, and materials will be most valuable in maximizing engagement and learning. Diagnostic tests can be **formal** or **informal** and include pre-tests, pre-reading activities, surveys, vocabulary inventories, and graphic organizers (such as KWL charts). These tests are used to assess student understanding prior to engaging in learning. Diagnostic tests are generally not graded, as there is little expectation that all students in a class possess the same baseline of proficiency at the start of a unit.

## Formative Assessments

Formative assessments are any assessments that take place in the **middle of a unit of instruction**. The goals of formative assessments are to help teachers understand where a student is in his or her progress toward **mastering** the current unit's content and to provide the students with **ongoing feedback** throughout the unit. The advantage of relying heavily on formative assessments in instruction is that it allows the teacher to continuously **check for comprehension** and adjust instruction as needed to ensure that the whole class is adequately prepared to proceed at the end of the unit. To understand formative assessments well, teachers need to understand that any interaction that can provide information about the student's comprehension is a type of formative assessment which can be used to inform future instruction.

Formative assessments are often a mixture of formal and informal assessments. **Formal formative assessments** often include classwork, homework, and quizzes. Examples of **informal formative assessments** include simple comprehension checks during instruction, class-wide discussions of the current topic, and exit slips, which are written questions posed by teachers at the end of class, which helps the teacher quickly review which students are struggling with the concepts.

## Summative Assessments

**Summative assessment** refers to an evaluation at the end of a discrete unit of instruction, such as the end of a course, unit, or semester. Classic examples of summative assessments include end-of-course assessments, final exams, or even qualifying standardized tests such as the SAT or ACT. Most summative assessments are created to measure student mastery of particular **academic standards**. Whereas formative assessment generally informs current instruction, summative assessments are used to objectively demonstrate that each individual has achieved adequate mastery of the standards in question. If a student has not met the benchmark, he or she may need extra instruction or may need to repeat the course.

These assessments usually take the form of **tests** or formal portfolios with rubrics and clearly defined goals. Summative assessments are usually high-stakes, heavily-weighted, and they should always be formally graded. These types of assessments often feature a narrower range of question types, such as multiple choice, short answer, and essay questions to help with systematic grading.

**Project-based** assessments are beneficial in evaluating achievement, as they incorporate several elements of instruction and highlight real-world applications of learning. This allows students to demonstrate understanding through a hands-on, individualized approach that reinforces connections to learning and increases retainment. **Portfolios** of student work over time serve as a valuable method for assessing individual progress toward reaching learning targets. Summative assessments provide insight regarding overall instructional effectiveness and are necessary for guiding future instruction in subsequent years but are not usually used to modify current instruction.

**Review Video: Assessment Reliability and Validity**
Visit mometrix.com/academy and enter code: 424680

## Benchmark Assessments

**Benchmark assessments** are intended to quantify, evaluate, and compare individual and groups of students' achievement of school-wide, district, and state **academic standards.** They are typically administered in specific intervals throughout the school year and encompass entire or large units of curriculum to determine student mastery and readiness for academic advancement. Benchmark assessments provide data that enable the teacher to determine students' progress toward reaching academic goals to guide current and continued instruction. This data can be utilized by the school and individual teachers to create learning goals and objectives aligned with academic standards. It can also be used to plan instructional strategies, activities, and assessments to support students in achieving these academic standards. In addition, benchmark assessments provide feedback regarding understanding and the potential need for remediation to allow the teacher to instill necessary supports in future instruction that prepare students for success in achieving learning targets.

## Alignment of Assessments with Instructional Goals and Objectives

To effectively monitor student progress, assessments must align with **instructional goals** and **objectives**. This allows the teacher to determine whether students are advancing at an appropriate pace to achieve state and district academic standards. When assessments are aligned with specific learning targets, the teacher ensures that students are learning relevant material to establish a foundation of knowledge necessary for growth and academic achievement. To achieve this, teachers must determine which instructional goals and objectives their students must achieve and derive instruction, content, and activities from these specifications. Instruction must reflect and reinforce learning targets, and the teacher must select the most effective strategies for addressing students' needs as they work to achieve them. Assessments must be reflective of content instruction to ensure they are aligned with learning goals and objectives, as well as to enable the teacher to evaluate student progress in mastering them. The teacher must clearly communicate learning goals and objectives throughout all stages of instruction to provide students with clarity on expectations. This establishes a clear purpose and focus for learning that enhances relevancy and strengthens connections to support student achievement.

## Clearly Communicating Assessment Criteria and Standards

Students must be clear on the purpose of learning throughout all stages of instruction to enhance understanding and facilitate success. When assessment **criteria** and **standards** are clearly communicated, the purpose of learning is established, and students are able to effectively connect instructional activities to learning goals and criteria for assessment. Communicating assessment criteria and standards provides students with clarity on tasks and learning goals they are expected to accomplish as they prepare themselves for assessment. This allows for more **focused instruction** and engagement in learning, as it enhances relevancy and student motivation. Utilizing appropriate forms of **rubrics** is an effective strategy in specifying assessment criteria and standards, as it informs students about learning goals they are working toward, the quality of work they are expected to achieve, and skills they must master to succeed on the assessment. Rubrics indicate to students exactly how they will be evaluated, thus supporting their understanding and focus as they engage in learning to promote academic success.

### *Rubrics for Communicating Standards*

The following are varying styles of rubrics that can be used to communicate criteria and standards:

- **Analytic:** Analytic rubrics break down criteria for an assignment into several categories and provide an explanation of the varying levels of performance in each one. This style of rubric is beneficial for detailing the characteristics of quality work as well as providing students with feedback regarding specific components of their performance. Analytic rubrics are most effective when used for summative assessments, such as long-term projects or essays.
- **Holistic:** Holistic rubrics evaluate the quality of the student's assignment as a whole rather than scoring individual components. Students' scores are determined based upon their performance across multiple performance indicators. This style of rubric is beneficial for providing a comprehensive evaluation but limits the amount of feedback that students receive regarding their performance in specific areas.
- **Single-point:** Single-point rubrics outline criteria for assignments into several categories. Rather than providing a numeric score to each category, however, the teacher provides written feedback regarding the students' strengths and ways in which they can improve their performance. This style of rubric is beneficial in providing student-centered feedback that focuses on their overall progress.
- **Checklist:** Checklists typically outline a set of criteria that is scored using a binary approach based upon completion of each component. This style increases the efficiency of grading assignments and is often easy for students to comprehend but does not provide detailed feedback. This method of grading should generally be reserved for shorter assignments.

### *Communicating High Academic Expectations in Assessments*

The attitudes and behaviors exhibited by the teacher are highly influential on students' attitudes toward learning. Teachers demonstrate belief in students' abilities to be successful in learning when they communicate **high academic expectations**. This promotes students' **self-concept** and establishes a **growth mindset** to create confident, empowered learners that are motivated to achieve. High expectations for assessments and reaching academic standards communicates to students the quality of work that is expected of them and encourages them to overcome obstacles as they engage in learning. When communicating expectations for student achievement, it is important that the teacher is aware of students' individual learning needs to provide the necessary support that establishes equitable opportunities for success in meeting assessment criteria and standards. Setting high expectations through assessment criteria and standards while supporting students in their learning enhances overall achievement and establishes a foundation for continuous academic success.

### *Effective Communication and Impact on Student Learning*

Communicating high academic expectations enhances students' self-concept and increases personal motivation for success in learning. To maximize student achievement, it is important that the teacher set high academic expectations that are **clearly** communicated through **age-appropriate** terms and consistently reinforced. Expectations must be reflected through learning goals and objectives and must be **visible** at all times to ensure student awareness. Teachers must be **specific** in communicating what they want students to accomplish and clearly detail necessary steps for achievement while assuming the role of facilitator to guide learning and provide support. Providing constructive **feedback** throughout instruction is integral in reminding students of academic expectations and ensuring they are making adequate progress toward reaching learning goals. When high academic expectations are communicated and reinforced, students are empowered with a sense of confidence and self-responsibility for their own learning that promotes their desire to learn. This ultimately enhances achievement and equips them with the tools necessary for future academic success.

## Analyzing and Interpreting Assessment Data

Teachers can utilize multiple techniques to effectively analyze and interpret assessment data. This typically involves creating charts and graphs outlining different data subsets. They can list each learning standard that was assessed, determine how many students overall demonstrated proficiency on the standard, and identify individual students who did not demonstrate proficiency on each standard. This information can be used to differentiate instruction. Additionally, they can track individual student performance and progress on each standard over time.

Teachers can take note of overall patterns and trends in assessment data. For example, they can determine if any subgroups of students did not meet expectations. They can consider whether the data confirms or challenges any existing beliefs, implications this may have on instructional planning and what, if any, conclusions can be drawn from this data.

Analyzing and interpreting assessment data may raise new questions for educators, so they can also determine if additional data collection is needed.

### *Using Assessment Data to Differentiate Instruction for Individual Learners*

By analyzing and interpreting assessment data, teachers can determine if there are any specific learning standards that need to be retaught to their entire classes. This may be necessary if the data shows that all students struggled in these specific areas. Teachers may consider reteaching these standards using different methods if the initial methods were unsuccessful.

Teachers can also form groups of students who did not demonstrate proficiency on the same learning standards. Targeted instruction can be planned for these groups to help them make progress in these areas. Interventions can also be planned for individual students who did not show proficiency in certain areas. If interventions have already been in place and have not led to increased learning outcomes, the interventions may be redesigned. If interventions have been in place and assessment data now shows proficiency, the interventions may be discontinued.

If assessment data shows that certain students have met or exceeded expectations in certain areas, enrichment activities can be planned to challenge these students and meet their learning needs.

## Aligning Assessments with Instructional Goals and Objectives

Assessments that are congruent to instructional goals and objectives provide a **clear purpose** for learning that enhances student understanding and motivation. When learning targets are reflected in assessments, instructional activities and materials become more **relevant**, as they are derived from these specifications. Such clarity in purpose allows for more focus and productivity as students engage in instruction and fosters connections that strengthen overall understanding for maximized success in learning. Aligning assessments with instructional goals and objectives ensures that students are learning material that is relevant to the curriculum and academic standards to ensure **preparedness** as they advance in their academic careers. In addition, it enables the teacher to evaluate and monitor student progress to determine whether they are progressing at an ideal pace for achieving academic standards. With this information, the teacher can effectively modify instruction as necessary to support students' needs in reaching desired learning outcomes.

### Norm-Referenced Tests

On **norm-referenced tests**, students' performances are compared to the performances of sample groups of similar students. Norm-referenced tests identify students who score above and below the average. To ensure reliability, the tests must be given in a standardized manner to all students.

Norm-referenced tests usually cover a broad range of skills, such as the entire grade-level curriculum for a subject. They typically contain a few questions per skill. Whereas scores in component areas of the tests may be calculated, usually overall test scores are reported. Scores are often reported using percentile ranks, which indicate what percentage of test takers scored lower than the student being assessed. For example, a student's score in the 75th percentile means the student scored better than 75% of other test takers. Other times, scores may be reported using grade-level equivalency.

One advantage of norm-referenced tests is their objectivity. They also allow educators to compare large groups of students at once. This may be helpful for making decisions regarding class placements and groupings. A disadvantage of norm-referenced tests is that they only indicate how well students perform in comparison to one another. They do not indicate whether or not students have mastered certain skills.

### Criterion-Referenced Tests

**Criterion-referenced tests** measure how well students perform on certain skills or standards. The goal of these tests is to indicate whether or not students have mastered certain skills and which skills require additional instruction. Scores are typically reported using the percentage of questions answered correctly or students' performance levels. Performance levels are outlined using terms such as *below expectations, met expectations*, and *exceeded expectations*.

One advantage of criterion-referenced tests is that they provide teachers with useful information to guide instruction. They can identify which specific skills students have mastered and which skills need additional practice. Teachers can use this information to plan whole-class, small-group, and individualized instruction. Analyzing results of criterion-referenced tests over time can also help teachers track student progress on certain skills. A disadvantage of criterion-referenced tests is that they do not allow educators to compare students' performances to samples of their peers.

### Ways That Standardized Test Results Are Reported

- **Raw scores** are sometimes reported and indicate how many questions students answered correctly on a test. By themselves, they do not provide much useful information. They do not indicate how students performed in comparison to other students or to grade-level expectations.
- **Grade-level equivalents** are also sometimes reported. A grade-level equivalent score of 3.4 indicates that a student performed as well as an average third grader in the fourth month of school. It can indicate whether a student is performing above or below grade-level expectations, but it does not indicate that the student should be moved to a different grade level.
- **Standard scores** are used to compare students' performances on tests to standardized samples of their peers. Standard deviation refers to the amount that a set of scores differs from the mean score on a test.
- **Percentile ranks** are used on criterion-referenced tests to indicate what percentage of test takers scored lower than the student whose score is being reported.
- **Cutoff scores** refer to predetermined scores students must obtain in order to be considered proficient in certain areas. Scores below the cutoff level indicate improvement is needed and may result in interventions or instructional changes.

### Formal and Informal Assessments

Assessments are any method a teacher uses to gather information about student comprehension of curriculum, including improvised questions for the class and highly-structured tests. **Formal assessments** are assessments that have **clearly defined standards and methodology** and which are applied consistently to all students. Formal tests should be objective and scrutinized for validity and reliability since they tend to carry higher weight for the student. Summative assessments, such as end-of-unit tests, lend themselves to being formal tests because it is necessary that a teacher test the comprehension of all students in a consistent and thorough way.

Although formal assessments can provide useful data about student performance and progress, they can be costly and time-consuming to implement. Administering formal assessments often interrupts classroom instruction and may cause testing anxiety.

**Informal assessments** are assessments that do not adhere to formal objectives, and they do not have to be administered consistently to all students. As a result, they do not have to be scored or recorded as a grade and generally act as a **subjective measure** of class comprehension. Informal assessments can be as simple as asking the students to raise their hands if they are ready to proceed to the next step or asking a particular question of an individual student.

Informal assessments do not provide objective data for analysis, but they can be implemented quickly and inexpensively. Informal assessments can also be incorporated into regular classroom instruction and activities, making them more authentic and less stressful for students.

## Using Various Assessments

The goal of **assessment** in education is to gather data that, when evaluated, can be used to further student learning and achievement. **Standardized tests** are helpful for placement purposes and to reflect student progress toward goals set by a school district or state. If a textbook is chosen to align with district learning standards, the textbook assessments can provide teachers with convenient, small-scale, regular checks of student knowledge against the target standard.

In order be effective, teachers must know where their students are in the learning process. Teachers use a multitude of **formal and informal assessment methods** to do this. Posing differentiated discussion questions is an example of an informal assessment method that allows teachers to gauge individual student progress rather than their standing in relation to a universal benchmark.

Effective teachers employ a variety of assessments, as different formats assess different skills, promote different learning experiences, and appeal to different learners. A portfolio is an example of an assessment that gauges student progress in multiple skills and through multiple media. Teachers can use authentic or performance-based assessments to stimulate student interest and provide visible connections between language-learning and the real world.

## Assessment Reliability

**Assessment reliability** refers to how well an assessment is constructed and is made up of a variety of measures. An assessment is generally considered **reliable** if it yields similar results across multiple administrations of the assessment. A test should perform similarly with different test administrators, graders, test-takers, and over multiple iterations. Factors that affect reliability include the day-to-day wellbeing of the student (students can sometimes underperform), the physical environment of the test, the way it is administered, and the subjectivity of the scorer (with written-response assessments).

Perhaps the most important threat to assessment reliability is the nature of the **exam questions** themselves. An assessment question is designed to test knowledge of a certain construct. A question is reliable in this sense if students who understand the content answer the question correctly. Statisticians look for patterns in student marks, both within the single test and over multiple tests, as a way of measuring reliability. Teachers should watch out for circumstances in which a student or students answer correctly a series of questions about a given concept (demonstrating their understanding) but then answer a related question incorrectly. The latter question may be an unreliable indicator of concept knowledge.

### *MEASURES OF ASSESSMENT RELIABILITY*

- **Test-retest reliability** refers to an assessment's consistency of results with the same test-taker over multiple retests. If one student shows inconsistent results over time, the test is not considered to have test-retest reliability.
- **Intertester reliability** refers to an assessment's consistency of results between multiple test-takers at the same level. Students at similar levels of proficiency should show similar results.
- **Inter-rater reliability** refers to an assessment's consistency of results between different administrators of the test. This plays an especially critical role in tests with interactive or subjective responses, such as Likert-scales, cloze tests, and short answer tests. Different raters of the same test need to have a consistent means of evaluating the test-takers' performance. Clear rubrics can help keep two or more raters consistent in scoring.
- **Intra-rater reliability** refers to an assessment's consistency of results with one rater over time. One test rater should be able to score different students objectively to rate subjective test formats fairly.
- **Parallel-forms reliability** refers to an assessment's consistency between multiple different forms. For instance, end-of-course assessments may have many distinctive test forms, with different questions or question orders. If the different forms of a test do not provide the same results, the test is said to be lacking in parallel-forms reliability.
- **Internal consistency reliability** refers to the consistency of results of similar questions on a particular assessment. If there are two or more questions targeted at the same standard and at the same level, they should show the same results across each question.

## ASSESSMENT VALIDITY

**Assessment validity** is a measure of the relevancy that an assessment has to the skill or ability being evaluated and the degree to which students' performance is representative of their mastery of the topic of assessment. In other words, a teacher should ask how well an assessment's results correlate to what it is looking to assess. Assessments should be evaluated for validity on both the **individual question** level and as a **test overall**. This can be especially helpful in refining tests for future classes. The overall validity of an assessment is determined by several types of validity measures.

An assessment is considered **valid** if it measures what it is intended to measure. One common error that can reduce the validity of a test (or a question on a test) occurs if the instructions are written at a reading level the students can't understand. In this case, it is not valid to take the student's failed answer as a true indication of his or her knowledge of the subject. Factors internal to the student might also affect exam validity: anxiety and a lack of self-esteem often lower assessments results, reducing their validity as a measure of student knowledge.

An assessment has content validity if it includes all the **relevant aspects** of the subject being tested—if it is comprehensive, in other words. An assessment has **predictive validity** if a score on the test is an accurate predictor of future success in the same domain. For example, SAT exams purport to have validity in predicting student success in a college. An assessment has construct validity if it accurately measures student knowledge of the subject being tested.

### *MEASURES OF ASSESSMENT VALIDITY*

- **Face validity** refers to the initial impression of whether an assessment seems to be fit for the task. As this method is subjective to interpretation and unquantifiable, it should not be used singularly as a measurement of validity.
- **Construct validity** asks if an assessment actually assesses what it is intended to assess. Some topics are more straightforward, such as assessing if a student can perform two-digit multiplication. This can be directly tested, which gives the assessment a strong content validity. Other measures, such as a person's overall happiness, must be measured indirectly. If an assessment asserted that a person is generally happy if he or she smiles frequently, it would be fair to question the construct validity of that assessment because smiling is unlikely to be a consistent measure of all peoples' general happiness.

- **Content validity** indicates whether the assessment is comprehensive of all aspects of the content being assessed. If a test leaves out an important topic, then the teacher will not have a full picture as a result of the assessment.
- **Criterion validity** refers to whether the results of an assessment can be used to **predict** a related value, known as **criterion**. An example of this is the hypothesis that IQ tests would predict a person's success later in life, but many critics believe that IQ tests are not valid predictors of success because intelligence is not the only predictor of success in life. IQ tests have shown validity toward predicting academic success, however. The measure of an assessment's criterion validity depends on how closely related the criterion is.
- **Discriminant validity** refers to how well an assessment tests only that which it is intended to test and successfully discriminates one piece of information from another. For instance, a student who is exceptional in mathematics should not be able to put that information into use on a science test and gain an unfair advantage. If the student is able to score well due to his or her mathematics knowledge, the science test did not adequately discriminate science knowledge from mathematics knowledge.
- **Convergent validity** is related to discriminant validity, but takes into account that two measures may be distinct but correlated. For instance, a personality test should distinguish self-esteem from extraversion so that they can be measured independently, but if an assessment has convergent validity, it should show a correlation between related measures.

## Practicality

An assessment is **practical** if it uses an appropriate amount of human and budgetary resources. A practical exam doesn't take very long to design or score, nor does it take students very long to complete in relation to other learning objectives and priorities. Teachers often need to balance a desire to construct comprehensive or content-valid tests with a need for practicality: lengthy exams consume large amounts of instruction time and may return unreliable results if students become tired and lose focus.

## Assessment Bias

An assessment is considered biased if it disadvantages a certain group of students, such as students of a certain gender, race, cultural background, or socioeconomic class. A **content bias** exists when the subject matter of a question or assessment is familiar to one group and not another. For example, a reading comprehension passage that discusses an event in American history would be biased against students new to the country. An **attitudinal bias** exists when a teacher has a pre-conceived idea about the likely success of an assessment of a particular individual or group. A **method bias** arises when the format of an assessment is unfamiliar to a given group of students. **Language bias** occurs when an assessment utilizes idioms, collocations, or cultural references unfamiliar to a group of students. Finally, **translation bias** may arise when educators attempt to translate content-area assessments into a student's native language—rough or hurried translations often result in a loss of nuance important for accurate assessment.

## Authentic Assessments

An authentic assessment is an assessment designed to closely resemble something that a student does, or will do, in the real world. For example, students will never encounter a multiple-choice test requiring them to choose the right tense of a verb, but they will encounter contexts in which they have to write a narration of an event that has antecedents and consequents spread out in time—like narrating their version of what caused a traffic accident. The latter is an example of a potential **authentic assessment**.

Well-designed authentic assessments require a student to exercise **advanced cognitive skills** (e.g., solving problems, integrating information, performing deductions), integrate **background knowledge**, and confront **ambiguity**. Research has demonstrated that mere language proficiency is not predictive of future language success—learning how to utilize knowledge in a complex context is an essential additional skill.

The terms "authentic" and "performance-based" are often used interchangeably when describing assessments; however, a performance-based assessment doesn't necessarily have to be grounded in a possible authentic experience.

## PERFORMANCE-BASED ASSESSMENTS

A performance-based assessment is one in which students demonstrate their learning by performing a **task** rather than by answering questions in a traditional test format. Proponents of **performance-based assessments** argue that they lead students to use **high-level cognitive skills** since they focus on how to put their knowledge to use and plan a sequence of stages in an activity or presentation. They also allow students more opportunities to individualize their presentations or responses based on preferred learning styles. Research suggests that students welcome the chance to put their knowledge to use in real-world scenarios.

Advocates of performance-based assessments suggest that they avoid many of the problems of language or cultural bias present in traditional assessments, allowing more accurate assessment of how well students learned the underlying concepts. In discussions regarding English as a second language, they argue that performance assessments come closer to replicating what should be the true goal of language learning—the effective use of language in real contexts—than do more traditional exams. Critics point out that performance assessments are difficult and time-consuming for teachers to construct and for students to perform. Finally, performative assessments are difficult to grade in the absence of a well-constructed and detailed rubric.

## TECHNOLOGY-BASED ASSESSMENTS

**Technology-based assessments** provide teachers with multiple resources for evaluating student progress to guide instruction. They are applicable in most formal and informal instructional settings and can be utilized as formative and summative assessments. Technology-based assessments simplify and enhance the efficiency of determining comprehension and instructional effectiveness, as they quickly present the teacher with information regarding student progress. This data enables the teacher to make necessary adjustments to facilitate student learning and growth. Implementing this assessment format simplifies the process of aligning them to school and district academic standards. This establishes objectivity and uniformity for comparing results and progress among students. It also helps ensure that all students are held to the same academic expectations. While technology-based assessments are beneficial, there are some shortcomings to consider. This format may not be entirely effective for all learning styles in demonstrating understanding, as individualization in technology-based assessment can be limited. These assessments may not illustrate individual students' growth over time but rather their mastery of an academic standard, thus hindering the ability to evaluate overall achievement. As technology-based evaluation limits hands-on opportunities, the real-world application and relevancy of the assessment may be unapparent to students.

### *ADVANTAGES AND DISADVANTAGES OF TECHNOLOGY-BASED ASSESSMENTS*

Technology-based assessments can have many advantages. They can be given to large numbers of students at once, limited only by the amounts of technological equipment schools possess. Many types of technology-based assessments are instantly scored, and feedback is provided quickly. Students are sometimes able to view their results and feedback at the conclusion of their testing sessions. Data can be quickly compiled and reported in easy-to-understand formats. Technology-based assessments can also often track student progress over time.

Technology-based assessments can have some disadvantages as well. Glitches and system errors can interfere with the assessment process or score reporting. Students must also have the necessary prerequisite technological skills to take the assessments, or the results may not measure the content they are designed to measure. For example, if students take timed, computer-based writing tests, they should have proficient typing skills. Otherwise, they may perform poorly on the tests despite strong writing abilities. Other prerequisite skills include knowing how to use a keyboard and mouse and understanding how to locate necessary information on the screen.

## Portfolio Assessments

A **portfolio** is a collection of student work in multiple forms and media gathered over time. Teachers may assess the portfolio both for evidence of progress over time or in its end state as a demonstration of the achievement of certain proficiency levels.

One advantage of **portfolio assessments** is their breadth. Unlike traditional assessments, which focus on one or two language skills, portfolios may contain work in multiple forms, such as writing samples, pictures, and graphs designed for content courses, video and audio clips, student reflections, teacher observations, and student exams. A second advantage is that they allow a student to develop work in authentic contexts, including in other classrooms and at home.

In order for portfolios to function as an objective assessment tool, teachers should negotiate with students in advance of what genres of work will be included and outline a grading rubric that makes clear what will be assessed, such as linguistic proficiency, use of English in academic contexts, and demonstrated use of target cognitive skills.

## Curriculum-Based Assessments

Curriculum-based assessments, also known as **curriculum-based measurements (CBM)**, are short, frequent assessments designed to measure student progress toward meeting curriculum **benchmarks**.

Teachers implement CBMs by designing **probes**, or short assessments that target specific skills. For example, a teacher might design a spelling probe, administered weekly, that requires students to spell 10 unfamiliar but level-appropriate words. The data from these assessments can be tracked over time to measure student progress toward defined grade-level goals.

CBM has several clear advantages. If structured well, the probes have high reliability and validity. Furthermore, they provide clear and objective evidence of student progress—a welcome outcome for students and parents who often grapple with less-clear and subjective evidence. Used correctly, CBMs also motivate students and provide them with evidence of their own progress; however, while CBMs are helpful in identifying areas of student weaknesses, they do not identify the causes of those weaknesses or provide teachers with strategies for improving instruction.

## Textbook Assessments

Textbook assessments are the assessments provided at the end of a chapter or unit in an approved textbook. **Textbook assessments** present several advantages for a teacher: they are already made; they are likely to be accurate representations of the chapter or unit materials; and, if the textbook has been prescribed or recommended by the state, it is likely to correspond closely to Common Core or other tested standards.

Textbook assessments can be limiting for students who lag in the comprehension of academic English or whose preferred learning style is not verbal. While textbooks may come with DVDs or recommended audio links, ESOL teachers will likely need to supplement these assessment materials with some of their own findings. Finally, textbook assessments are unlikely to represent the range of assessment types used in the modern classroom, such as a portfolio or performance-based assessments.

## Peer Assessment

A peer assessment is when students grade one another's work based on a teacher-provided framework. **Peer assessments** are promoted as a means of saving teacher time and building student metacognitive skills. They are typically used as **formative** rather than summative assessments, given concerns about the reliability of student scoring and the tensions that can result if student scores contribute to overall grades. Peer assessments are used most often to grade essay-type written work or presentations. Proponents point out that peer assessments require students to apply metacognition, build cooperative work and interpersonal skills, and broaden the sense that the student is accountable to peers and not just the teacher. Even advocates of the practice agree that students need detailed rubrics in order to succeed. Critics often argue that low-performing students have little to offer high-performing students in terms of valuable feedback—and this disparity may be more pronounced in ESOL classrooms or special education environments than in mainstream ones. One way to overcome this weakness is for the teacher to lead the evaluation exercise, guiding the students through a point-by-point framework of evaluation.

# Developmental Screening

## Types of Developmental Assessments

Developmental assessments measure the development of infants, toddlers, and preschoolers. These **norm-referenced tests** measure fine and gross motor skills; communication and language; and social, cognitive, and self-help milestones that young children should achieve at certain ages. When a child is suspected of having a **developmental delay**, a developmental assessment is useful in identifying the child's strengths and weaknesses. These assessments map out the **progress** of a child compared to the progress of similar-aged children. Developmental assessments are also useful in identifying if the delay is significant or can be overcome with time. These assessments can be used to determine what **educational placement** is most appropriate for a child with a developmental delay. Developmental assessments are administered via observations and questionnaires. Parents, legal guardians, caregivers, and instructors who are most familiar with the child provide the most insight on developmental strengths and weaknesses.

**Review Video: Identifying Appropriate Evaluation Strategies**
Visit mometrix.com/academy and enter code: 100353

## Screening Tests for Identifying Students Who Need Special Education

When determining if a child needs special education, **screening tests** are the first step. The Individuals with Disabilities Education Act offers guidance for schools to implement screening tests. Districts and schools often have school-wide processes in place for screening students for **special education**. Screening tests can also be used to identify students who are falling behind in class. The advantage of screening tests is that they are easily administered. They require few materials and little time and planning in order to administer. Additionally, they can be used to quickly assess students' strengths and weaknesses, they do not have to be administered one-on-one, and they can be used for everyone in the class. Screening tests can be as simple as paper-and-pencil quizzes assessing what students know. They are used for measuring visual acuity, auditory skills, physical health, development, basic academic skills, behavioral problems, risk of behavioral problems, language skills, and verbal and nonverbal intelligence.

## Individual Intelligence Tests vs. Individual Academic Achievement Tests

Intelligence tests measure a student's capacity for abstract thinking, mental reasoning, judgment, and decision-making. These **norm-referenced tests** help determine a student's **overall intelligence**, which correlates with **potential academic performance**. Intelligence tests can be used to determine if a student's deficits are due to intellectual disabilities or related to specific learning disabilities or emotional disorders. They can also measure verbal skills, motor performance, and visual reasoning. Intelligence tests are also known as **intelligence quotient tests (IQ tests)**. IQ tests should be administered by trained professionals to ensure the tests are administered accurately. Unlike intelligence tests, individual academic achievement tests measure a student's strengths and weaknesses in individual skills. They are also norm referenced and used to determine if a student needs **special education services**. Results from individual academic tests help determine areas of concern or possible deficits for an individual student. Unlike intelligence tests, individual academic tests can be administered by teachers.

## Adaptive Behavior Scale Assessments

Adaptive behavior scales are useful for diagnosing a student with an **intellectual disability** that affects the development or progression of adaptive behavior. They are used in preschools and for determining eligibility for **special education** in grade schools. They are also used in planning the **curriculum** for students with intellectual disabilities. Adaptive behavior scales are standardized but not always norm referenced because of difficulties comparing expectations for some adaptive and maladaptive skills exhibited by similar-aged peers. In terms of curriculum planning, these assessments can determine the type and quantity of assistance a student may need. Adaptive behavior scale assessments identify a student's level of **independence**. Adaptive behavior scales can be used to determine **skill abilities** associated with daily living, community functioning, social skills, communication, motor functions, and basic academic skills. Teachers and other professionals can administer adaptive behavior scales to students with intellectual disabilities to determine starting points for improving their adaptive behavior deficits.

## Curriculum-Based Measurement of Student Academic Progress

Curriculum-based measurement (**CBM**) is a way for teachers to track how students are **progressing** in mathematics, language arts, social studies, science, and other skills. It is also useful for communicating progress to parents or legal guardians. CBM results can determine whether or not current **instructional strategies** are effective for particular students. In the same respect, CBM can determine if students are meeting the **standards** laid out in their Individualized Education Program goals. If CBM results show that instructional strategies are not effective or goals are not being met, teachers should change instructional strategies. CBM can be revisited to determine whether or not the newly implemented strategies are effective. Progress can sometimes be charted to present a visual for how a student is progressing in a particular content area or with a specific skill.

## Woodcock-Johnson Tests

### *High-Incidence Disabilities*

Woodcock-Johnson tests can be used as diagnostic tools for identifying children with **high-incidence disabilities**. The Woodcock-Johnson Tests of Achievement, the Woodcock-Johnson Tests of Cognitive Abilities, and the Woodcock-Johnson Tests of Oral Language are comprehensively useful for assessing children's:

- Intellectual abilities
- Cognitive abilities
- Aptitude
- Oral language
- Academic achievements

These norm-referenced tests are valuable in understanding children's strengths and weaknesses and how they compare to cohorts of normally progressing, similar-aged peers. For example, **Woodcock-Johnson tests (WJ tests)** are useful in identifying children with language disorders because children with language disorders typically score lower on the listening comprehension and fluid reasoning test sections. The WJ tests are useful diagnostic tools for identifying children with attention-deficit/hyperactivity disorder (ADHD) as well. While children with ADHD may perform similarly to children with learning disabilities, their key deficits are in the cognitive efficiency, processing speed, academic fluency, short-term memory, and long-term retrieval test sections.

## Prenatal, Perinatal, and Neonatal Disabilities

Prenatal, perinatal, and neonatal risk factors can be genetic or environmental. These factors put infants at risk for developing **intellectual disabilities** that affect their day-to-day lives. An intellectual disability is a disability that significantly limits a child's overall cognitive abilities. **Prenatal** risk factors include genetic syndromes (e.g., Down syndrome), brain malformation, maternal diseases, and environmental influences. Drugs, alcohol, or poison exposure can all affect an unborn child. **Perinatal** (during delivery) risk factors include labor and delivery trauma or anoxia at birth. **Neonatal** (post-birth) risk factors include hypoxic ischemic brain injury, traumatic brain injury, infections, seizure disorders, and toxic metabolic syndromes. Early screening and applicable assessments are tools used to identify young children with intellectual disabilities and can assist with providing special education services under the Individuals with Disabilities

Education Act. These tools can also help assess the severity of deficits and the need for special services, such as occupational therapy.

### *Learning Disabilities in Reading and Mathematics*

The Woodcock-Johnson tests (WJ tests) include tests of achievement, cognitive abilities, and oral language. Together, these assessments are useful in the diagnostic process of identifying a student with a **disability**. Additionally, they are helpful for identifying specific **deficits** in a student's reading or math skills. WJ tests are norm-referenced and compare the results of a child's performance to that of a cohort of children of similar age and average intellectual abilities. These assessments provide information about **reading disorders**, such as dyslexia, because they measure phonological awareness, rapid automatized naming, processing speed, and working memory. WJ tests report on a child's cognitive functioning in these test areas. These assessments also provide useful information for students with learning deficits in **mathematics**. Performance on the math calculation skills and math reasoning test sections provides information on specific deficits in general comprehension, fluid reasoning, and processing speed. Deficits in these areas are correlated with learning disabilities in mathematics.

## The Wechsler Intelligence Scales

The Wechsler Intelligence Scales are assessments that measure the cognitive abilities of children and adults. The **Wechsler Intelligence Scale for Children (WISC)**, now in its fifth edition (WISC-V), is used for children ages 6–16 and measures the child's intellectual ability through 10 primary subtests and 6 secondary subtests. The result is an overall composite score, the Full-Scale Intelligence Quotient (FSIQ), as well as index scores in subcategories such as verbal comprehension, fluid reasoning, and quantitative reasoning. WISC-V results are useful tools for evaluating a student with a disability. Test results can be used to measure and report on a student's general intelligence and provide insight into the student's cognitive abilities in order to determine an appropriate educational pathway. Results can be reported in a student's Evaluation Team Report (ETR) and Individualized Education Program (IEP) in order to justify special education services or have a starting point for IEP goals. WISC-V results are especially important in an ETR, and they are generally completed at least once every three years, because they contribute to describing the **overall performance profile** of a student with a disability.

## Kaufman Assessment Battery for Children

The Kaufman Assessment Battery for Children (KABC), updated to a second edition in 2008 with a normative update in 2014 (**KABC-II NU**) is a unique standardized test because it is used to evaluate preschoolers, minority groups, and children with learning disabilities. The KABC-II NU can be used to assess children ages 3–18 and is meant to be used with children who are nonverbal, bilingual, or English-speaking. However, it is especially useful in assessing the abilities of students who are **nonverbal**. The KABC-II NU can be used to help determine students' educational placements and assist with their educational planning. This assessment consists of subtests that may be combined and interpreted according to one of two different models depending on the child's language background. The subtests lead to both individual scaled scores and a global score. The scales are:

- Simultaneous
- Sequential
- Planning
- Learning
- Knowledge

The KABC-II NU is also unique because it includes a **nonverbal scale** that can be administered to children with hearing or speech impairments and children who do not speak English.

### Vineland Adaptive Behavior Scales

The Vineland Adaptive Behavior Scales, Third Edition (**Vineland-3**), assesses the personal and social skills of children and adults. **Adaptive behavior** refers to the skills needed for day-to-day activities and independent living. Children with disabilities sometimes have deficits in adaptive behavior, and the Vineland-3 is useful for planning their **educational pathways**. It is an especially useful tool for developing **transition plans and goals** for students of appropriate ages on Individualized Education Programs. The Vineland-3 is a process that involves people who know the students best, like parents and teachers. The teacher version and parent version of this assessment can be delivered via interview or survey. The parent version focuses on a student's adaptive behavior at home, while the teacher version focuses on adaptive behavior in the school setting. Vineland-3 assesses four **domains**: communication, activities of daily living, social relationships, and motor skills. A student's parents or caregivers fill out a form pertaining to home life, and a teacher fills out a form pertaining to school settings. The comprehensive score from both the teacher and parent version are used to report abilities in the four domains.

### Types of Cognitive Assessments

Cognitive tests assess the **cognitive functioning abilities** of children and adults. They are useful tools for diagnosing or identifying children with disabilities who are eligible for **special education services** under the Individuals with Disabilities Education Act. Examples of cognitive tests used in diagnosing or identifying children with disabilities include aptitude tests and intelligence quotient (IQ) tests. There are also cognitive assessments that measure verbal reasoning, numerical reasoning, abstract reasoning, spatial ability, verbal ability, and more. Children's cognitive abilities are related to how quickly they **process** information. Assessment results can be good measurements of how quickly children may learn new information or tasks. Cognitive assessments provide specific information about children's cognitive functioning by providing measurements of their intelligence, attention, concentration, processing speed, language and communication, visual-spatial abilities, and short- and long-term memory capabilities. Results can also be used on a child's Evaluation Team Report or to develop goals for an Individualized Education Program.

### Advantages and Disadvantages of Curriculum-Based Assessments

Curriculum-based assessments (**CBAs**) determine if students are making adequate progress through the curriculum. They can be administered by a teacher, special educator, or school psychologist. CBAs have advantages over norm-referenced assessments, like developmental assessments, because they are not used to compare performance between students. Other types of assessments measure a student's cumulative abilities across multiple skills instead of assessing individual skills. CBAs measure student progress in more **individualized** ways. They are especially useful for measuring IEP goal progress. Since CBAs are **teacher-created assessments**, they provide opportunities to assess students informally and formally on IEP goals. For example, a teacher may verbally quiz a student on ten addition problems to determine if the student is making progress on math IEP goals. CBAs are also used in the "response to intervention" process to identify students with special needs by measuring the effectiveness of interventions provided to them.

# Assessment for Students with Disabilities

## Alternate Assessments

Students with and without disabilities are typically expected to take the same standardized tests, sometimes with accommodations and modifications. Some students with disabilities take **alternate assessments**, which are forms of the standardized tests that other students take. Students that participate in alternate assessments are unable to participate in state standardized tests even with accommodations. Less than one percent of students in public school districts participate in alternate assessments. They are mostly intended for students with **intellectual disabilities** or **severe cognitive delays**. Alternate assessments are based on **alternate achievement standards**, which are modified versions of state achievement standards. Alternate assessments are a way for students' progress to be assessed with standards that are more appropriate for their skills. For example, a state standard for math may not be appropriate for a student with an intellectual disability. Instead, the student may have the alternate standard of demonstrating the ability to count money to make a purchase. Teachers, parents, and students work collaboratively to demonstrate that the achievement standards are met.

## Role of Formal Assessments in the Education of a Student with Disabilities

Formal assessments measure how well a student has mastered learning material and are useful in detecting if a student is **falling behind** in general or at the end of a unit. Formal test results can be used to compare the performance of a student with disabilities against other students of similar demographics. **Developmental assessments** are norm-referenced tests that are designed to assess the development of young children. Developmental assessments are used to identify the strengths and weaknesses of a child suspected of having a disability. **Intelligence tests** are another type of norm-referenced test that can determine a student's potential to learn academic skills. Intelligence tests, sometimes called IQ tests, also indicate a student's specific level of intelligence. This is helpful in knowing if a student's learning problems are associated with sub-average intellectual abilities or other factors, such as an emotional disturbance. A student with an emotional disturbance or specific learning disability would have an average or above-average intelligence score, whereas a student with intellectual disabilities would have a sub-average score. **Curriculum-based assessments** are also helpful in determining where, specifically, a student needs the most help within a content area.

## Interest Inventories

Interest inventories are tools for measuring people's interests or preferences in activities. They are useful for gathering information about a student's likes and dislikes. In special education, interest inventories are sometimes used to help develop the **transition portion** of an Individualized Education Program (IEP). A student's interests as determined by an interest inventory can be used to drive the entire IEP. For an older student with a driving interest in mind, interest inventories can also be reflected in the annual IEP goals. Interest inventories can come in the form of observations, ability tests, or self-reported inventories. They can also work as age-appropriate **transition assessments** used in the transition statement section of the IEP. An advantage of interest inventories is that they help students get to know their own strengths and interests. They are also useful in guiding students with disabilities into thinking about postsecondary careers, education, or independent living.

## Role of Informal Assessments in the Education of a Student with Disabilities

Informal assessments are a little more flexible for teachers, particularly in the ways they can be administered in the classroom. In special education, informal assessments play an important role in **adjusting instruction** to meet the specific needs of a student. Using informal assessment outcomes to drive instruction helps ensure that academic or behavioral student needs are met. Informal assessments are also helpful in adjusting instruction to meet **specific goals or objectives** on a student's IEP. Checklists, running records, observations, and work samples are all informal assessments from which data for IEP goals can be collected. **Checklists** can include behaviors or academic skills the student is meant to achieve. **Running records** help provide insight into student behavior over time by focusing on a sequence of events. **Work samples** are helpful in providing a concrete snapshot of a student's academic capabilities.

## Chapter Quiz

Ready to see how well you retained what you just read? Scan the QR code to go directly to the chapter quiz interface for this study guide. If you're using a computer, simply visit the online resources page at **mometrix.com/resources719/gacesegcelemed** and click the Chapter Quizzes link.

# Foundations and Professional Responsibilities

## Disability Education Laws

### Individuals with Disabilities Education Act

The Individuals with Disabilities Education Act (**IDEA**) includes six major principles that focus on students' rights and the responsibilities public schools have for educating children with **disabilities**. One of the main principles of IDEA is to provide a **free and appropriate public education** suited to the individual needs of a child with a disability. This requires schools to provide special education and related services to students identified as having disabilities. Another purpose of IDEA is to require schools to provide an appropriate **evaluation** of a child with a suspected disability and an **Individualized Education Program (IEP)** for a child with a disability who qualifies under IDEA. Students with IEPs are guaranteed **least restrictive environment**, or a guarantee that they are educated in the general education classroom as much as possible. IDEA also ensures **parent participation**, providing a role for parents as equal participants and decision makers. Lastly, **procedural safeguards** also serve to protect parents' rights to advocate for their children with disabilities.

**Review Video:** Development of the Individuals with Disabilities Education Act
Visit mometrix.com/academy and enter code: 100350

### People Protected by Parts B and C of IDEA

Early intervention services are provided to children with special needs from birth to age three under **IDEA Part C**. Children from birth to age 3 who are identified as having disabilities and qualify under IDEA receive **Individualized Family Service Plans (IFSPs)**.

Special education and related services are provided to children with disabilities from ages 3 to 21 under **IDEA Part B**. Children ages 3 to 21 who are identified as having disabilities and qualify under IDEA receive educational documents **IEPs**.

### Individualized Education Programs vs. Individualized Family Service Plans

IFSPs and IEPs are both educational documents provided under the Individuals with Disabilities Education Act to service the rights of children with disabilities and their families. The major differences between IEPs and IFSPs, aside from the ages they service, is that **IFSPs** cover **broader services** for children with disabilities and their families. IFSP services are often provided in the children's homes. **IEPs** focus on special education and related services within the children's **school settings**.

### Purpose of IEPs and Function of the PLOPs

An IEP is a written statement for a child with a disability. Its primary purposes are to establish **measurable annual goals** and to list the **services** needed to help the child with a disability meet the annual goals.

The Individuals with Disabilities Education Act mandates that a statement of the child's academic achievement and functional performance be included within the IEP. This statement is called **Present Levels of Performance**. It provides a snapshot of the student's current performance in school. Present Levels of Performance should also report how a student's disability is affecting, or not affecting, progress in school.

IDEA mandates that an **Annual Goals section** be provided within the IEP. Annual goals outline what a student is expected to learn within a 12-month period. These goals are influenced by the student's PLOPs and are developed using objective, measurable data based on the student's previous academic performance.

**Review Video: 504 Plans and IEPs**
Visit mometrix.com/academy and enter code: 881103

## Child Find Law

Child Find is part of the Individuals with Disabilities Education Act and states that schools are legally required to find children who have **disabilities** and need **special education** or other services. According to the **Child Find law**, all school districts must have processes for identifying students who need special education and related services. Children with disabilities from birth to age 21, children who are homeschooled, and children in private schools are all covered by the Child Find law. Infants and toddlers can be identified and provided with services so that parents have the right tools in place to meet their children's needs before they enter grade school. The Child Find law does not mean that public schools need to agree to evaluate students when evaluations are requested. Schools may still refuse evaluation if school professionals do not suspect the children of having disabilities.

## Steps to Implementing IEPs

The five most important steps in the IEP process are the identification via "Child Find" or the referral for special education services; evaluation; determination of eligibility; the first IEP meeting at which the IEP is written; and the ongoing provision of services during which progress is measured and reported. The referral can be initiated by a teacher, a special team in the school district, the student's parent, or another professional. The evaluation provides a snapshot of a student's background history, strengths, weaknesses, and academic, behavioral, or social needs. An IEP team of professionals as well as the student's parents/guardians use the evaluation and any other reports regarding a student's progress to determine if the student is eligible for special education services. Once a student has been found eligible for special education, the first IEP meeting is held during which an IEP is written by a special education teacher or other specialist familiar with the student. The IEP meeting, either initial or annual, is held before the new IEP is implemented. Once the IEP meeting has occurred, services will be provided as detailed in the written IEP, during which the student's progress will continually be measured and reported. The IEP team includes the student, parents/guardians, special education teacher, general education teacher, school psychologist, school administrator, appropriate related service professionals, and any other professionals or members that can comment on the student's strengths.

## Manifestation Determination

Manifestation determination is a process defined by IDEA. The **manifestation determination process** is put into effect when a student receiving special education needs to be removed from the educational setting due to a suspension, expulsion, or alternative placement. Manifestation determination is the process that determines if the **disciplinary action** resulted from a **manifestation of the student's disability**. This is important because if the action was a manifestation of the disability, the outcome of the disciplinary action may change. During the initial part of this process, relevant data is collected about the student and the circumstances of the offending behavior. The student's Individualized Education Program team determines whether or not the student's behavior was related to the disability. If they determine that the behavior was not related to the disability, the disciplinary action is carried out. If the behavior is determined to be related to the disability, the student is placed back into the original educational setting.

## Provision of Title III of the Americans with Disabilities Act

Title III of the Americans with Disabilities Act (ADA) prohibits discrimination against people with disabilities in **public accommodations.** Title III seeks to level the playing field of access for people with disabilities participating in public activities. Businesses open to the public, such as schools, restaurants, movie theaters, day care facilities, recreation facilities, doctor's offices, and restaurants, are required to comply with **ADA standards**. Additionally, commercial facilities, such as privately-owned businesses, factories, warehouses, and office buildings, are required to provide access per ADA standards. Title III of the ADA outlines the general requirements of the **reasonable modifications** that businesses must provide. Title III also provides detailed, specific requirements for reasonable modifications within businesses and requires new construction and building alterations to abide by ADA regulations. Title III also outlines rules regarding **enforcement of ADA regulations**, such as the consequences for a person or persons participating in discrimination of a person with a disability. Title III provides for **certification of state laws or local building codes**. This means that a state's Assistant Attorney General may issue certification to a place of public accommodation or commercial facility that meets or exceeds the minimum requirements of Title III.

## LARRY P. V. RILES

The *Larry P. v. Riles* (1977) court case examined possible **cultural discrimination** against African-American students. The court case questioned whether an intelligence quotient (IQ) test was an accurate measurement of a student's true intelligence. The case argued that a disproportionate number of African-American students identified as needing special education services; the term at the time was "educable mentally retarded" (EMR) program services. The court plaintiff, Larry P., argued that IQ tests were **biased** against African-American students, which resulted in their placements in limiting educational settings. The defendant, Riles, argued that the prevalence of African-American students in the EMR classes was due to genetics and social and environmental factors. The court ultimately ruled that the IQ tests were discriminatory and resulted in the disproportionate placement of African-American students in the EMR setting. It was determined that these particular assessments were **culturally biased**, and the students' performances would be more accurately measured using adaptive behavior assessments, diagnostic tests, observations, and other assessments.

## DIANA V. STATE BOARD OF EDUCATION

*Diana v. State Board of Education* (1970) was a court case involving a student who was placed in special education after results of the Stanford-Binet intelligence test indicated she had a mild case of "mental retardation." This class-action lawsuit was developed on behalf of nine **Mexican-American children**, arguing that IQ scores were not an adequate measurement to determine special education placement. The case argued that Mexican-American children might be at a disadvantage because the IQ tests were written and administered in English. This might possibly constitute **discrimination**. The plaintiffs in the case argued that IQ scores were not a valid measurement because the children might have been unable to comprehend the test written in English. In the conclusive results of this case, the court ordered children to be tested in their primary language, if it was not English. As a result of this case, IQ tests were no longer used as the sole assessments for determining **special education placement**. There was also increased focus on **cultural and linguistic diversity** in students.

## WINKELMAN V. PARMA CITY SCHOOL DISTRICT

This court case began as an argument against a **free and appropriate public education** (FAPE) as required by IDEA. The parents of Jacob Winkelman believed their son was not provided with a FAPE in his special education setting in Parma City Schools. The disagreement became about whether or not children can be **represented by their parents** per IDEA in federal court. The U.S Court of Appeals for the Sixth Circuit argued that IDEA protected the rights of the children and not the parents. In the end, the District Court ruled that parents could represent their children within disputes over a free and appropriate public education as constituted by IDEA. Ultimately, this settled the question of whether or not **parents have rights under IDEA**, in addition to their children. The court case determined that parents play a significant role in the education of their children on IEPs and are IEP team members. Therefore, parents are entitled to litigate *pro se* for their children.

## HONIG V. DOE

*Honig v. Doe* (1988) was a Supreme Court case examining the violation of the **Education for All Handicapped Children Act** (EAHCA, an earlier version of the Individuals with Disabilities Education Act) by the California School Board. The offense occurred when a child was suspended for a violent behavior outburst that was related to his disability. The court case centered on two plaintiffs. Both were diagnosed with an emotional disturbance and qualified for special education under EAHCA. Following the violent incident, the school suspended the students and recommended them for expulsion. The plaintiff's case argued that the suspension/expulsion went against the **stay-put provision of the EAHCA**, which states that children with disabilities must remain in their current educational placements during review proceedings unless otherwise agreed upon by both parents and educational representatives. The defendant argued that the violence of the situation marked an exception to the law. The court determined that schools are able to justify the placement removal of a student when maintaining a **safe learning environment** outweighs a student's right to a free and appropriate public education.

## Pennsylvania Association for Retarded Children v. Commonwealth of Pennsylvania

The Commonwealth of Pennsylvania was accused by the Pennsylvania Association for Retarded Children (PARC 1971), now known as the Arc of Pennsylvania, of denying a **free and appropriate public education** to students with disabilities. The Commonwealth of Pennsylvania was accused of refusing to educate students who had not reached the "mental age of 5." The groups argued before the District Court of the Eastern District of Pennsylvania. This case was significant because PARC was one of the first institutions in the country to challenge the **placement of students with special needs**. The plaintiffs argued that all children should and would benefit from some sort of educational instruction and training. Ultimately, this was the beginning of instituting the state requirement of a free and appropriate public education (**FAPE**) for all children in public education from ages 6–21. The Commonwealth of Pennsylvania was tasked with providing a FAPE and sufficient education and training for all eligible children receiving special education. They could no longer deny students based on their mental ages. This triggered other state institutions to make similar decisions and led to the creation of similar federal policies in the **Education for All Handicapped Children Act** (1974).

## 1990 Amendments to IDEA

The Individuals with Disabilities Education Act (IDEA) replaced the Education for All Handicapped Children Act in 1990. IDEA amendments changed the **age range** for children to receive special education services to ages 3–21. IDEA also changed the language of the law, changing the focus onto the **individuals with disabilities** rather than the **handicapped children**. Therefore, the focus shifted from the conditions or disabilities to the individual children and their needs. IDEA amendments also **categorized** different disabilities. IDEA 1997 increased the emphasis on IEPs for students with disabilities and increased parents' roles in the educational decision-making processes for their children with disabilities. Part B of the 1997 amendment provided services to children ages 3–5, mandating that their learning needs be outlined in **IEPs** or **Individualized Family Service Plans**. Part C of IDEA provided **financial assistance** to the families of infants and toddlers with disabilities. Part C states that educational agencies must provide **early intervention services** that focus on children's developmental and medical needs, as well as the needs of their families. Part C also gives states the option to provide services to children who are at risk for developmental disabilities.

## Disabilities Education Improvement Act of 2004

In 2004, the Individuals with Disabilities Education Act (IDEA) implemented the **Individuals with Disabilities Education Improvement Act**; IDEA was reauthorized to better meet the needs of children in special education programs and children with special needs. As a result of these changes:

- Special educators are required to achieve **Highly Qualified Teacher status** and be **certified in special education**.
- Individualized Education Programs must contain measurable **annual goals** and descriptions of how progress toward the goals will be **measured and reported**.
- Schools or agencies must provide science or research-based **interventions** as part of the evaluation process to determine if children have specific learning disabilities. This may be done in addition to assessments that measure achievement or intelligence.

The changes made to require science or research-based interventions resulted in many districts implementing **Response to Intervention procedures**. These procedures meet IDEA 2004 requirement of providing interventions in addition to achievement reports or intelligence tests on the Individualized Education Programs for children with disabilities.

## Development of Educational Laws Like Goals 2000 and No Child Left Behind

President Bill Clinton signed the **National Educational Goals Act**, also known as Goals 2000: Educate America Act, into effect in the 1990s to trigger standardized educational reform. The act focused on **outcomes-based education** and was intended to be completed by the year 2000. The goals of this act included ensuring that children are ready to learn by the time they start school; increasing high school graduation rates; demonstration of competency by students in grades 4, 8, and 12 in core content areas; and positioning the United States as first in the world in mathematics and science achievement. Goals 2000 was withdrawn when President George W. Bush implemented the **No Child Left Behind Act (NCLB)** in 2001. The NCLB also supported standards-based reform, and it mandated that states develop more **skills-based assessments**. The act emphasized state testing, annual academic progress, report cards, and increased teacher qualification standards. It also outlined changes in state funding. The NCLB required schools to meet **Adequate Yearly Progress (AYP)**. AYP was measured by results of achievement tests taken by students in each school district, and consequences were implemented for school districts that missed AYP during consecutive years.

## Every Student Succeeds Act of 2015

The NCLB was replaced in 2015 by the Every Student Succeeds Act (**ESSA**). The ESSA built upon the foundations of NCLB and emphasized **equal opportunity** for students. The ESSA currently serves as the main K–12 educational law in the United States. The ESSA affects students in public education, including students with disabilities. The purpose of the ESSA is to ensure a **quality education** for all students. It also aims to address the achievement of **disadvantaged students**, including students living in poverty, minority groups, students receiving special education services, and students with limited English language skills. The ESSA determined that states may decide educational plans as long as they follow the government's framework. The ESSA also allows states to develop their own educational standards and mandates that the curriculum focus on preparing students for postsecondary educations or careers. The act requires students to be tested annually in math and reading during grades 3–8 and once in high school. Students must also be tested in science once in elementary school, middle school, and high school. **School accountability** was also mandated by the ESSA. The act requires states to have plans in place for any schools that are underperforming.

## ESL Rights for Students and Parents

As public schools experience an influx of English as a Second Language (ESL) students, knowledge of their **rights** becomes increasingly important. The **Every Student Succeeds Act (ESSA)** of 2015 addresses funding discrepancies for ESL students and families. The ESSA allocates funds to schools and districts where low-income families comprise 40 percent or more of the enrollment. This is intended to assist with ESL students who are underperforming or at risk for underperforming. The ESSA also provides funding for ESL students to become English proficient and find academic success. However, in order for schools and districts to receive this funding, they must avoid discrimination, track ESL student progress, assess ESL student English proficiency, and notify parents of their children's ESL status. Avoiding discrimination includes preventing the over-identification of ESL students for special education services. The referral and evaluation process must be carried out with caution to ensure that students' perceived disabilities are actual deficits and not related to their English language learning abilities.

## Rehabilitation Act of 1973

The Rehabilitation Act of 1973 was the law that preceded the Individuals with Disabilities Education Act of 1975. The Rehabilitation Act protects the rights of people with disabilities in several ways.

- It protects people with disabilities against discrimination relating to **employment**.
- It provides students with disabilities equal access to the **general education curriculum** (Section 504).

## AMERICANS WITH DISABILITIES ACT OF 1990 (ADA)

The Americans with Disabilities Act (1990) also protects the rights of people with disabilities.

- The ADA provides **equal employment** for people with disabilities. This means employers must provide reasonable accommodations for people with disabilities in their job and work environments.
- It provides **access** for people with disabilities to both public and private places open to the public (e.g., access ramps and automatic doors).
- It provides **telecommunications access** to people with disabilities. This ensures people with hearing and speech disabilities can communicate over the telephone and Internet.

## ELEMENTARY AND SECONDARY EDUCATION ACT (ESEA)

The Elementary and Secondary Education Act (ESEA) also protects the rights of people with disabilities.

- Passed by President Johnson in 1965, the ESEA was part of the president's "War on Poverty." The law sought to allow **equal access to a quality education**.
- The ESEA extended more funding to secondary and primary schools and emphasized high **standards and accountability**.
- This law was authorized as the **No Child Left Behind** (2001) under President Bush, then reauthorized as the **Every Student Succeeds Act** under President Obama.

## SECTION 504

A Section 504 Plan comes from the civil rights law, Section 504 of the Rehabilitation Act of 1973, and protects the rights of individuals with disabilities. A 504 Plan is a formal plan or blueprint for how the school will provide services to a student with a disability. This essentially removes barriers for individuals with disabilities by ensuring that **appropriate services** are provided to meet their special needs. A 504 Plan includes:

- **Accommodations**: A 504 Plan includes accommodations a student with a disability may need to be successful in a regular education classroom. For example, a student with ADHD may need to sit near the front of the room to limit distractions.
- **Related Services**: A 504 Plan includes related services, such as speech therapy or occupational therapy, a student may need to be successful in the general education classroom.
- **Modifications**: Although it is rare for a 504 Plan to include modifications, sometimes they are included. Modifications change what the student is expected to do, such as being given fewer homework assignments.

## 504 PLANS VS. INDIVIDUALIZED EDUCATION PROGRAMS

- A 504 Plan and an IEP are similar in that they serve as a blueprint for a student with a disability. However, a 504 Plan serves as a blueprint for how the student will have **access to school**, whereas the IEP serves as a blueprint for a student's **special education experience**.
- A 504 Plan helps level the playing field for a student with a disability by providing services and changes to the **learning environment**. An IEP provides individualized special education and related services to meet the **unique needs of a student with a disability**. Both IEPs and 504 Plans are provided at no cost to parents.
- The 504 Plan was established under the **Rehabilitation Act of 1973** as a civil rights law. The Individualized Education Program was established under the **Individuals with Disabilities Education Act** (1975 and amended in 2004).
- Unlike an IEP, a 504 Plan does **not** have to be a planned, written document. An IEP is a **planned, written document** that includes unique annual learning goals and describes related services for the student with a disability.

## Informed Parental Consent

IDEA requires that parents be **informed** before a student is evaluated for special education services. IDEA mandates that a school district receive **parental consent** to initiate an evaluation of a student for special education services. Consent means the school district has fully informed the parent of their intentions or potential reasons for evaluation of the student. Legally, the request must be written in the parent's native language. This consent does not mean the parent gives consent for a student's placement in special education. In order for a student to be initially placed in special education or receive special education services, parental consent must be given for this issue separately. At any time, parents can withdraw consent for special education placement or special education services. Schools are able to file **due process** if they disagree with the parental withdrawal of consent. Parents also have a right to consent to parts of a student's IEP, but not necessarily all of the IEP. Once parental consent is granted for all parts of the IEP, it can be implemented.

## Tiers of the Response to Intervention Model

- **Tier 1: High Quality Classroom Instruction, Screening, and Group Interventions**: In Tier 1, **all students** are screened using universal screening and/or the results of statewide assessments. Students identified as at risk receive supplemental instruction. Students who make adequate progress are returned to their regular instruction. Students who do not make adequate progress move to Tier 2.
- **Tier 2: Targeted Interventions**: These interventions are designed to improve the progress of the students who did not make adequate progress in Tier 1. Targeted instruction is usually in the areas of reading and math and does not last longer than one grading period. This is applied generally to smaller groups and not the full classroom as in Tier 1.
- **Tier 3: Intensive Interventions and Comprehensive Evaluation**: Students who are not successful in Tier 2 move on to Tier 3. They receive intensive interventions that target their specific deficits. Students who do not meet progress goals during intensive interventions are referred to receive comprehensive evaluations and are considered to be eligible for special education under the Individuals with Disabilities Education Act.

## Stakeholders in Special Education

Stakeholders that play roles in educating students with disabilities include the students, parents, general educators, administrators, and community members. Students should receive an educational **curriculum** based on strict standards, such as the Common Core Content Standards. This ensures that they receive good educational foundations from which to grow and expand upon during their school careers. Parents, legal guardians, and sometimes agencies act in the best interests of their children. If they do not think the IEPs suit the needs of their children, they can request **due process hearings** in court. Requirements for a free and appropriate public education and least restrictive environment ensure that students are educated alongside peers in general education classrooms by general educators. General educators collaborate with special educators to create **successful inclusion classrooms**. When inclusion is done successfully, the students with disabilities meet their IEP goals.

## Multi-Factored Evaluations or Evaluation Team Reports

Multi-Factored Evaluations (MFEs) are processes required by the Individuals with Disabilities Education Act to determine if a student is eligible for special education. When a student is suspected of having a disability, the parent or school district can initiate the evaluation process. **Student information** that is evaluated in an MFE includes background information, health information, vision testing, hearing testing, social and emotional development, general intelligence, past and current academic performance, communication needs, gross and fine motor abilities, results of aptitude or achievement tests, academic skills, and current progress toward IEP goals. Progress reporting on IEP goals is only appropriate during an annual MFE when a student has already qualified for special education services. The purpose of an MFE is to provide **comprehensive information** about a student for professionals working with the student. An MFE also helps determine what academic or behavioral **goals** or related services might be appropriate for a student with disabilities.

## Free and Appropriate Public Education Components

IDEA defines free and appropriate public education (FAPE) as an educational right for children with disabilities in the United States. FAPE stands for:

- **Free**: All students found eligible for special education services must receive free services, expensed to the public instead of the parents.
- **Appropriate**: Students are eligible for educations that are appropriate for their specific needs, as stated in their IEPs.
- **Public**: Students with disabilities have the right to be educated in public schools.
- **Education**: An education must be provided to any school-aged child with a disability. Education and services are defined in a student's IEP.

Ideally, FAPE components are put in place in order to guarantee the best education possible that also suits the individual needs of a student with a disability. FAPE should take place in the least restrictive environment, or the environment with the fewest barriers to learning for the individual student with a disability.

**Review Video: Legal and Ethical Issues in Special Education**
Visit mometrix.com/academy and enter code: 934372

## Multi-Factored Evaluation or Evaluation Team Report

A Multi-Factored Evaluation (**MFE**), sometimes referred to as an Evaluation Team Report (**ETR**), serves as a snapshot of a child's abilities, strengths, and weaknesses. An MFE is conducted to determine a student's eligibility for special education. Once a student with a disability qualifies for special education, an MFE is conducted at least every three years after the initial MFE date. MFEs are conducted for students ages 3 to 21 who are on IEPs. The purpose of the MFE is to influence a student's IEP. An MFE reports on a student's **current abilities** and how the disability may affect **educational performance**. MFEs can also determine if a student qualifies for related services, such as occupational therapy or speech-language therapy. An MFE can be requested by a parent or school district when a child is suspected of having a disability. The school district typically has 30 days or less to respond to a parental request to evaluate a student, giving consent or refusal for an evaluation. While initial MFEs are conducted as a means to determine special education qualification, annual MFEs are conducted to address any changes in the needs or services of a student already receiving special education services.

## Least Restrictive Environments to Deliver Special Education Services

Special education services are delivered to students that qualify with a **disability** defined by IDEA. IDEA also requires that students who qualify for special education must receive special education services in **least restrictive environments** that provide the fewest barriers to their learning. A student's most appropriate instructional setting is written out in the **IEP**. Some special education instructional settings include:

- No instructional setting
- Mainstream setting
- Resource room
- Self-contained classroom
- Homebound instruction

With **no instructional setting**, students participate in the general education curriculum but may receive related services, such as speech-language therapy or occupational therapy. In the **mainstream setting**, students are instructed in the general education classroom for most or part of the day and provided with special education supports, accommodations, modifications, and related services. A **resource room** is an environment where students receive remedial instruction when they cannot participate in the general curriculum for one or more subject areas. A **self-contained classroom** is a setting for students who need special education and related services for more than 50 percent of the day. **Homebound instruction** is for students who are homebound or hospitalized for more than four consecutive weeks.

## Due Process Rights Available to Parents and Legal Guardians

When parents or legal guardians and school districts cannot agree on components of IEPs for students with disabilities, parents and legal guardians have a right to **due process**. Due process is a legal right under IDEA that usually involves the school district violating a legal rule. Examples of these violations include a school district not running an IEP meeting, failing to conduct a triannual evaluation, or failing to implement a student's IEP. Disputes often involve a student's instructional placement, appropriate accommodations or modifications, related services, or changes to IEPs. School districts' due process policies vary depending on the district. IDEA, however, mandates that a **due process legal form** be completed by the parent or legal guardian in order to move forward. This form must be completed within two years of a dispute. **Mediation**, or the process of coming to an agreement before filing due process, can be a solution to the dispute. IEP meetings, even when it is not time for an annual review, are also appropriate options for resolving a dispute before filing due process.

## Purpose of Mediation in Lieu of a Parent or Legal Guardian Filing for Due Process

Mediation is a process used to address a dispute prior to a parent or legal guardian filing for due process. The purpose of mediation is to **resolve a dispute** between the parent or legal guardian of a student with a disability and the school district. Disputes occur when the parent or legal guardian does not agree with an IEP component, such as what related services are provided or the way a student's IEP is being implemented. Mediation is not a parent or legal guardian's legal right, but school districts often support mediation to offset a **due process filing**. Mediation involves the attempt to resolve a dispute and includes a meeting between the parent or legal guardian, school district member, and a neutral third party, such as a mediator provided by the state. States have lists of **mediators** available for these situations. Agreements that come out of the mediation process are put into writing and, if appropriate, put into a student's IEP. Disagreements can continue to be mediated, or the decision may be made to file due process. Prior to mediation, parents or legal guardians and school districts have the option of holding IEP meetings (outside of annual meetings) to resolve disputes.

## Maintaining Confidentiality and Privacy of Student Records

Similar to the Health Insurance Portability and Accountability Act of 1996 (HIPAA), the **Family Educational Rights and Privacy Act (FERPA)** is a law that protects privacy. However, the FERPA is specific to the privacy of students. The FERPA law applies to any school or agency that receives funds from the US Department of Education. This ensures that schools or agencies cannot share any confidential information about a student without a parent or student's written consent. **Student educational records** can be defined as records, files, documents, or other materials which contain a student's personal information. **IEPs** and **ETRs** are examples of private documents under the FERPA law. The responsibility of a school covered by the FERPA is to maintain confidentiality and privacy. The members of an IEP team, such as special educators, related service professionals, general educators, or other professionals, cannot share any identifying, private information about a student. Information addressing the needs of individual students found on an IEP, ETR, or other identifying document must remain confidential unless express written consent is given by the parent or legal guardian.

## Pre-Referral/Referral Process for a Student with a Disability

The purpose of a pre-referral process for a child with a suspected disability is to attempt **reasonable modifications and accommodations** before the child is referred for special education services. Schools often have **pre-referral teams** whose purpose is to identify the strengths and needs of a child, put reasonable strategies into action, and evaluate the results of this pre-referral intervention. If the results do not show any change, another intervention can be attempted, or the student can be referred for a special education evaluation.

If a child is suspected of having a disability and did not succeed with pre-referral interventions, the school or parent can request an **evaluation**. During the evaluation process, the school compiles information to see if the student needs special education or related services. This information is used to determine if the student's disability is affecting school performance and if the student qualifies for special education. The evaluation lists and examines the student's strengths, weaknesses, and development and determines what supports the student needs in order to learn. An evaluation must be completed before special education services can be provided.

## Role of a School Psychologist in Special Education

School psychologists are certified members of school teams that **support the needs of students and teachers**. They help students with overall academic, social, behavioral, and emotional success. School psychologists are trained in data collection and analysis, assessments, progress monitoring, risk factors, consultation and collaboration, and special education services. In special education, school psychologists may work directly with students and collaborate with teachers, administrators, parents, and other professionals working with particular students. They may also counsel students' parents, participate in the Response to Intervention process, and perform initial evaluations of students who are referred for special education services. School psychologists also work to improve academic achievement, promote positive behavior and health by implementing school-wide programs, support learning needs of diverse learners, maintain safe school environments, and strengthen and maintain good school-parent relationships.

## Overrepresentation of Students from Diverse Backgrounds

**Disproportionate representation** occurs when there is not an equal representation of students from different **cultural and linguistic backgrounds** identified for special education services. Students from different cultural and linguistic groups should be identified for special education services in similar proportions. This ensures that no one group is **overrepresented** and **overidentified as having special needs** due to their cultural or linguistic differences. Disproportionality can occur based on a child's sex, language proficiency, receipt of free and reduced lunch, or race and ethnicity. Historically, most disproportionality has been a civil rights issue and due to a child's cultural or linguistic background. Recently, the focus has been on the disproportionate number of students who spend time in special education classrooms instead of being educated alongside regularly educated peers.

The referral process, **Response to Intervention (RTI)**, provides safeguards against disproportionality. The RTI process requires instruction and intervention catered to the unique, specific needs of the individual student. The purpose of RTI is not the identification of a disability or entitlement to services. Instead, it focuses on data used to make educational decisions about individuals, classrooms, schools, or districts. Models like RTI address disproportionate representation, but they are not perfect.

## Collaborating with IEP Team Members

It is important for Individualized Education Program (IEP) team members to **collaborate** with each other in order to ensure that students are receiving educational plans that are suitable to their needs in the least restrictive environments. **IEP team members** include special education teachers, general education teachers, parents or legal guardians, students, school district representatives, and others knowledgeable about the students' performances. Each member brings a valuable piece of information about the students for instructional planning and IEP planning meetings. It is important for special educators to establish good relationships and collaborate with the students and parents or legal guardians in order to gauge the students' strengths and weaknesses. Collaboration is essential between the general and special educators in order to ensure that students' IEP goals and needs are being met in the appropriate settings. Collaboration with district team members or others like school psychologists is helpful for gaining insight on special education procedures or assessment results.

**Review Video: Collaborating with Other Professionals**
Visit mometrix.com/academy and enter code: 100351

### Communicating with Service Members Across All Special Education Settings

In order to provide the best educations possible for students with disabilities, it is important for special educators and related service members to **communicate** effectively. Communication is important due to the degree of collaboration required between the special educators and the related service members. Related service members are often IEP team members and help students meet their IEP goals and objectives. **Related service members**, like speech pathologists and occupational therapists, also work on a consultation basis with special educators. They may also consult with general education teachers to ensure that students receive required related services in the general education or inclusive classroom settings. Special educators and related service members must collaborate in order to ensure the needs of the students are met, especially when IEP goals or objectives are out of the scope of the special educators' knowledge bases. For example, a speech pathologist might help a teacher address a student's fluency goal.

### Communicating with Parents of Students with Disabilities

It is good practice to communicate with parents outside of progress reporting times and Individualized Education Program meetings. This is especially important for students with **communication deficits** who may not be able to communicate with their parents or legal guardians. Communication also helps prevent potential crises or problem behaviors and alerts parents or legal guardians before any major issues arise. Special educators should find methods of communication that work best for parents or legal guardians, such as phone calls, emails, or writing in daily communication logs. Email is beneficial for creating paper trails, especially for any discussions about educating students. However, email lacks tone and body language and can sometimes be misunderstood. Phone calls fulfill an immediate need to speak with a parent or legal guardian. However, there are no paper trails with phone calls, and they can also lead to misunderstanding. Phone calls may be time consuming, but they can be conducted on special occasions or when behavioral issues need to be discussed. Written communication logs are useful for writing brief summaries about students' days. With any mode of communication, it is essential to **document** what is communicated between the parents or legal guardians and the educators.

### The Roles and Rights Families have in the Education of Children with Disabilities

Under the Individuals with Disabilities Education Act, parents and legal guardians of children with disabilities have **procedural safeguards** that protect their rights. The safeguards also provide parents and legal guardians with the means to resolve any disputes with school systems. **Parents and legal guardians** may underestimate their importance to IEP teams. However, they are important members of IEP teams and integral parts of the decision-making processes for their children's educational journeys. Parents and legal guardians often work more closely with their children than other adults. Therefore, as part of IEP teams, they serve as **advocates** and can often provide insight regarding the children's backgrounds, educational and developmental histories, strengths, and weaknesses. Parents and legal guardians are also important decision-makers in transition meetings, when students with disabilities move from one level of school to another. Their input in transition meetings helps ensure that appropriate services and supports are in place at the next levels of school so that students can succeed.

### Roles of Parents/Legal Guardians and the School District During Evaluation

If parents or legal guardians suspect their children have disabilities, they can request that the school districts **evaluate** the children for special education. A parent or legal guardian can send a **written evaluation request** to the child's school, principal, and the school district's director or director of special education services. In some states, parents and legal guardians may be required to sign a school district form requesting the evaluation. Parents should follow up on the request and/or set a time frame for the school district to respond. The school district may choose to implement the **Response to Intervention (RTI) pre-referral process**. RTI is a process by which the school gives the student special academic support before determining whether or not to move forward with the evaluation process. Not all states or school districts have the same method for applying RTI. Under the Individuals with Disabilities Education Act, the time frame for completion of RTI is 60 days. However, some states can set their own timelines. RTI should not be the only means by which the school district collects data on the student and should be part of a comprehensive evaluation conducted by the student's school.

### Speech Language Pathologist

Speech language pathologists (**SLPs**) provide interventions for children with communication disorders. They can assist, evaluate, prevent, and diagnose a variety of **speech issues**, from fluency to voice disorders. Before children reach grade school age, it is important that they receive early interventions for suspected communication disorders. SLPs are helpful with targeting speech or language issues, identifying at-risk students, or providing interventions for children and adults. SLPs also play a role in helping children develop good reading and writing skills, especially when deficits are evident. SLPs work collaboratively with special educators to deliver **interventions** to children with speech and language disorders in grade school. In schools, SLPs play a role in prevention, assessment, intervention, program design, data collection and analysis, and Individualized Education Program compliance. SLPs work with special educators, parents, students, reading specialists, occupational therapists, school psychologists, and others in order to provide effective services to students who require them.

### Occupational Therapist

Students with special needs may need **occupational therapy services**. The number of services students receive is defined on their IEPs. **Occupational therapists (OTs)** may help students on IEPs refine their fine motor skills, improve sensory processing deficits, improve visual skills, and improve self-care skills. OTs can also assist with behavior management, social skills, and improving attention and focus. When a student is identified as possibly needing occupational therapy, the OT spends time observing the student in a variety of settings where the skill or skill deficit will be demonstrated. Prior to the student's IEP meeting, the OT typically meets with the student's teachers, parents, and other professionals in order to discuss observations, assessment results, and determinations. **Determinations** are then put into the IEP and implemented as related services. Fine motor skill instruction begins with the OT instructing the student on a particular skill. OTs can set up regimens for teachers and parents to generalize using the fine motor skills in the classroom and home environments.

### Paraprofessional

The US Department of Education requires paraprofessionals to have high school diplomas or the equivalent under Title I law. Paraprofessionals (paras), sometimes called **paraeducators**, assist classroom teachers with classroom activities and help students with special needs. In a special education setting, a para works with a certified teacher to help deliver **instruction** and help students meet **Individualized Education Program goals and objectives**. Paras are not responsible for teaching new skills or introducing new goals and objectives to students. In this respect, special educators generally work alongside the paras and students to introduce new skills, goals, or objectives. At times, paras may be responsible for helping students maintain behavior plans, working with students who may be aggressive or violent, and providing physical assistance if necessary. Training is usually provided by the school district for situations when physical assistance is a possible necessity. Paras can also help take notes on students' progress toward meeting their goals or objectives. They can also discuss how students are progressing with behavior plans.

# Special Education Models

## Purpose of Special Education

Special education is specially designed instruction delivered to meet the individual needs of children with disabilities. Special education includes a free and appropriate education in the least restrictive environment. In the past, a special education model might consist of a self-contained classroom of students with special needs whose needs were addressed in that setting. Today, students who qualify for special education must receive instruction in **free and appropriate settings**. This means they receive special education services in settings that provide the **fewest barriers** to their learning. The most appropriate setting varies, depending on the student and the disability. The purpose of special education is to ensure that the unique needs of children with disabilities are addressed. In the public-school setting, the Individuals with Disabilities Education Act mandates that students with disabilities receive free and appropriate public educations. The goal of special education is to create **fair environments** for students with special needs to learn. Ideally, the settings should enable students to learn to their fullest potential.

## Co-Teaching Models

Co-teaching models are utilized in collaborative, inclusive teaching settings that include students with and without disabilities. General educators teach alongside special educators and hold all students to the same educational standards. In the **one teach/one support model**, one instructor teaches a lesson while the other instructor supports students who have questions or need assistance. A **parallel teaching model** involves a class being split into two groups, with one instructor teaching each group. The **alternative teaching model** may be appropriate in situations where it is necessary to instruct small groups of students. In this model, one instructor teaches a large group of students while the other provides instruction to a smaller group of students. In **station teaching**, students are split into small groups and work in several teaching centers while both instructors provide support. Teachers participating in **team teaching** collaboratively plan and implement lesson content, facilitate classroom discussions, and manage discipline. Successful co-teaching uses all of these models as appropriate to meet the needs of diverse groups of learners in the inclusive classroom setting.

## Remedial Instruction vs. Special Education

Though the terms are sometimes used interchangeably, remedial instruction does not always equal special education. The difference between remedial instruction and special education has a lot to do with the intellectual levels of the students. In **remedial instruction**, a student has average or better-than-average intellectual abilities but may struggle with **skills** in one or more content areas. Remedial instruction provides one-on-one instruction to students who are falling behind. Remedial programs are often mainstreamed into general education classrooms to address the varying learning abilities of students. Remedial instruction can be delivered by general education teachers. **Special education** programs address the needs of students who may have lower intellectual abilities and require individualized instruction. Students in special education have **disabilities** specified by the Individuals with Disabilities Education Act and use Individualized Education Programs. Unlike remedial instruction, special education requires qualified and credentialed special educators to decide how to best provide interventions in classroom settings for students with disabilities.

## Remedial Instruction vs. Compensatory Approaches to Intervention

Compensatory interventions can be offered in the form of programs or services that help students with special needs or students who are at risk. The compensatory approach is different from remedial instruction because remedial instruction involves the breaking of concepts or tasks into smaller chunks and reteaching information. The **remedial approach** focuses on repetition and developing or reinforcing certain skills. The **compensatory approach** is implemented when a remedial approach is not working. It focuses on building upon students' strengths and working with or around their weaknesses. Tools such as audiobooks, text-to-speech software, speech recognition software, and other types of assistive technology are compensatory accommodations that help provide a free and appropriate education for students with disabilities who might otherwise continue to demonstrate skill deficits without these tools. Compensatory approaches and remedial instruction can and should be delivered at the same time to help ensure that students with disabilities are meeting their potential.

## Chapter Quiz

Ready to see how well you retained what you just read? Scan the QR code to go directly to the chapter quiz interface for this study guide. If you're using a computer, simply visit the online resources page at **mometrix.com/resources719/gacesegcelemed** and click the Chapter Quizzes link.

# GACE Practice Test

Want to take this practice test in an online interactive format?
Check out the online resources page, which includes interactive practice questions
and much more: **mometrix.com/resources719/gacesegcelemed**

**1. Among the following, a child with which type of disability is likely to be best at focusing attention on one thing for a long time?**

a. Down syndrome
b. Developmental delay
c. Attention-deficit/hyperactivity disorder
d. Autism spectrum disorder

**2. When transitioning from one subject to another and when she becomes anxious, a student always taps her front tooth 5 times then opens and closes her eyes 11 times before leaving her desk. The child most likely has:**

a. Tic Disorder
b. Obsessive Compulsive Disorder
c. Anxiety Disorder
d. Depression

**3. A resource room teacher has a student recently diagnosed with depression. The student has been put on an antidepressant. The teacher knows the student may develop certain transitory reactions to the medication. One reaction might be:**

a. Persistent nausea that lasts for several months
b. Increased thirst and a dry mouth
c. Sudden memory loss or inability to focus for hours at a time
d. Severe, unexplained bruising

**4. Which of the following is true about learned helplessness and students with disabilities?**

a. Students with disabilities typically do not suffer from learned helplessness.
b. Students with disabilities often learn to control situations.
c. Students with disabilities tend to reach out for help before they get to learned helplessness.
d. Students with disabilities often feel like they have no control.

**5. According to Piagetian theory, how does learning occur?**

a. Naturally
b. Through discrete and predictable stages
c. Through repetition
d. With a good teacher

**6. Compared to a child with typical development, a child with spina bifida would be most likely to demonstrate deficits in:**

a. Intellectual development
b. Language development
c. Motor development
d. Social development

**7. Which of the following terms represents an older umbrella term that encompassed autism spectrum disorder?**

a. Pervasive developmental disorder
b. Asperger's syndrome
c. Variable developmental disorder
d. Artistic continuum syndrome

**8. Ms. Wright, a speech-language pathologist, sees Tommy, a first grader, for therapy sessions focusing on his delayed language development. Tommy has a diagnosis of a seizure disorder and takes anticonvulsant medications for this. Ms. Wright has observed that, in the past three sessions, Tommy appeared inattentive, his eyelids were drooping, and she had to prompt him often to get him to attend to what she was saying. What is the most likely explanation for this?**

a. Tommy is bored with the therapy sessions.
b. Tommy is not getting a good night's sleep at home.
c. Tommy is sleepy due to his anti-seizure medications.
d. Tommy is behaving this way to get more attention.

**9. Alex is a ninth-grade student who receives services as a student with a traumatic brain injury. In order to be eligible to receive services under this disability category, which of the following causes of the injury can be ruled out?**

a. Birth trauma
b. Combat injuries
c. Violence
d. Sports-related injuries

**10. Rachel teaches in a resource room with students of various ages and different grade levels. One student, Peter, has mastered addition, subtraction, multiplication, and short division. He is just beginning long division. Joe is a year older, has mastered long division, and is working on fractions. How could Rachel apply Vygotsky's principle of the zone of proximal development with these two students?**

a. Have Peter and Joe both do Joe's fraction problems together to accelerate Peter's progress.
b. Have Peter and Joe split the work and do Peter's long division problems together to give Peter confidence.
c. Have Joe help Peter with long division, as Joe is just slightly more advanced than Peter is.
d. Have each student work long division problems separately and compare their answers.

*Refer to the following for question 11:*

> Dante is a seventh-grade student who seems to have given up on schoolwork and always talks about dropping out when he is old enough. He is currently being evaluated for special education services due to his failing grades in multiple classes. His assessment results reveal that he scored in the average range on his IQ test and in the low range on his achievement test.

**11. Which strategy would be the LEAST likely to succeed in helping Dante get on the right track and care more about school?**

a. Amending his Individualized Education Program (IEP) to include a goal that focuses on graduating
b. Speaking to the counselors about activities he could get involved in at school
c. Checking in with him each day to see how he is doing
d. Lightening the load of the work he has to complete

**12. Mary Frances is moving to a group home. In her current medical facility placement, the nurse has always administered her daily medications. Mary Frances has a calendar and always knows what day it is. How can her teacher most effectively help her learn to take her medications on her own?**

a. She will not need to learn this because caregivers in her group home will give them to her.
b. Remind her every day to take her pills instead of having the nurse give them to her.
c. Give her a pill holder with compartments marked for each day and teach her to use it.
d. Instruct her to mark on her calendar or a chart every day after she has taken her pills.

**13. Rebecca has intellectual disabilities and has lived at home with her parents all her life. She has no job skills. Her parents are getting older and would like her to have a job when she finishes school. She has been placed in a group home and a day habilitation training program. Which scenario is most suitable for her?**

a. Attend academic classes in the training center and work in a workshop part time.
b. Receive job training in classes at the training center and transition to a workshop.
c. Be placed in a sheltered workshop immediately instead of in the training center.
d. Learn work skills at the training center and then have a job at the training center.

**14. Jason is a second-grade student with an intellectual disability. Which of the following characteristics would you most expect to impact his educational performance?**

a. Significantly subaverage general intellectual functioning
b. Concomitant impairments that cause severe educational needs
c. Disorder in one or more of the basic psychological processes
d. An injury to the brain caused by an external force

**15. Cory is a 10th-grade student with an OHI due to attention-deficit/hyperactivity disorder. Which one of the following social influences is likely to have the most impact on his academic performance?**

a. The education levels of his parents
b. The composition of his household
c. His race or ethnic background
d. The friends he spends time with

**16. Which of the following best describes the primary goal of a behavior plan?**

a. To increase desired behaviors
b. To diagnose problem behaviors
c. To develop punishments for problem behaviors
d. To challenge behaviors

**17. Which of the following is the best example of an independent living skills goal for a high school student with a specific learning disability?**

a. The student will be able to access the city bus.
b. The student will live with a roommate in an apartment.
c. The student will live in a group home.
d. The student will attend community college.

**18. Which of the following characteristics would be the LEAST common in students who receive special education services under the multiple disabilities category?**

a. Hampered speech and communication skills
b. Challenges with mobility
c. Requiring assistance with everyday tasks
d. Loss of vision and hearing

**19. Which one of the following environmental factors is likely to have the greatest impact on students who receive special education services due to mental health concerns?**

a. Sleep deprivation
b. Smoking
c. Exposure to toxins
d. Substance abuse

**20. Which of the following learning theories views motivation as extrinsic and intrinsic?**

a. Behaviorism
b. Cognitivism
c. Constructivism
d. Humanism

**21. A young boy in the first grade is struggling to stay on task and keep his body under control during class. His constant movements are distracting other students and keeping him from completing the day's work. How should the situation be handled in the classroom?**

a. Sit with him and break down the day's work into smaller segments. Help him alternate between physical activities just outside the classroom (such as jumping jacks or running errands in the hallway) and completing his segmented activities for the day.
b. Agree upon a nonverbal signal. When the signal (clearing the throat, touching the nose) is given, the boy is reminded to sit down and focus on his work.
c. Call his name sharply in class to get his attention. Clearly communicate the expectations for behavior and work completion so that he knows what he should be doing.
d. Call his parents to discuss the problem. Suggest having him evaluated for certain learning difficulties so that all adults involved in his care can work together to help him.

**22. What is an example of a learning objective that is NOT measurable?**

a. Students will be able to sound out each letter in the alphabet in six weeks.
b. Students will be able to understand 20% of the English language in six months.
c. Students will be able to complete half of their reading packets in one week.
d. Students will be able to read a chapter of a novel in one day.

**23. Which of the following is most accurate regarding textbooks that elementary school teachers use when teaching culturally diverse students?**

a. Textbooks introduce many new concepts in a short time for such students.
b. Teacher editions commonly offer tips for meeting diverse students' needs.
c. The reading levels of most textbooks are appropriate for diverse students.
d. Most textbooks eliminate the need for much differentiation of instruction.

**24. Which of the following is most accurate about what teachers need to consider in planning lessons in reading and math for both special needs students and the class as a whole?**

a. They already know which skill or concept they want to teach.
b. They assume students have prerequisites for a skill/concept.
c. They must determine what mastery of a skill/concept requires.
d. They are premature in thinking how to expand/apply learning.

**25. Behavior problems in special education students are most effectively handled with:**

a. Zero tolerance
b. Positive Behavioral Support (PBS)
c. Acceptance and tolerance
d. Positive Behavioral Control (PBC)

**26. A new teacher is faced with a difficult student. The teacher has provided the appropriate warnings and stated classroom discipline methods. What is the next step for the teacher?**

a. Continue to discipline the student.
b. Send the student in the hall.
c. Send the student to the principal.
d. Contact the student's parents.

**27. Having a print-rich environment includes all of the following EXCEPT:**

a. Writing classroom labels in only one language to avoid confusion
b. Making sure print is at the children's eye level
c. Displaying the students' work around the classroom
d. Having the teacher prepare materials in front of the students to model writing

**28. Which consequence would be the LEAST appropriate for a third-grade student with behavioral issues?**

a. Having the student stay in during recess
b. Having the student go to a time-out area during class
c. Having the student fill out a points sheet when they display poor behavior
d. Having the student skip a fun activity at the end of the day

**29. Which time-out strategy is most effective for very young students?**

a. None; time-out has been proven ineffective for young students.
b. Warn the student of the consequences before delivering it; make him or her sit silently and alone for a set amount of time; warn him or her that repeated offenses will result in the same consequence; allow him or her to rejoin activity.
c. Make the student sit away from the group, ideally facing away from activity, and then require the child to apologize for his or her actions before rejoining the group; failure to apologize results in longer time spent away from the group.
d. Warn the student of the consequence; if action is repeated, make him or her sit away from the group for a set amount of time; debrief with student about the reasons for the time out; communicate expectation for behavior before rejoining activity.

**30. Ms. Case is planning field trips in the spring for some of her high school classes. One of her groups includes Sarah, who has a diagnosis of severe autism. Which of these would be a suitable activity?**

a. A trip to a local Renaissance festival
b. A nature hike to examine local flora
c. A community mixer for her age group
d. An outing to attend a rock concert

**31. Ms. Lewis has a resource room with students who have a variety of different disabilities. One student, Jonathan, has a very slow response time to any stimulus. Another student, Michelle, can work very quickly but needs help focusing her attention. Corey and Jennifer work at a similar pace but are using very different instructional materials. Ms. Lewis has one teacher's aide in her room. Which is the most efficient use of instructional time in this setting?**

a. Ms. Lewis works with Jonathan for the first half of the period while the teacher's aide rotates among the other students, then Ms. Lewis works with each of the others for the second half of the period.
b. Ms. Lewis gives Jonathan a stimulus and lets him process it while the aide monitors him and Ms. Lewis then attends to each other student in turn, giving all students equal time.
c. Ms. Lewis works with Corey and Jennifer, since they work at a similar pace, while the aide goes between Jonathan and Michelle.
d. Ms. Lewis concentrates on helping Michelle to focus while the aide goes between the other students.

**32. Ms. George has some new students in her special education class this year. After she has assigned individual seatwork, she notices that two Chinese girls are helping each other. What should she do?**

a. She should punish them for cheating and tell them to do the assignment over individually.
b. She should acknowledge potential cultural factors and explicitly teach classroom expectations.
c. She should separate the girls' seats so they can continue seatwork but not work together.
d. She should report their activity to the school principal and let her address it with the girls.

**33. Ms. Hutchinson is supervising her small class at lunch. Ann, who has Down syndrome, displays some rude behaviors at times. On this day, she deliberately breaks wind at the table, which offends and "grosses out" the others, who complain about it. Ann does not seem concerned and does not apologize. Later, the other students are still upset with her, and Ann does not understand why. In a one-on-one conversation with Ann, Ms. Hutchinson asks her, "What if one of the other students passed gas at the table while you were eating?" Ann looks surprised and then disgusted as she imagines this. "Oh!" she responds, "that would be awful!" "Yes," Ms. Hutchinson agrees, "so now do you see why they were upset when you did it?" "Yes," says Ann, and she apologizes to the others, promising not to do this again. What is the best description of what Ms. Hutchinson did here?**

a. She enforced more proper manners by inducing guilt in Ann at her inappropriate behavior.
b. She modeled some more appropriate behavior for Ann by demonstrating a better example.
c. She aided self-awareness, self-control, and self-management by enabling perspective-taking.
d. She increased self-reliance and self-confidence in Ann by treating her as a respected equal.

**34. Elise is a behavior specialist with a group of students who have various disabilities. One student has memory deficits. Another student has perceptual problems. A third student is diagnosed with difficulties in language processing. And a fourth student has IEP objectives to learn better problem-solving skills. In her research, which of the following would be a useful class of publications for Elise to read?**

a. Journals of cognitive psychology
b. Journals of applied behavior analysis
c. Journals of the American Medical Association
d. Journals of neuroscience research

**35. Which of the following strategies would be LEAST effective in structuring an inclusive classroom environment?**

a. Providing multisensory approaches to learning
b. Enforcing a rigidly structured routine
c. Developing clear rules and expectations
d. Using station learning opportunities

*Refer to the following for question 36:*

> Christina is an 11th-grade student who receives special education services due to an emotional disturbance and has a hard time completing any work due to frustration. When Christina becomes frustrated enough, she tends to lash out verbally at nearby people.

**36. Which of the following would be the most appropriate strategy to include in her behavior plan to help her calm down when frustrated so she can complete her schoolwork?**

a. Teaching her stress management techniques
b. Allowing her to complete work in a separate setting
c. Providing rewards for completing work
d. Giving her choices about what work she does

**37. How might a lesson introduction be most beneficial when teaching students with learning disabilities about math?**

a. To provide students with additional information
b. To ensure that students understand the curriculum
c. To connect the learning from the previous lesson
d. To challenge the students to learn as much as possible

**38. When teaching a classroom with students with disabilities, which of the following would be most effective in building self-esteem?**

a. Giving them work that does not challenge them
b. Being patient with their learning needs
c. Allowing students to work in groups
d. Using positive nonverbal communication

**39. Which of the following classroom organization methods would be most beneficial for a teacher who includes a lot of classroom discussions?**

a. Including a meeting area in the classroom
b. Arranging the desks facing toward each other
c. Having tables instead of desks
d. Ensuring that each student can move around

**40. Which of the following would be the best example of a learning objective that is appropriately challenging for a third-grade student with a disability in reading fluency?**

a. The student will be able to identify 25 letters in one minute.
b. The student will be able to identify 25 letter sounds in one minute.
c. The student will be able to read 50 sight words in one minute.
d. The student will be able to read 100 words in one minute.

**41. Which of the following best explains why learning objectives should be time-bound?**

a. Objectives should explain the progress toward achievement.
b. Objectives should require a reasonable amount of resources.
c. Objectives should lead to a desired goal.
d. Objectives should include a date in relation to the accomplishment.

**42. Gordon is a seventh-grade student with an intellectual disability. Which of the following is likely most important in ensuring that Gordon has a meaningful learning experience in the class?**

a. Linking the content to real-life experiences
b. Making the content student-centered
c. Promoting self-knowledge
d. Using a variety of resources

**43. Which of the following would be the most effective communication strategy when working with a student who has frequent misbehaviors due to his disability at school?**

a. Sending home a weekly behavior report
b. Asking general education teachers to contact parents
c. Asking the school psychologist to contact parents
d. Sending home a daily behavior report

**44. When developing a lesson plan for a small group of students to specifically address IEP goals in writing, which one of the following should be the primary focus of the lesson?**

a. Ensuring that the students are accessing their accommodations
b. Ensuring that the students are working on their IEP goals
c. Ensuring that the students have access to the general education curriculum
d. Ensuring that the students have access to an alternate curriculum

**45. Which of the following issues would be most likely to arise when teaching a large group of students with a wide range of disabilities?**

a. The teacher may not be able to meet each student's IEP goals.
b. The teacher may not be able to provide accommodations.
c. The teacher may not be able to incorporate assistive technology.
d. The teacher may not be able to appropriately differentiate.

**46. Which of the following is the best example of how the results of an adaptive behavior scale can drive instruction?**

a. To determine which problem behaviors the student engages in
b. To determine whether or not a student needs a behavior plan
c. To determine which independent living skills a student needs to work on
d. To determine how to adapt the curriculum to a student's needs

**47. Emma is a nonverbal student who is assigned an oral presentation in her history class. Which of the following alternatives best allows her to access the curriculum?**

a. Allowing Emma to present a slideshow instead
b. Allowing Emma to skip this assignment
c. Allowing Emma's aide to present the information
d. Allowing Emma to write a paper on a similar topic

**48. Mr. Stewart's students show good reading comprehension of any given paragraph in any chapter of their textbook, but they have trouble organizing, recalling, or applying the main points of a chapter. Which of the following is the simplest, most direct, and most efficient way to help?**

a. Point out and explain the text's informational structure and features.
b. Create separate handouts with simplified organization of main points.
c. Identify, select, procure, duplicate, and distribute graphic organizers.
d. Create and deliver a slide show presentation for each text chapter.

**49. Ms. Ross introduces new vocabulary words to her class daily. She then assigns reading that includes these words, uses these words in her speech as she presents lessons, and points them out when they appear in other contexts. Which instructional method does this represent?**

a. Appropriate word choice
b. Teaching of word analysis
c. Using contextual analysis
d. Multiple word exposures

**50. Which of the following is the most efficient and effective method for teaching word recognition to a class with a variety of student levels and needs?**

a. Providing individualized direct instructions
b. Using multilevel teaching practices
c. Teaching to the class median
d. Creating smaller groups at each level

**51. Components of explicit instruction include:**

a. Clarifying the goal, modeling strategies, and offering explanations geared to a student's level of understanding
b. Determining the goal, offering strategies, and asking questions designed to ascertain whether understanding has been reached
c. Reassessing the goal, developing strategies, and determining whether further reassessing of the goal is required
d. Objectifying the goal, assessing strategies, and offering explanations geared toward a student's level of understanding

**52. A teacher has a student with dyscalculia who has trouble organizing addition and subtraction problems on paper. She can best help him by:**

a. Encouraging memorization of number families. Committing them to memory is the only way.
b. Demonstrating a problem in different ways. Write a problem on the board: 11-3. Gather 11 books and take 3 of them away. Draw 11 Xs on the board and erase 3 of them.
c. Use graph paper to help him organize. Show him how to write the problems, keeping each number in a box aligned with other numbers.
d. Make a game of addition and subtraction problems. Divide the class into groups and let them compete to see which group can solve the most problems.

**53. What is an example of a modification of the curriculum?**

a. Access to textbooks with larger print
b. Access to a computer to type assignments
c. Access to manipulatives
d. Access to alternative books

**54. What strategy listed here is most designed to promote generalization of learning?**

a. Having a student practice a new skill in a variety of different settings/contexts
b. Having a student practice a new skill regularly and periodically testing that skill
c. Having a student practice a complex skill one step at a time, and then adding steps
d. Having a student practice a new skill in class before applying it in real-life tasks

**55. Joseph has Down syndrome. He can communicate with short, simple verbal phrases. He can read only a few words that he learned over a long time. He lives just a few blocks from his school. His area is not served by the school bus system. His teacher has a goal for Joseph to learn the directions to and from school so his mother will no longer need to accompany him. Which of these would be a good way for the teacher to work with him on this goal?**

a. Send Joseph out first with a map, monitoring him remotely.
b. Send Joseph out first with written directions and shadow him from a distance.
c. Walk with Joseph, prompting him to verbalize the route until he learns it.
d. Gradually decrease the number of days his mother walks with him

**56. Bert and Nan are first graders receiving special education. They each have an IEP objective in reading/phonological awareness to produce rhyming words and distinguish rhyming from non-rhyming words. Bert is blind, and Nan has cerebral palsy with poor fine motor skills. Which of the following would be the best plan for both students to work on this objective?**

a. Give both a worksheet with a list of word pairs and have each student circle the pairs that rhyme and cross through the pairs that do not rhyme.
b. Read a list of word pairs to both students and have each raise the left hand if the words do not rhyme and the right hand if they do rhyme.
c. Give Nan a worksheet with a list of word pairs, having her circle the rhyming pairs and cross out the non-rhyming pairs; read word pairs to Bert and have him raise his right or left hand to indicate if they rhyme or not.
d. Give Nan a list of word pairs, have her read them to Bert, and have him indicate by which hand he raises whether they rhyme or not.

**57. Which of the following research-based intervention strategies would be most appropriate for a third-grade student who is working on basic decoding skills?**

a. Multisensory techniques
b. Metacognitive strategies
c. Text structuring
d. Explicit teaching

**58. Fred is deaf and autistic and does not speak. He has had periodic outbursts of anger in the past. This year, his teacher got him a computer. He learned to use it quickly and types very well. Fred has always had good receptive language skills and vocabulary knowledge. During this school year, the teacher and school psychologist have observed that the frequency and severity of Fred's outbursts have decreased significantly. What is the most likely reason for this improvement?**

a. Fred is a year older now and is growing out of having outbursts.
b. Having a computer to occupy him, Fred is happier and less bored.
c. The improvement cannot be explained with the information given.
d. Fred is less frustrated now that he has a means of communicating.

**59. Lori is a 10th-grade student with a postsecondary goal of becoming an artist. Which of the following would likely be most productive in helping Lori reach this goal?**

a. Setting up an appointment with the art teacher at school
b. Giving her a list of schools to research
c. Having her call local art galleries in town
d. Allowing her to take an online vocational test

**60. When working with a group of eighth-grade students with writing deficiencies who struggle to stay on topic when writing, which of the following intervention strategies would be most appropriate?**

a. Providing a graphic organizer for the students to use
b. Modeling the writing for the students
c. Providing opportunities for the students to practice
d. Allowing students to collaborate with peers

**61. A student with a disability takes online courses and struggles with communication and seeking help in social situations. Which of the following instructional strategies would be most effective in supporting the student in online instruction?**

a. Supplementing online instruction with face-to-face instruction
b. Assisting the student in seeking support from the online teacher
c. Providing opportunities to demonstrate the knowledge learned online
d. Ensuring the student's accommodations are documented in the student's IEP

**62. Which of the following best describes how technology can be included in a small group of students with disabilities working on reading comprehension?**

a. Accessing audiobooks to listen to the story
b. Using computers to research the author of the story
c. Accessing speech-to-text software to answer questions
d. Using tablets to read a story and answer questions

**63. In order for students to make progress on their IEP goals, which of the following makes the most sense when grouping students for a math intervention group?**

a. Grouping students based on their ability level
b. Grouping students based on their grade level
c. Grouping students based on their teachers
d. Grouping students based on their maturity level

**64. Which of the following best describes when it would be appropriate to provide one-on-one in-class support to a fifth-grade student who receives special education services and has been demonstrating an inability to attend to his general education teachers?**

a. As soon as the student demonstrates these behaviors
b. At the student's annual IEP meeting
c. After data have been collected and analyzed
d. When the student gets suspended from school

**65. Jeffrey is an eighth-grade student with a deficiency in reading fluency. Which of the following assistive technology devices would be LEAST appropriate in supporting his needs?**

a. Text-to-speech device
b. Speech-to-text device
c. Audiobooks
d. Graphic organizers

**66. Which of the following is the most appropriate use of technology to provide assistance with reading a story for a high school student who struggles with reading comprehension?**

a. Allowing the student to use text-to-speech programs
b. Allowing the student to watch videos of the stories
c. Allowing the student to complete an online activity
d. Allowing the student to complete an electronic worksheet

**67. Bobby is an 11th-grade at-risk student with a specific learning disability who rarely sees either of his parents. He will likely need to be self-sufficient after graduation. Which of the following instructional strategies is likely to be most effective for Bobby to become self-sufficient?**

a. Helping Bobby research colleges he might want to attend
b. Giving Bobby extra support to pass all of his classes
c. Teaching Bobby executive functioning skills
d. Assisting Bobby in applying and interviewing for jobs

**68. Carter is a sixth-grade student with an intellectual disability. Why would the use of manipulatives be an appropriate instructional strategy when teaching a math lesson?**

a. Manipulatives can stimulate the sense of touch in students with intellectual disabilities.
b. Manipulatives can make math lessons more enjoyable for students with intellectual disabilities.
c. Manipulatives can help students with intellectual disabilities learn classroom rules.
d. Manipulatives can aid in communication for students with intellectual disabilities.

**69. Which instructional strategy would be most beneficial in working with a small group of seventh graders who struggle with math calculations?**

a. Using worksheets
b. Using flash cards
c. Using visual aids
d. Using group projects

**70. Which of the following is an instructional strategy that is LEAST likely to be effective when working with a group of sixth-grade students with ADHD?**

a. Offering choices of task completion to the students
b. Providing hands-on learning activities
c. Providing a task above the students' current skill level
d. Repeating instructions often throughout the task

**71. What would be the MOST effective instructional strategy in teaching a reading lesson to students with dyslexia?**

a. Using a whole-word approach
b. Using multisensory strategies
c. Using modeling
d. Using graphic organizers

*Refer to the following for question 72:*

Bobby is a fifth-grade student who struggles with reading comprehension and writing. For an English unit, students will be reading a story independently and then participating in classroom activities based on the story for the next few weeks.

**72. Which of the following instructional strategies would be LEAST effective for Bobby's ability to learn the subject matter?**

a. Assigning Bobby an easier story
b. Including hands-on activities
c. Offering choices for learning
d. Using technology

**73. Which of the following is true regarding teaching spelling?**

a. Students who have an understanding of letter-sound association do not need to be taught to spell. If they can sound out a word, they can spell it.
b. Students who are able to determine the origin of a root word (Latin, Greek, Indo-European, etc.) can usually deduce the correct spelling of a word and do not require direct instruction in spelling.
c. Drilling spelling exercises is the most effective long-term method of teaching spelling.
d. By applying spelling patterns found in word families, the spelling of many words can be deduced.

**74. A teacher explicates a poet's use of symbolism and metaphor in a short poem to a high school class, showing how he uses an animal to represent an idea ("The Thought-Fox" by Ted Hughes). She is pleasantly shocked when a student who had seemed thoroughly unimpressed with her poetry unit suddenly expresses appreciation by saying, "So this is really good." When she asks him to elaborate, he responds, "It's really good because you can relate it to something that's real in your life." Which teaching strategy that enhances reading proficiency is most related to this outcome?**

a. Making reading material meaningful to the student
b. Making the activity of reading fun for the students
c. Making reading include choices made by a student
d. Making ample opportunities for students to read

**75. The school psychologist is explaining assessment results to Clifford's parents and other IEP team members. She says that Clifford has difficulties with planning, organizing, keeping track of time, and relating a current lesson to earlier learning. She also says that he talks out of turn in class. These all relate most to deficits in...**

a. Executive function
b. Self-regulation
c. Sequencing
d. Memory

**76. In the first week of school, a resource teacher asks her high school students to make lists of things they know how to do well. How is this activity most useful to the teacher?**

a. It establishes a feeling of success in her students from the start.
b. It is an informal assessment of their writing skills and gives the teacher an idea of each student's interests and abilities.
c. It is a formal assessment of prior knowledge.
d. It invites further discussion of each student's unique contributions and will help the class bond with mutual respect.

**77. For students with IEP goals to improve auditory comprehension, which of the following is the best assessment method to monitor their progress?**

a. Retelling a story they heard
b. Informal reading inventory
c. Curriculum-based testing
d. Periodic fluency checking

**78. What is the primary purpose of universal newborn hearing screenings?**

a. Educational planning
b. Disability diagnosis
c. Early identification
d. IDEA eligibility

**79. With regard to testing and assessment, what type of test compares students against a set of pre-determined standards or objectives?**

a. Norm-referenced tests
b. Criterion-referenced tests
c. Subject assessment tests
d. Performance-based tests

**80. All the following statements are true about the evaluation component of a lesson except:**

a. Evaluation may be groupwide instead of individual.
b. Evaluation must occur in some form with every lesson.
c. Evaluation may occur on an ongoing basis.
d. Evaluation may occur again—for example, during a unit test.

**81. On an achievement test, a standard score reflects:**

a. Where the student's rank falls compared to other students
b. Where the student's score falls relative to the average or mean
c. How the student's score compares only within the same grade
d. How the student's score compares only to students the same age

**82. Stephanie is a middle school student with a variety of maladaptive behaviors that are disruptive to the classroom. Her IEP team is meeting to address these. What should their first step be?**

a. Remove Stephanie from the classroom to stop these disruptions.
b. Differentially reinforce alternative behaviors.
c. Conduct a functional behavior assessment to learn why she behaves as she does.
d. Write a different instructional plan to address her needs better.

**83. Which of the following best describes a developmental assessment?**

a. A norm-referenced scale
b. A quick identifier
c. A behavior rating scale
d. An alternate assessment

**84. Brittany is a four-year-old preschool student who is administered a developmental assessment as part of her special education evaluation. Which of the following disability categories would LEAST likely be considered as a result of these assessments?**

a. Development disability
b. Speech or language impairment
c. Specific learning disability
d. Autism spectrum disorder

**85. Which one of the following is NOT typically used to collect data as a curriculum-based assessment?**

a. DIBELS
b. AIMSweb
c. EasyCBM
d. TerraNova

**86. When evaluating a sixth-grade student for a specific learning disability, which of the following is an academic achievement test that can be administered?**

a. CogAT
b. Woodcock-Johnson
c. Myers-Briggs Type Indicator
d. SAT

**87. Which of the following examples is LEAST likely to be considered a formative assessment technique?**

a. Analyzing student work
b. Using strategic questioning
c. Giving unit pretests
d. Using exit tickets

**88. Gerald is a fifth-grade student with a deficiency in reading fluency. How can the results of a diagnostic assessment in this area help to guide his instruction?**

a. To figure out how much progress Gerald has made
b. To help decide which areas to focus on the most
c. To compare Gerald to his peers in the class
d. To understand which accommodations will work for Gerald

**89. Which of the following is NOT one of the benefits of using curriculum-based assessments?**

a. To measure short-term student growth
b. To match all the standards on the classroom curriculum
c. To inform a teacher's instruction
d. To motivate students to improve

**90. Mary is a 10-year-old student who has a developmental disability due to a physical impairment. Why would she NOT be eligible for special education services as a student with a developmental delay?**

a. The developmental delay category does not include physical impairments.
b. The developmental delay category does not include students older than age 9.
c. The developmental delay category does not include students with developmental disabilities.
d. The developmental delay category does not include students younger than age 12.

**91. Which of the following is NOT one of the purposes of the prereferral process when evaluating students for special education services?**

a. To evaluate student strengths and weaknesses
b. To put accommodations and interventions into place
c. To evaluate accommodations and interventions
d. To obtain consent to begin the evaluation process

**92. Which of the following best describes the purpose of the standard score when interpreting assessment data?**

a. To determine how spread out the numbers are
b. To determine how far a score is from the average
c. To determine the rank of the score compared to others
d. To determine the hypothetical range of scores

**93. Samuel is a student with a specific learning disability in the area of oral expression. What kind of assessment would be most appropriate in order to evaluate his continued eligibility?**

a. Expressive language
b. Receptive language
c. Auditory discrimination
d. Verbal intelligence

**94. Which of the following would be the LEAST appropriate for a special education teacher to use to evaluate the progress of their students on their IEP goals?**

a. Standardized assessment data
b. Curriculum-based assessments
c. Classroom observations
d. End-of-quarter grades

**95. How can state standardized tests be beneficial in determining the proper instruction for students with disabilities?**

a. Using the results of the tests to determine accommodations
b. Using the results of the tests to determine class placement
c. Using the results of the tests to determine all IEP goals and objectives
d. Using the results of the tests to determine the least restrictive environment

**96. Which of the following is most important in writing nondiscriminatory assessments?**

a. Getting to know the background of each student in the class
b. Ensuring the inclusion of multicultural questions
c. Eliminating biases associated with certain topics
d. Evaluating each student based on their identity

**97. A student has been identified with a cluster of learning disabilities. She will be joining a special education classroom. She is understandably nervous about making the change to a different teacher and group of classmates. In order to help her make the transition, the child should:**

a. Have a party to which her new classmates are invited along with some friends from the fifth-grade class she is leaving.
b. Prepare to begin classes with her new teacher the next day. Once the decision has been made, nothing will be gained by postponing the inevitable.
c. Be brave and understand life will be full of transitions. This is an opportunity to learn new skills that will serve her well in the future.
d. Visit the classroom, meet the teacher and her new classmates, and be given the opportunity to ask questions about the change she is about to make.

**98. During which step of the IEP process are classroom accommodations and modifications tested for effectiveness?**

a. Identification
b. Prereferral
c. Eligibility
d. Review

**99. A major review of an exceptional student's IEP is required:**

a. Once every year
b. Once every three years
c. In one or three years depending on the state
d. In varying periods by each state

**100. By law, a child with a disability is defined as:**

a. A child with intellectual disabilities; hearing, speech, language, visual, orthopedic, or other health impairments; emotional disturbance; autism; brain injury caused by trauma; or specific learning disabilities who needs special education and related services.
b. A child with intellectual disabilities, emotional disturbance, autism, brain injury caused by trauma, or specific learning disabilities who needs special education and related services.
c. A child who is unable to reach the same academic goals as his peers, regardless of cause, and needs special education and related services.
d. The term disability is no longer used. The correct term is other ability.

**101. As defined by the Individuals with Disabilities Education Act (IDEA), Secondary Transition is a coordinated set of activities that are:**

a. Results-oriented and include post-school activities, vocational education, employment support and adult services and considers the individual's strengths, preferences and interests
b. Socially structured and consider the individual's strengths, preferences and interests and vocational requirements
c. Designed to support vocational training, results-oriented and have a strong social component
d. Selected by the parent(s) or guardian because the student cannot choose for himself

**102. Which of the following is the most common disability in children aged 5-21 according to the IDEA annual reports to Congress?**

a. Specific learning disability
b. Speech or language impairment
c. Intellectual disability
d. Emotional disturbance

**103. A third-grade boy is new to the school. His teacher has noticed he happily plays with other children, redirects his attention without upset when another child rejects his offer to play and doesn't mind playing on his own. However, the boy doesn't pay attention when academic instruction is given. He continues to speak with other children, draws, or distracts himself. The teacher reminds him repeatedly to listen and follow instruction. When he does not, she moves him to a quiet desk away from the others. When isolated, the boy puts his head on the desk and weeps uncontrollably, or he stares at a fixed spot and repeats to himself, "I hate myself, I hate myself. I should be dead." During these episodes, the teacher cannot break through to the student; his disconnection seems complete. The teacher has requested a conference with his parents, but they do not speak English and have not responded to her offer of a translator. The teacher should:**

a. Establish a consistent set of expectations for the child. He needs to understand there are appropriate times for play and for learning.
b. Isolate the boy first thing. His behavior suggests manipulation. By third grade, children fully understand they are expected to pay attention when the teacher is speaking. The boy is punishing the teacher with tears and repetitive self-hate, consciously or unconsciously attempting to make the teacher feel guilty.
c. Immediately refer him to the counselor. The boy is exhibiting serious emotional distress suggesting an underlying cause that should be evaluated.
d. Recognize the child's highly sensitive nature; offer comfort when he acts out self-loathing. Carefully explain why he must learn to pay attention so he will use reason instead of emotion when making future choices.

**104. What is not included in an Individual Education Plan?**

a. Medical issues or information
b. The student's interests
c. Family history of disability
d. Test results

**105. What recent legislation has placed additional accountability on schools?**

a. No Child Left Behind Act
b. Americans with Disabilities Act
c. Family Educational Rights and Privacy Act
d. Human Equity Act

**106. The school psychologist can be a crucial member of the Individualized Education Program team. Which responsibility does the psychologist typically hold?**

a. Administering IQ tests
b. Administering achievement tests
c. Administering progress monitoring probes
d. Administering transition planning inventories

**107. Which of the following is true?**

a. Pre-service training is adequate preparation for the teachers to do their work
b. The school district is in the business of educating students, not teachers
c. Teachers should spend some of their work time in professional study and collaborative work
d. To avoid taking time away from students, teachers should pursue professional development on their own time

**108. According to the Individuals with Disabilities Education Act (IDEA), which condition could fall under the umbrella term of specific learning disability?**

a. Speech or language impairment
b. Auditory processing disorder
c. Attention deficit disorder
d. Bipolar disorder

**109. A teacher suspects one of her kindergarteners has a learning disability in math. Why would the teacher suggest intervention to the child's concerned parents rather than assessment as the first step?**

a. She wouldn't; assessment should precede intervention
b. She wouldn't; kindergarteners develop new skills at radically different rates. Suggesting either intervention or assessment at this point is premature. The teacher would more likely observe the child over a three month period to note her development before including the parents about her concern
c. Assessing a young child for learning disabilities often leads to an incorrect conclusion because a student must be taught the subject before it's possible to assess her understanding of it. Intervention teaches the child specific skills to correct her misconceptions. If the intervention fails, assessment is the next step
d. Assessment at this stage is unnecessary and wastes time and money. Since an assessment that resulted in a diagnosis of a learning disability would recommend intervention to correct it, it is more efficient to proceed directly to intervention

**110. Which of the following is true about stakeholder rights and an Independent Educational Evaluation (IEE)?**

a. The testing is administered by someone who is not employed by the school district.
b. The IEP team must accept the results of the IEE.
c. The parents must pay for the IEE to be conducted.
d. The parents must explain the reason for the IEE.

**111. Which of the following would be the most appropriate for a student who was evaluated for special education services and provided accommodations, but was later found to not have a disability?**

a. Referring the student back to general education without accommodations
b. Referring the student back to general education with accommodations
c. Referring the student to the 504 team
d. Referring the student to supports outside of school

**112. A kindergarten teacher has received a community outreach referral. She asks the school's speech-language pathologist to evaluate a preschool child for delayed language development, as the parents cannot afford to pay a private practitioner's fees. The parents bring their child to the school. The speech-language pathologist assesses the child and privately has a strong suspicion that this child is displaying many signs of early autism. The speech-language pathologist takes the appropriate action. What does she do?**

a. Tells the parents what she suspects and recommends treatment
b. Refers the parents to a free community clinic for a complete behavioral assessment
c. Asks the referring kindergarten teacher to tell the parents that she suspects autism
d. Recommends that the parents take their child to their pediatrician for a checkup

**113. Lee, a student in a residential facility, has severe physical disabilities including cerebral palsy with spastic quadriplegia and severe scoliosis. He is unable to sit up, and due to his scoliosis, he cannot lie straight. He is accommodated with a large, very wide, bedlike reclining wheelchair with high wooden sides, which was built by Kim, the occupational therapist (OT). Lee is a very good-natured and cooperative individual who enjoys performing any activity his physical limitations will allow. Gigi, the behavior specialist, needs to give Lee an IQ test. Ordinarily she would take an individual student into her office for private testing. But when they arrive, they discover that Lee's chair is too wide to fit through the doorway. Also, some tasks in the test include marking on paper with a pen and pointing to things on the paper. Lee can grasp a pen put into his hand and can manipulate it. He can also point to things. But the only position possible for Lee is lying on his back, making it difficult for him to mark on the paper. The office area is empty and quiet at this time of day. The school's funds are limited at present, and Kim is the only OT for a large group of students. Tom, the chief of psychological services, is helping Gigi with the logistics of administering the test. He suggests solutions to both of these problems. What does he suggest?**

a. Give Lee the test in the classroom, with the teacher and other students engaged in many different activities around them, and omit the pointing and marking tasks.
b. Ask Kim to come up with some temporary seating device that is narrow enough to fit through the doorway, with an adaptive paper holder attached to it.
c. Give Lee the test in the hallway outside Gigi's office, and put the papers on a clipboard that Tom will hold above Lee so he can do the marking and pointing portions of the test.
d. Come up with a different IQ test that does not include marking and pointing tasks, and administer it in the hall outside the classroom.

**114. Frank has dyslexia and is in a general education classroom. He has reading and writing sessions with his special education teacher, Ms. Miller, for one hour a day. She has taught him a number of techniques to help him decipher letters and words more easily, to distinguish between "b" and "d" in his writing, to keep his "s" going in the right direction, etc. Ms. Miller meets with Frank's general education classroom teacher, Ms. Phillips, to give her some insights and recommendations to facilitate his education. Of the following, which is NOT one of the things she might do?**

a. Ask Ms. Phillips to grade Frank's papers on content but not on spelling and to excuse him from taking spelling tests.
b. Ask her to grade Frank's papers on the same basis as other students' but to highlight his reversed letters and numbers.
c. Ask her to allow Frank some additional time to complete in-class reading assignments.
d. Ask her to keep Ms. Miller informed of his progress and of areas needing more work.

**115. Frank has developmental disabilities and mental illness and was raised by a private caregiver who was not a trained professional. The caregiver is deceased, so he cannot be consulted. Frank has now been placed in a group home and attends a school specifically for students with intellectual disabilities. He is cooperative but needs training in some areas. For example, he needs to learn to use utensils and wipe his mouth at meals. How should this be addressed?**

a. The house parents at the group home should teach him at home.
b. The teachers at his school should teach him this during the day.
c. Both group home staff and schoolteachers should teach him this.
d. It should be an IEP goal carried out both at home and at school.

**116. Sammy is blind and deaf and has spent his preschool, kindergarten, and first and second grade years in a special school for blind and deaf students. He has been very successful as a student. Because of his success and his family's relocation to another city, he has been recommended for placement in a general education school. Who should be involved in designing and implementing transition plans?**

a. Sammy's former teacher and his new teacher
b. Sammy's new teacher and his parents
c. Sammy's former teacher, new teacher, and parents
d. Sammy's parents, former and new teachers, and Sammy

**117. Of the following criteria for defining intellectual disabilities, which was NOT used before 1961?**

a. IQ score
b. Social incompetence
c. Impaired adaptive behavior
d. Essentially incurable

**118. Mr. Price has a multicultural class. Michael's family is Jehovah's Witness, so he abstains from saying the pledge of allegiance. Ellen's family is Christian Scientist, so her parents object to her being sent to the school nurse. Both Mai's family and River's family object to school competitions and do not view students helping one another as cheating. Fatima's family and Nobu's family both believe in a tradition of arranged marriages at early ages for their children. Mr. Price is perplexed about how to navigate the vast cultural differences. What can he do?**

a. Ask the school psychologist to help explain abnormal psychology to him.
b. Ask the school social worker to help him arrange family counseling for his students.
c. Ask the school librarian for sources to educate himself on cultural variations.
d. Ask the school principal to reassign him to a more culturally homogenous class.

**119. Donna is a speech therapist who has just moved to a new school. She inherits a caseload from the previous person who was not a speech therapist but a general education teacher with some course credits in special education. She discovers that one student, Erin, has been placed in a special education classroom with other "speech therapy students." However, the other students in this group all have delayed language development, whereas Erin stutters. Erin reads and writes above grade level, has a high IQ score and a large vocabulary, and gets good grades in all subjects. What action should Donna take?**

a. Keep Erin in the same group but also does a lot of one-on-one stuttering therapy with her.
b. Find two other students who stutter and form a new group with them and Erin.
c. Advocate for Erin to be in the general classroom with speech therapy sessions.
d. Work individually with Erin, as her stutter would humiliate her in the classroom.

**120. Which of these is true regarding the relationships between state agencies and local health departments?**

a. Each state has a centralized structure, and the state agency controls local public health services.
b. Each state is decentralized, letting local health departments make decisions and deliver services.
c. Each state has mixed/shared authority, with a combination of centralized and decentralized structure.
d. Some states are centralized, some are decentralized, and some have mixed/shared authority.

# Answer Key and Explanations

**1. D:** Children with autism spectrum disorder often have deficits in social skills, communication skills, and joint or shared attention. They tend to prefer focusing individual attention on one activity or subject for sustained periods and may have difficulty with transitions. Children with attention-deficit/hyperactivity disorder (C) have difficulty focusing and sustaining their attention, are easily distracted, and tend to jump from one thing to another. Children with intellectual disabilities secondary to Down syndrome (A) and those with overall developmental delays (B) are likely to have shorter attention spans and less ability to focus.

**2. B:** Obsessive Compulsive Disorder (OCD). Children and adults with OCD typically engage in a series of highly ritualized behaviors that are rigidly performed when they feel stressed. Behaviors include tapping, snapping fingers, blinking, counting and so forth.

**3. B:** Although there are a number of antidepressants available, most of them share the side effect of a dry mouth and increased thirst that lasts for a few weeks after beginning treatment. The student is likely to ask for water frequently because this type of thirst isn't easily quenched. The teacher and the student should understand this side effect will ease and disappear with time. Answer A is incorrect because persistent nausea is unlikely to be transitory and likely would require medical attention. Answer C is incorrect because sudden memory loss is not a common immediate reaction. Answer D is incorrect because severe bruising is not a typical reaction to antidepressants.

**4. D:** Students with disabilities often suffer from learned helplessness, or a condition in which they feel like they have no control. These students will often give up because they think that nothing can be done to improve their condition. This is something that impacts individuals with disabilities as they are learning about themselves and what they are able to accomplish. Answer A is incorrect because students with disabilities will often suffer from learned helplessness. Answer B is incorrect because these students with learned helplessness have a difficult time controlling situations. Answer C is incorrect because students with disabilities do not always have the chance to reach out for help before they get to learned helplessness.

**5. B:** According to Piaget's theory, four stages of development occur in sequence and result in learning. These stages begin at birth with the sensorimotor stage, which continues until the child is approximately two years old. During this stage, an infant learns about himself or herself and the environment through motor reflexes. The preoperational stage, which begins when the child is two years old and ends when they are approximately six years old, includes language development. The next stage is the concrete operational stage, which begins at approximately six years old and continues into early adolescence. During this stage, learning continues, and the ability for abstract thought begins to develop. Finally, in adolescence a person enters the formal operational stage. At this point, according to Piaget, abstract thought is fully functional, and individuals are able to utilize deductive reasoning skills.

**6. C:** The effects of spina bifida vary in severity with the type of spina bifida and the individual who has it. The most likely effect is on motor development because the spinal column does not fuse completely, leaving an opening. Many children with spina bifida cannot walk, and the strength and mobility of the upper limbs and body can also be affected. Intellectual development (A) can be affected if cerebrospinal fluid backs up into the brain and the fluid buildup, called hydrocephalus, is not relieved by shunting; spina bifida without hydrocephalus does not cause brain damage. As long as intellectual development is not affected, language development (B) is not affected by spina bifida. This condition does not affect social development (D) as, for example, autism often does.

**7. A:** Pervasive developmental disorder (PDD) is an old name that roughly mapped onto and encompassed syndromes now recognized as autism spectrum disorder and some other related syndromes. PDD causes disabilities in language, thought, emotion, and empathy.

**8. C:** While a student who is very bored could certainly nod off, this is not the most likely explanation in the case of a child taking medications for a seizure disorder. Boredom should not be the first reason to consider. Therefore, option A is incorrect.

Whereas some children may not get a good night's sleep at home, there is no reason to assume that as the first possibility in this case. Ms. Wright has no background information that Tommy's parents let him stay up late, that he lives in an environment that is noisy at night, or that his sleep is disrupted by parents working different shifts, sharing a bedroom with an infant, or any other such factors. Therefore, option B is incorrect.

Many anti-seizure medications are known to cause drowsiness as a side effect. Different drugs can be tried, but some will not control an individual's seizures. So, some medications will make those who use them very sleepy. Therefore, option C is correct.

There is no reason to assume Tommy is deliberately acting sleepy to get more attention. He is in individual therapy sessions with Ms. Wright, has her individual attention, and has no other students with whom to compete. Whereas first graders are certainly capable of engaging in attention-seeking behavior, at this age the most likely kinds of attention-seeking behavior would not usually be pretending to fall asleep. Anti-seizure medications are a more obvious source of daytime sleepiness in a child this age. Therefore, option D is incorrect.

**9. A:** According to IDEA, birth trauma would not be considered one of the causes of traumatic brain injury. Students with birth trauma would likely be considered under a different eligibility category. Students who receive services under the traumatic brain injury category will typically have a medical diagnosis of a traumatic brain injury. Answer B is incorrect because combat injuries can be one of the causes of traumatic brain injuries, even at a young age. Answer C is incorrect because violence is often associated with students who are impacted by traumatic brain injuries. Answer D is incorrect because sports-related injuries can also cause damage to the brain and cause traumatic brain injuries.

**10. C:** Vygotsky's zone of proximal development describes that a child benefits from exposure to knowledge that is only slightly beyond what they currently know. This implies that a student can benefit from receiving help from another child who is just slightly ahead in development. Peter is just starting long division, so having Joe help is fitting as his knowledge is slightly more advanced than Peter's. Joe may be able to explain long division in a fitting way that is accessible to Peter. Choice A is incorrect as Peter is not ready to do any fraction problems at this time. Choice B is incorrect as Peter does not need a reduction in work, he just needs some assistance. Choice D is incorrect because having the students work separately and then compare answers does not provide the direct scaffolding as in Vygotsky's theory.

**11. A:** Although adding a goal to his IEP may be helpful in getting his teachers to focus on Dante graduating, it likely will not have much of an impact on what he actually does and is unlikely to improve his motivation without a more particular plan. Answer B is incorrect because it may be a good idea to get him involved with some activities. Answer C is incorrect because a daily check-in will likely make him feel needed and welcome. Answer D is incorrect because lightening his load may encourage him to do the work and pass the classes.

**12. C:** It is true that in many group homes caregivers have the duty of giving medications to disabled individuals, but this option does not foster independence for an individual who can learn to take her own pills. Rather than simply letting her continue to depend on caregivers, staff should try to teach Mary Frances to take the medications on her own to see if she can comply. If it turns out she cannot remember or gets confused and it is a health risk, she has caregivers as a backup. But she will be more self-sufficient if she can learn to manage her medication herself. Therefore, option A is incorrect.

Reminding Mary Frances every day might be the first step toward her learning to take her pills on her own. Doing so would require her to take slightly more action than simply accepting pills from the nurse, but it is not an end in itself. To learn, Mary Frances may need to be prompted at first, but this could gradually be phased out. Reminding her every day is not that much different from just giving her the pills every day. Therefore, option B is incorrect.

Giving Mary Frances a pill holder marked with the days of the week and instructing her how to use it is a good way to foster independence. Once she masters putting the pills into the holder, she can tell if she has taken them yet by whether that day's compartment is empty or full. Therefore, option C is correct.

Marking on the calendar or on a chart when Mary Frances has taken her pills is a very good way to reinforce independent self-medication. It is also a good way for her to keep track of whether she is taking her medication daily. However, it would not be effective initially because she would only mark the calendar or chart after taking her pills, so there is nothing to cue her to take them until she gets into the habit. The pill holder is a concrete reminder to take her pills, and she can be instructed to place it where she will see it every day (on her bedside table or on the kitchen table). The pill holder is more concretely and closely associated with pills than a calendar or even a pill chart. Marking a chart or calendar after taking her pills would be an ideal strategy to pair with the pill holder, but by itself might be insufficient. Therefore, option D is incorrect.

**13. B:** Taking academic classes would provide no job training and no transition to the workshop. Rebecca would need more training at the workshop to get up to speed. This is not the best plan. Therefore, option A is incorrect.

Rebecca can learn job skills first in the training center and then, when she is ready, she can be transitioned to the workshop, where she can actually do work and earn some money. Therefore, option B is correct.

If she were placed directly in the workshop, Rebecca would not be prepared since she has no job skills. She needs training first. Therefore, option C is incorrect.

A classroom at the training center is a good place for Rebecca to learn some job skills. However, staying there indefinitely would be like staying in school indefinitely. The workshop, though sheltered for disabled individuals, is still closer to a real workplace than a school, and she can earn money there. After going to school, she should make the transition to having a job. Therefore, option D is incorrect.

**14. A:** A student with an intellectual disability will have a significantly subaverage general intellectual functioning. This will typically be combined with deficits in adaptive behavior and will be manifested during the developmental period. This is something that likely would be noticed in Jason starting from an early age. Answer B is incorrect because a concomitant, or accompanying, disability would fall under the category of multiple disabilities. Answer C is incorrect because a disorder in basic psychological processes would fall under a specific learning disability. Answer D is incorrect because an injury to the brain by an outside force would be in the "traumatic brain injury" category.

**15. D: Although all these choices can have positive and negative impacts, high school students commonly have the strongest social influences on academic engagement and performance coming from their peer groups. As a student enters high school, the locus of influence frequently moves from family involvement to friends. That said, when a child comes from a household in which both parents are present and supportive, it can have a huge impact on the access they have to educational support. Children who have little support in the home or come from broken homes have a high chance of struggling academically. The locus of influence for students is extremely variable, however, so it is important that teachers recognize that not all students will have a strong influence from either peer groups or family, and each student should be considered individually.**

**16. A:** The primary goal of a behavior plan is to increase certain behaviors that students may not be exhibiting. Students that struggle with participating in the class or social group may need a behavior plan that is targeted at increasing participation in the class. It is important to identify not only students who exhibit negative behaviors but also students who do not exhibit positive behaviors. Answer B is incorrect because the behavior plan is not designed to diagnose behaviors but rather to develop a plan for what to do when these behaviors occur or do not occur. Answer C is incorrect because the behavior plan is not focused on developing punishments. Answer D is incorrect because the behavior plan does not challenge any behaviors.

**17. A: Independent living skills goals focus on functional, teachable behaviors that support daily life after high school. Being able to access public transportation is a specific, measurable skill that can be taught and practiced. Answer B is incorrect because living with a roommate is a life outcome rather than a skill-based goal. Answer C is incorrect because living in a group home is a placement decision, not an instructional goal. Answer D is incorrect because attending community college is an educational outcome, not an independent living skill.**

**18. D:** When students suffer from deafness and blindness, they will receive services under the "deaf-blindness" category, according to the Individuals with Disabilities Education Act. Students who are either deaf or blind and also have a different disability would be considered under the multiple disabilities category. It is important to consider the impact that a disability has on a student so they can receive the services they need and are appropriately identified. Answer A is incorrect because speech issues are common with students who suffer from multiple disabilities. Answer B is incorrect because mobility issues are common when one of the impairments is physical. Answer C is incorrect because students with multiple disabilities are often impacted to the point where they need assistance throughout their lifetime.

**19. D:** Substance abuse can be an extremely detrimental environment factor, especially for those with mental health concerns. Substance abuse can either lead to mental health concerns in family members, or it can be a cause of concern in the student. It is important to understand some of the causes of the concerns that students are reporting in order to intervene as early as possible. Answer A is incorrect because although sleep deprivation can impact students with mental health concerns, it likely does not have the same impact as substance abuse. Answer B is incorrect because smoking is likely to have more of an impact on a person's physical health. Answer C is incorrect because although exposure to toxins can be detrimental to a person's health, it likely has more of an impact on physical health.

**20. C:** The constructivism theory states that learning motives are determined by the learner and by outside rewards from the community. Motivation comes not just from the learners themselves based on their knowledge but also through communicating with others. It is important to understand which approach to take when motivating students to achieve their highest potential. Answer A is incorrect because the behaviorism theory states that motivation is extrinsic. Answer B is incorrect because the cognitivism theory states that motivation for learning is intrinsic. Answer D is incorrect because the humanism theory states that motivation comes from inside the learner and is therefore intrinsic.

**21. A:** Several aspects of this prompt are important in understanding the best approach. It is common for students at this age to have trouble staying seated and focused for long periods of time. Therefore, all approaches should be based on the assumption that the child is not necessarily abnormal until the behavior becomes patterned and debilitative despite creative classroom strategies. The student is not only neglecting his own work but keeping others from focusing as well. Alternating physical activity and schoolwork will give the boy breaks to release physical energy and help "ground" himself for the work at hand. He may also feel more able to complete the work if it is broken down into smaller, more manageable segments.

**22. B:** For learning objectives to be measurable, they must be written in a way that can be quantifiably described. Answer B isn't measurable because it is impossible to quantify 20% of the English language. Answers A, C, and D are incorrect because they are all measurable. There are 26 letters in the alphabet, so answer A can be quantified. Half of a reading packet and one chapter of a book are also measurable quantities.

**23. A:** One general problem that elementary school teachers face when teaching culturally diverse students is that most textbooks introduce a large number of new concepts to be taught within a short time frame. Another problem is that many of these texts' teacher editions do not offer tips for meeting the needs of culturally diverse students (B). An additional problem is that the reading levels of most texts are too difficult for many diverse students (C). As a result, teachers must differentiate their instruction for diverse students in general education classrooms because the books they use will not preclude this need (D).

**24. C:** In planning lessons, teachers need to consider the skill or concept they want to teach and be sure to define it and not assume they already know what it is (A). They need to identify the prerequisites that students need to learn the new material, not assume that they already have them (B). They need to consider what is required for the students to master the material being taught (C). They should also think about how they can expand what they have taught and how to show students to apply their new learning in useful ways. Such planning is not premature (D) and should be part of the lesson plans.

**25. B:** Positive Behavioral Support is the most widely recommended and effective approach. The Individuals with Disabilities Education Act of 1997 requires schools to consider positive behavioral interventions and supports.

**26. C:** Each teacher should have a list of school and classroom rules posted in their classroom. Also, students should be fully aware of the consequences of not following the rules. If a student is unruly, the teacher should act according to their stated rules and consequences, and if the student's behavior does not improve, sending that student to the principal's office is the next step. A teacher must keep in mind that while they need to enforce the rules, they are responsible for the safety and educational needs of the other students, as well.

**27. A:** Making labels in more than one language is not confusing to the children. Rather, it is supportive of their home language (if it is not English), and bilingual or multilingual labels send the message that writing comes in a variety of shapes and languages. A print-rich environment includes labels to identify objects and work areas, print that is at a child's eye level so it can be seen easily, and print that was created by the children themselves so that they can make the connection between print and their own work. That connection between individual creation and print is reinforced when the teacher models writing by preparing posters and other written materials in front of the children.

**28. A:** Although each of these choices could be beneficial consequences for a third-grade student, having them skip recess is usually the least appropriate. Students with behavior needs often need sensory stimulation, which recess provides. It is also likely this student's favorite part of the day, and behavior may escalate if they have to skip it. Answer B could be an effective strategy in changing their behavior quickly. Answer C is beneficial in that a point sheet keeps them aware of and responsible for their own behavior. Answer D has the benefit of using behavioristic negative punishment that can help condition a reduction in negative behaviors, but it can be hard to make effective with students at this age as it is far removed from the action itself. For instance, if the student acts up at 9am, but the punishment does not take place until 2pm, the response may not be as strong as intended.

**29. D:** Students should always be warned that time-out is a potential consequence of their actions. The purpose behind this approach should always be to give the student time to think about his or her actions and to understand that certain behaviors are unacceptable in class. This consequence should never be used to shame or torture the child; therefore, it should always be connected to the undesired behavior before and after the event. By warning and then debriefing the child, he or she will have a better understanding of why the removal from the group was necessary. Forcing the child to apologize or to sit in repeated time-outs defeats the purpose of engaging the child in understanding and striving for better behavior.

**30. B:** A Renaissance festival would be crowded and noisy, with many different smells, sights, and sounds. The magnitude and variety of sensory stimuli would be overwhelming to most individuals with autism. Therefore, option A is incorrect.

A nature hike is likely to be in a quiet and tranquil environment. With plants as the main sensory stimuli, an autistic individual would have the opportunity to focus on examining them closely. Many autistic individuals are susceptible to sensory overload from environmental stimuli; many are also very good at focused, circumscribed activities wherein they can apply their intellectual abilities to specific tasks. Therefore, option B is correct.

A community mixer is a social event. Most people with autism have difficulty with social interactions. Typically, they have difficulty recognizing and interpreting social cues such as facial expressions and body language. In addition to the social emphasis, a mixer would also be noisy and crowded, which would be over-stimulating to an autistic student. Therefore, option C is incorrect.

A rock concert would involve over-amplified music, which can be painful to many individuals with autism. And it would be crowded with many people. Therefore, option D is incorrect.

**31. B:** Spending half the period with one student is not an efficient use of time. The extra attention does not speed up Jonathan's response time so it does not benefit him and it deprives other students of Ms. Lewis' attention. Therefore option A is incorrect.

Ms. Lewis should give the benefit of her instructional skills equally to all students. It is a good use of the aide's time to monitor Jonathan. She can make sure he is on task and let Ms. Lewis know when he has made a response. She can then monitor and help whichever other students Ms. Lewis is not working with at the time. Therefore option B is correct.

The fact that Corey and Jennifer simply work at the same speed is not a valid reason for Ms. Lewis to spend all her time with them, although it might be convenient. Each student should get equal time. Therefore option C is incorrect.

Though Michelle needs individual attention to stay focused, this does not mean Ms. Lewis should spend all her time with her. The aide can monitor and help her when Ms. Lewis is working with other students. Therefore option D is incorrect.

**32. B:** Because these two students come from a different culture, the two girls' behavior may be a result of differing cultural expectations instead of deliberate cheating. Given their backgrounds, Ms. George should be cognizant of these cultural differences and avoid penalizing them for their behavior. Punishing what is normal to them will only confuse them, so option A is incorrect. Since individual work is important in school settings, the teacher should work to properly explain classroom expectations in a culturally sensitive manner, so choice B is correct. The teacher could also consider assigning more group work, which the students may be more comfortable with.

Separating the girls would not be the best first action, as this could be seen as a punishment and make it harder for them to adapt to the new school setting. Due to their similar cultural backgrounds, the students are likely more comfortable working with each other, and separating them could lead to greater discomfort in the classroom.

Reporting the girls to the principal is punitive and unnecessary in this situation, so choice D is incorrect.

**33. C:** Ms. Hutchinson's technique was not accusatory or scolding. It would not likely induce guilt in someone as unrepentant as Ann. She asked a question that got Ann to consider others' points of view. Therefore, option A is incorrect.

Ms. Hutchinson did not model any behavior for Ann. She did not provide any examples of alternative behaviors. She simply asked Ann two questions. Therefore, option B is incorrect.

By asking Ann how she would feel if another student had done to her what she did, Ms. Hutchinson helped her overcome her egocentric thinking. Due to her intellectual disabilities, Ann thinks on a concrete operational level, and it will frequently not occur to her on her own to take another's perspective. She does have the ability to do this, though, with some help. Via this dialogue, Ms. Hutchinson got Ann to realize how the other students felt. Therefore, option C is correct.

Though Ms. Hutchinson did treat Ann with respect in this interaction and spoke to her as an equal, self-reliance and self-confidence were not issues that needed to be addressed in this case. Ann's rude behavior at the table did not show a lack of self-confidence. It showed a lack of self-management and self-awareness because she did not realize the impact of her actions on others. Therefore, option D is incorrect.

**34. A:** Journals of cognitive psychology are concerned with research in the study of memory, language processing, perception, problem-solving, and thinking. These are the exact areas in which Elise's students have educational needs. Therefore, option A is correct.

Applied behavioral analysis means applying experimentally-derived principles of behavior with the goal of improving social behavior. Journals on this subject would not address the cognitive needs of Elise's students. Therefore, option B is incorrect.

The Journal of the American Medical Association (JAMA) is a professional medical journal publishing peer-reviewed original medical research. It is a very popular journal among doctors. Its research articles would not typically address cognitive concerns. Therefore, option C is incorrect.

Journals of neuroscience research publish research results about the development, functions, and diseases of the nervous system, using molecular, cellular, and systems approaches. Diseases of the nervous system can affect cognitive processes. However, this research is not as directly related to studying the particular cognitive deficits of Elise's students as the journals of cognitive psychology are. Therefore, option D is incorrect.

**35. B:** Although some students may thrive in a structured routine, it is important for the teacher to be open to change and be flexible. It is possible that lesson plans or teaching strategies don't go as planned, so it is important for the teacher to be able to change the routine when needed. An overly rigid or structured routine could force the teacher and class into an ineffective plan. Students with disabilities will especially need flexibility from the teacher on a daily basis. Answer A is incorrect because every student in the class can benefit from a multisensory approach. Answer C is incorrect because developing clear rules and expectations allows the students to understand what they can and cannot do in the class. Answer D is incorrect because station learning can allow students to work with peers and learn using a variety of techniques.

**36. B:** A variety of emotional disturbances can impact the way students learn and process in both stressful and typical environments. The most generally appropriate strategy for helping Christina complete her work is to modify the environment by allowing her to work in a separate setting if she is unable to focus in the typical setting. Stress management techniques should also be taught, but they are a less direct method of helping Christina complete her classwork. Rewards for completing work may be additionally helpful in strengthening Christina's ability to stay calm and focused under stress, but they are generally not helpful in reducing stress after it has already occurred. Rewards are a method of cognitive-behavioral therapy, which can be an effective method of teaching a student how to handle stressful situations or redirect their own thinking patterns. Implemented incorrectly, behavior reinforcement can backfire and cause the negative behavior to be reinforced, rather than the intended behavior management skill. Providing Christina with choices about what work she does is not likely to be the best option; she needs to complete the work that is required by the curriculum. If she is able to accomplish the work that is assigned with less drastic modification, that is the better option.

**37. C:** For students with learning disabilities in the area of math, it is important to break down their learning to demonstrate how everything fits together. If they struggled with the previous lesson, they may need some additional instruction before they can move on to the next lesson. It is important that they are instructed at a speed and level that meet their needs and ensure that there is a smooth transition between topics. Answer A is incorrect because simply providing students with learning disabilities with more information may overwhelm them. Answer B is incorrect because ensuring that they understand the curriculum will likely occur as the lesson is being taught and not before. Answer D is incorrect because it may not be appropriate to challenge these students while learning is still occurring.

**38. B:** Although all of these choices may help in building a student's confidence, being patient and sticking with them can be valuable. Students with disabilities will often struggle with self-esteem and need someone to believe in them and that they can do it. Being patient with them and their needs allows them to make progress at their own pace without any pressure. Answer A is incorrect because if the material is too easy for students, they might not give their best effort. Answer C is incorrect because although working in groups can support confidence and social belonging when structured well, it is not universally successful and not the single most effective strategy given. Answer D is incorrect because although positive nonverbal communication can support a positive classroom environment, it is less impactful than patience.

**39. B:** For teachers who like to use a lot of discussion in their class, one strategy is to have the desks facing each other. This allows the students to communicate directly to each other and have conversations rather than the teacher doing most of the talking. This can also allow everyone in the class, including students with disabilities, to feel needed and included in the group. Answer A is incorrect because most classrooms likely do not have enough space to accommodate a meeting area large enough for multiple students. Additionally, a meeting area would not support on-going classroom discussion throughout the day in the same way that having desks always facing each other would. Answer C is incorrect because although having tables might be helpful, it may be difficult for students to communicate with everyone in the class when they are at a table. Answer D is incorrect because although ensuring that students can move around is beneficial, it is more important that they can communicate with each other.

**40. D:** In order to measure reading fluency, it is essential to provide a student with a reading passage and record how many words they can read in one minute. This can help to determine how much progress a student has made and what they may still need to work on. Reading fluency is an important skill for a third grader to practice each day by reading passages and developing a clear understanding of words. Answer A is incorrect because identifying letters is a skill that students typically work on before third grade. Answer B is incorrect because although identifying letter sounds can be important, it is not always the best indicator of reading fluency ability. Answer C is incorrect because although reading sight words can help with reading fluency skills, it is not a measure of reading fluency by itself.

**41. D:** In order for objectives to be time-bound, there must be a date that the objective is to be reached. This is important for ensuring that students are making adequate progress in a timely manner. If the objectives are not bound by time, then it is harder to evaluate progress and determine whether they have been achieved within an appropriate time frame. Answer A is incorrect because the progress toward the achievement is considered the measure of the goal. Answer B is incorrect because using a reasonable amount of resources shows how achievable an objective may be. Answer C is incorrect because the use of objectives leading to a desired goal is a component of relevant or realistic objectives.

**42. A:** Although all these strategies may be helpful in creating a meaningful learning experience for Gordon, connecting the content to real-life experiences can have the most value. Students with intellectual disabilities often learn best by practicing the content they learn rather than simply hearing about it. Because of this, applying what they learn will likely help them remember more for longer. Answer B is incorrect because simply making the content student-centered may not always provide meaning to these students. Answer C is incorrect because promoting self-knowledge would likely be a better strategy for students who can explore opportunities independently. Answer D is incorrect because simply having many resources may not necessarily provide much meaning.

**43. D:** Although all of these choices may be beneficial in certain situations, it would likely be a good idea to send home a brief daily summary of how the student did in class that day. It would be a good practice to have the general education teachers report to the special education teacher each day about the student's positive and negative behaviors, which then would be communicated home. It is typically most effective to have just one person being the point of contact for the parents to make it more efficient. Answer A is incorrect because the student may have issues that need to be reinforced throughout the week, so this likely would not be often enough. Answer B is incorrect because it likely would not be as beneficial for the parents to be contacted multiple times throughout the day by different teachers. Answer C is incorrect because the school psychologist may or may not be able to contact the parents each day and there may be concerns or other areas that need to be communicated through the special education teacher.

**44. B:** When working with students in small-group pull-outs, it is important that the instruction is targeted to their IEP goals. Although each student may have a different goal, the teacher must plan the lesson in a way that fits in parts of each student's goal. Students may or may not have access to the special education teacher throughout the day, so it is vital to monitor and develop these goals when working with students in small groups. Answer A is incorrect because although it is important for students to access their accommodations, they would likely access these in the general education setting. Answer C is not the best answer because, in this particular small-group setting, the most important focus is intensive instruction on students' IEP writing goals; however, these goals and lessons should still be aligned with the general education curriculum so that students can make progress in it. Answer D is incorrect because students do not need to access an alternate curriculum to work on IEP goals.

**45. D:** Although all these choices could potentially be an issue for teachers who teach students with a wide range of needs, differentiating instruction is likely to be difficult. Differentiated instruction includes strategies to provide a curriculum that meets the needs of all the students in the class. It can be difficult to differentiate or change the curriculum for so many students in one class in a way that meets their needs. Answer A is incorrect because IEP goals can be monitored at various times and not necessarily in one class period. Answer B is incorrect because the teacher will still need to provide the accommodations for each student. Answer C is incorrect because the teacher must still incorporate the assistive technology if a student needs it in class to access the curriculum.

**46. C:** Adaptive behavior scales are used to determine which independent living skills a student has and what the student may need to work on. These assessments are typically used for students with intellectual disabilities or other severe disabilities to understand what instruction needs to be implemented. These tests typically consist of an evaluation of a student's social skills, daily living skills, communication skills, and other skills that the student will need after high school. Answer A is incorrect because the primary purpose of these scales is to identify skill deficits, not to diagnose behavior problems. Answer B is incorrect because the adaptive behavior scale is not used to determine whether or not a student needs a behavior plan. Answer D is incorrect because while adaptive behavior scales can inform curriculum, answer C is more specific about what needs to be taught (independent living skills).

**47. A:** Allowing Emma to give a slideshow presentation instead of presenting orally is the best way for her to access the same curriculum as her peers. This way, she is able to prepare and learn the same material as everyone else. Access to the curriculum involves providing opportunities for students with disabilities to learn the same material as their peers. Answer B is incorrect because if she skipped the assignment, she wouldn't gain the knowledge. Answer C is incorrect because having her aide present for her does not provide her with the opportunity to give a presentation. Answer D is incorrect because although she would still learn some of the same material as her peers, she wouldn't get a chance to present.

**48. A:** Textbooks incorporate informational structure, such as presenting items in chronological order, comparisons and contrasts, and pointing out causal relationships. They also use informational features such as boldface type, sub-headings, bullet points, review questions, glossaries, an index, etc., to assist students in organizing, remembering, and applying information, even though many students may not use them. The simplest, most direct, and most efficient way that Mr. Stewart can help his students is to point these out and explain how to use them. Creating separate handouts (B) takes more time and work and may duplicate what the text already does. Graphic organizers (C) are excellent aids, especially for students who learn more visually than verbally, but they also involve more work than using the text. Mr. Stewart's students have good reading comprehension but cannot organize whole chapters. A slide show is an excellent supplement to the text but should not replace an explanation of the text's informational aids.

**49. D:** Ms. Ross is presenting new words in multiple exposures to enhance vocabulary acquisition. Appropriate word choice (A) entails selecting words that are best suited to the particular instruction. Teaching word analysis (B) entails identifying word roots, prefixes, and suffixes, which greatly facilitates figuring out the meanings of new words. Contextual analysis (C) involves figuring out the meanings of new words by the context in which they occur.

**50. B:** Using multilevel teaching practices is an effective method to teach word recognition to a class of students with many reading levels and diverse needs. Giving direct instruction to individual students (A) is very effective but not efficient, and it can be impossible for one teacher to do this with typical class sizes. Creating smaller groups for each level (D) is similarly inefficient, as the teacher could end up with too many groups to teach in the time allowed. Teaching to the median (C) leaves out too many students who are below or above the medium range that the median targets. Multilevel practices address a variety of reading levels and allow adaptations for special student needs.

**51. A:** Explicit instruction involves clarifying the goal, modeling strategies, and offering explanations geared to a student's level of understanding. Explicit instruction is well organized and structured. It offers easily understood steps and depends in part on frequent reference to previously learned materials.

**52. C:** Use graph paper to help him organize. Show him how to write the problems, keeping each number in a box aligned with other numbers. This will help him determine which numbers are in the ones group, the tens group, the hundreds group, and so on.

**53. D:** Modifications of the curriculum alter the curriculum that is being taught, and these students are expected to complete assessments different than those of their peers. Access to alternative books changes what the student is learning and therefore would change the expectations for the assignment. Answers A, B, and C are all accommodations that allow students to access the same curriculum as their peers with alterations to how the material is presented. Textbooks with large print, computers for typing, and manipulatives are all accommodations to allow students to access the curriculum.

**54. A:** Generalization of learning is the ability to apply learning across multiple and varied contexts or settings. Regular practice and periodic testing (B) are designed to promote maintenance rather than generalization. Learning one step at a time (C) is a characteristic of task analysis, which breaks complex skills or tasks down into more achievable steps and is related to promoting skill acquisition rather than generalization. Practicing a new skill before applying it to real-life situations (D) is a way to promote both acquisition and maintenance of the skill before its application and generalization.

**55. C:** Since Joseph has never walked the route alone, he would get lost if sent out on his own now. Therefore, option A is incorrect.

Sending Joseph out with written directions is not a good idea since he does not have good reading skills. He would likely get lost if he went out alone without prior practice in finding his way. A teacher shadowing him would have to catch up with him to redirect him when he went the wrong way or stopped when he did not know which way to go. Therefore, option B is incorrect.

Since Joseph is used to walking the route with his mother, it would be better to accompany him at first. Doing so would provide a point from which to transition gradually to walking alone. Unlike his mother, the teacher will be prompting him to verbalize the route. Since his expressive language skills are better than his reading skills, this is a more effective modality to help him learn the directions. Therefore, option C is correct.

Gradually decreasing the days his mother goes with him, such as by having her go four days and having him go alone one day, then having her go three days and having him go alone two days, is not a good idea. Joseph's mother has never taught him the route, so he does not know the directions and cannot find his way independently. Since he has always relied on his mother, he would get lost the first time he tried to go on his own. Therefore, option D is incorrect.

**56. B:** Since he is blind, Bert could not read a printed or written worksheet or circle and cross out word pairs. Therefore, option A is incorrect.

Both students could listen to word pairs read aloud. Even with poor fine motor skills, Nan has the gross motor skills to raise her hands. Therefore, option B is correct.

As Nan has poor fine motor skills, she might have difficulty circling or crossing out words, especially since she is only in first grade. Therefore, option C is incorrect.

Having Nan read a list of word pairs aloud to Bert would give Bert but not Nan the opportunity to show recognition of rhymes. Therefore, option D is incorrect.

**57. A:** For a third-grade student working on basic decoding, multisensory techniques engage visual, auditory, and kinesthetic pathways to support accurate letter-sound decoding, helping students recognize and blend sounds into words. While explicit teaching, metacognitive strategies, and text structuring are valuable for reading comprehension and general instruction, they are less targeted to decoding skills. This realignment ensures the construct being tested (decoding) matches the correct answer.

**58. D:** The fact that Fred is a year older does not automatically imply that he would simply "grow out of" his outbursts, especially since he has a history of them. In other words, they do not reflect a new or temporary behavioral phase; therefore, option A is incorrect.

It is probably true that Fred is happier having the computer, but there is no way of knowing whether he was bored before or not. There is not enough information to know if his outbursts of anger were related to not having his attention sufficiently occupied; therefore, option B is incorrect.

It is not accurate to say that there is no information given to explain the improvement in Fred's behavior. It has been stated that he is deaf, autistic, and does not speak. From these facts, it can be inferred that he very well may not have enough ways to communicate in school; therefore, option C is incorrect.

Before, Fred could not express himself verbally despite his good receptive language skills. Now that he can type his thoughts and feelings, it is logical that his frustration would decrease and hence his outbursts; therefore, option D is correct.

**59. A:** Although all these choices may be beneficial to certain students, setting up an appointment with the school's art teacher will be a good way for her to get some information from an artist. This will allow her to see what options she may have to choose from and which paths she could potentially go down. Discussing this information with someone who has likely been in a similar situation can help to provide clarity and direction. Answer B is incorrect because simply researching schools may or may not help her narrow down what her plan and goal might be. Answer C is incorrect because just talking to employees at local art galleries may not provide much information about becoming an artist. Answer D is incorrect because although a vocational test might be helpful, it won't give her much specific information about becoming an artist.

**60. A:** Although all of these choices may be beneficial to certain students, providing a graphic organizer would be most beneficial for students who struggle with organizing their writing because it gives them a framework for how to set it up. Many students struggle to organize their writing and stay on topic, and the graphic organizer is designed to help with this. Answer B is incorrect because simply modeling the writing likely is not enough support for many students. Answer C is incorrect because practice without organizational support does not address the underlying difficulty. Answer D is incorrect because peer collaboration may support idea development, but it does not directly teach students how to structure and focus their writing.

**61. B:** Assisting the student in seeking support from the online teacher would likely be the most helpful for the student out of the options listed. Students who take online classes often struggle to understand how to seek help or who to contact if they need it. The question notes that the student often has trouble seeking help, so this would be a good first step.

The question also notes that the student struggles with communication in social situations, so face-to-face instruction likely would not be helpful. Option C focuses on assessment instead of instructional access. Option D focuses on administrative responsibility, which would not directly help the student access online instruction.

**62. D:** Although all these choices may be beneficial for students who struggle with reading comprehension, using a tablet allows the student to practice reading and answering questions. It is important for students to practice these skills as much as possible in order to improve them. For many students, using a tablet to read a story may yield better results than simply reading the story and taking a quiz or test. Answer A is incorrect because although audiobooks can be a useful accommodation, it would likely be more productive to have students practice the skill of reading independently when focusing on reading comprehension. Answer B is incorrect because although this may be helpful for students, practicing their comprehension skills is likely a better strategy. Answer C is incorrect because speech-to-text software would be more effective for students who struggle with writing.

**63. A:** Although all these choices certainly have an impact, it is best that the students are grouped by ability level. Each student will have different IEP goals and progress toward those goals, so it is important to place students in groups that will allow for this progress. It may be difficult for students to make progress on these goals if they are in small groups in which they are not working at an appropriate instructional level. Answer B is incorrect because grouping students on their grade level may not help them make progress on their IEP goals because students might be at various skill levels. Answer C is incorrect because simply grouping students based on their teachers also may involve grouping students at various ability levels. Answer D is incorrect because although grouping students based on maturity level might be important, some students with similar maturity levels function at different academic levels.

**64. C:** In order to understand why student behaviors have increased or declined, it is important to collect data before making major changes. Providing support to a student one on one is a significant change to the instruction that the student receives, so it should not be implemented until data have been collected on the student. These data might include what times of the day these behaviors arise or what kind of interactions may be involved with certain behaviors. Answer A is incorrect because the behavior may simply be a short-term situation in which the student does not display them consistently. Answer B is incorrect because although it may be a good thing to discuss at the annual IEP meeting, these do not always fall at the same time that changes need to be implemented. Answer D is incorrect because student suspensions do not necessarily dictate the level of support that a student receives in a class.

**65. B:** Speech-to-text devices are typically designed for students who struggle with writing rather than reading fluency. These speech-to-text devices are valuable in allowing students to speak what they might be thinking, and that is transferred into text. It is important to understand which technology is valuable and works for each student based on their individual needs and interests. Answer A is incorrect because text-to-speech devices can be beneficial in assisting students that may struggle to read the text without making mistakes. Answer C is incorrect because audiobooks provide students like Jeffrey a way to access the text without having to read it. Answer D is incorrect because graphic organizers can be beneficial in organizing the story for students who may struggle to put together what they have read.

**66. A:** Although all of these examples may help students who struggle with reading comprehension, text-to-speech programs are best in allowing the student to access the curriculum. Text-to-speech programs provide students with reading comprehension problems the opportunity to listen to the same story that the rest of the class is reading. It is important to provide students access to the general education curriculum whenever possible. Answer B is incorrect because watching videos of the story won't always give them all of the information that they need in the story. Answer C is incorrect because an online activity may leave out some of what the rest of the class is doing. Answer D is incorrect because electronic worksheets may be more beneficial after the story has been read.

**67. D:** Although all of these strategies may be useful for Bobby in the long term, having a job is something that he is likely going to need the most. Students who are at risk and infrequently see their parents need to develop some of these independent skills sooner than other students. Because of this, they are more likely to need a job in order to be able to provide for themselves. Answer A is incorrect because students like Bobby may or may not even be thinking about going to college. Answer B is incorrect because simply giving him extra support may not help him very much in the long-term. Answer C is incorrect; since Bobby will likely need to be self-sufficient after graduating high school, he will need the financial means to do so. Although teaching him executive functioning skills may be helpful, he is more likely to need immediate assistance in finding a job after graduation.

**68. A:** The use of manipulatives in which students get to use their hands can help them learn new concepts, especially in math. Being able to see where objects go and touching the objects allow students with intellectual disabilities to get more involved. Although these students are often visual learners, manipulatives can help in areas such as math and science. Answer B is incorrect because enjoyment is not an instructional justification. Answer C is incorrect because manipulatives are not designed to help students learn classroom rules. Answer D is incorrect because manipulatives typically do not help students communicate.

**69. C:** Students who struggle with math calculations will likely need an alternative teaching method in order to memorize facts. These students have likely used many of the traditional methods but continue to struggle. The use of visual aids allows students to see the numbers in a different way, which allows them to find a new approach to memorizing these facts. Answer A is incorrect because worksheets do not provide these students with an opportunity to practice an alternative teaching method that they have not already seen. Answer B is incorrect because flash cards tend to be difficult for students who struggle with math because they are unable to memorize facts easily. Answer D is incorrect because although group projects may be beneficial to some students, their use may not support students who struggle with memorizing facts.

**70. C:** Although each student may respond differently to challenging tasks, many students with ADHD will shut down if a task becomes too difficult. It is important to understand and recognize what the student is able to accomplish before challenging them. It can be embarrassing or cause anxiety for students who are unable to fulfill the challenge of the teacher. Answer A is incorrect because offering choices to the students allows them to feel like they are a part of the decision making. Answer B is incorrect because hands-on learning activities allow students to get up and move around. Answer D is incorrect because repeating the instructions often ensures that each student hears what is expected and does not forget.

**71. B:** Multisensory strategies, including the use of touch in manipulating letters or tapping the letters with their fingers, can be effective strategies for students with dyslexia. This sensory approach allows them to break down words and memorize them in different ways. Answer A is incorrect because the whole-word approach does not tend to be as effective for students with dyslexia. Answers C is incorrect because, while it may be useful, modeling is not as effective for addressing reading skills as using multisensory strategies. Answer D is incorrect because graphic organizers typically help students with comprehension and idea organization rather than with the reading challenges typically associated with dyslexia.

**72. A:** Assigning Bobby a separate, easier text would prevent him from engaging with the same content as his peers, not support him in accessing the subject matter. Answer B is incorrect because having more hands-on learning activities could make it easier for Bobby to learn. Answer C is incorrect because having choices and including each student in the selection process will likely make them more eager to learn. Answer D is incorrect because the use of technology, such as computers, may make the learning easier and more effective.

**73. D:** Students should be taught that writing is a process. By applying spelling patterns found in word families, the spelling of many words can be deduced. The other options are incorrect statements regarding teaching spelling. It is not true that knowing letter-sound association is enough alone to know how to spell. Simply knowing the origin of the root word, though potentially helpful, does not make instruction unnecessary. Drilling spelling exercises is often not the most effective long-term method of teaching spelling, as it can lead to frustration and a lack of interest on the part of the students.

**74. A:** The teacher's explication of the poem made its concept accessible to this student, who found it meaningful once he understood it. From his response, he found the message more meaningful than entertaining (B). While providing students with choices (C) and enough opportunities to read (D) are also teaching strategies that enhance reading proficiency, neither one was mentioned in this particular example. The teacher chose the short poem, and it was an example of only one small opportunity to read.

**75. A:** Executive function includes planning, organizing, keeping track of time, keeping track of multiple things, relating earlier learning to current learning, and other higher cognitive activities. Self-regulation (B) relates only to talking out of turn in class and is just one component of executive function. Sequencing (C) involves arranging items in the correct order (chronological, logical, etc.) and is also one specific aspect of executive function. Memory (D), or retaining and retrieving information, requires using mental strategies that are included in executive function.

**76. B:** It is an informal assessment of their writing and also gives the teacher an idea of each student's interests, abilities, and skills. This assignment gives the teacher an idea of her students' writing abilities at the beginning of the year. She can return to this piece of writing during the school year to assess progress.

**77. A:** A student's ability to retell a story they heard demonstrates the degree of auditory comprehension. An informal reading inventory (B) can assess a student's reading fluency, reading comprehension, etc., rather than assessing the student's understanding of what they hear. Curriculum-based assessment (C) tests whether students have learned the curriculum content taught through a broad approach, rather than focusing testing on a specific learning skill area like auditory comprehension, which is not a content area. Periodic fluency checking (D) is a way to monitor students' reading fluency rather than their listening comprehension.

**78. C:** The primary purpose of universal newborn hearing screenings is early identification of hearing loss, which affords early intervention. Professional organizations such as ASHA advocate universal screening because not all infants are screened even though hearing loss is the most common congenital disability. Educational planning (A) is a purpose of later educational testing of a child, not of newborn hearing screening. Disability diagnosis (B) requires a complete audiological evaluation defining type, degree, and configuration of hearing loss instead of just a screening, because that only identifies presence or absence of hearing loss. Eligibility for special education services under the IDEA (D) is a purpose of later, comprehensive assessments of preschool- and school-aged students, not infants.

**79. B:** Criterion-referenced tests are tests in which all students can achieve a score of 100%, assuming that they know all the material on the test. These tests measure only the students' knowledge of the material taught in the class. Often these tests will be "teacher made." Any subject test that is related directly to the material taught is considered a criterion-referenced test. Also, when taking a test of this type, students are not competing for the highest score, as all students have equal opportunity to achieve the highest score.

**80. A:** The teacher needs to know how well each student is doing and must teach each child. The teacher is striving for a quality learning experience for every child rather than averages or high percentages measured by a groupwide evaluation. It is true that evaluation must be part of every lesson, in some form or another, or else the teacher will not know if the objective was reached and if some or all students need a re-teach. This evaluation can continue with retention checks in other lessons—that is, on an ongoing basis—and may be repeated in overall unit tests.

**81. B:** The comparison of one student's rank to that of other students is called a percentile rank. Therefore, option A is incorrect.

Where the student's score falls relative to the average or mean score among all students is the definition of a standard score. It shows how far above or below the mean a student's score falls. Therefore, option B is correct.

Standard scores are not limited to assessing only how a student's score compares to others within the same grade. Because all scores are converted to the same numerical scale, standard scores can be used to compare students from different grades. Therefore, option C is incorrect.

Standard scores can be used to compare students of different age groups because scores are all converted to the same numerical scale. Therefore, option D is incorrect.

**82. C:** Removing Stephanie from the classroom is not the answer. This would deprive her of an education in the least restrictive setting. None of the given information indicates that her behaviors only occur in the classroom, so they could very well continue outside of class. Therefore, option A is incorrect.

Differential reinforcement of low behavior (DRL), of alternative behavior (DRA), or of other behavior (DRO) is a behavior modification technique that could be effective depending on the types of behaviors and why Stephanie is engaging in them. But the types of behaviors are not specified in the question. Without knowing why they are occurring, it is impossible to know if this is an appropriate intervention plan or not. Therefore, option B is incorrect.

Conducting a functional behavioral assessment is a way to find out the purposes of Stephanie's behaviors. Only when her team members know why she is doing what she does can they plan appropriate and effective intervention. The functional behavioral assessment should be their first step. Therefore, option C is correct.

Maladaptive behaviors have many different etiologies and serve many different purposes. It cannot be assumed from the information given that Stephanie's instructional plan is the reason for her behaviors. In the behavioral aspect, her IEP is not optimally meeting her needs or she may not have had an IEP written for her yet; this information is not given. In fact, the reason her IEP team is meeting may be to write her first IEP. It would do no good to write a different plan, or a new one, without first doing a functional behavior assessment to uncover the reasons behind Stephanie's behaviors. Therefore, option D is incorrect.

**83. A:** Developmental assessments are designed to find strengths and weaknesses in young students who may be exhibiting some delays. In order to do this, students are compared with what the average student is capable of doing in many developmental categories. These assessments can be effective in intervening in students early who may be struggling. Answer B is incorrect because a quick identifying assessment that would be used is typically referred to as a screener. Answer C is incorrect because a behavior rating scale typically identifies just the behavior of students of all ages. Answer D is incorrect because an alternative assessment is typically used for students with disabilities who cannot access standardized tests.

**84. C:** Developmental assessments typically do not include tests that would determine a student eligible for a specific learning disability. Although these developmental assessments are beneficial in determining what a student may struggle with, it is difficult to determine the academic skills of children at such a young age. Specific learning disabilities typically manifest as students have had more instruction in reading, writing, and math. Answer A is incorrect because the developmental disability category is common for preschool students who are struggling in certain developmental areas. Answer B is incorrect because speech or language impairments are also common with preschool students. Answer D is incorrect because students with a diagnosis of autism are often identified in the autism spectrum disorder category as a preschooler.

**85. D:** TerraNova is an example of a standardized test rather than a curriculum-based assessment. Curriculum-based assessments are designed to monitor the progress of students regularly, whereas standardized tests are given annually or semiannually to compare students to a norm. It is difficult to measure the progress of students on their IEP goals if they aren't monitored frequently. Answer A is incorrect because DIBELS is a common curriculum-based assessment that measures a student's abilities in reading. Answer B is incorrect because AIMSweb produces many curriculum-based assessment probes in the areas of reading, writing, and math. Answer C is incorrect because EasyCBM also assesses a student using curriculum-based assessment probes in many subjects.

**86. B:** The Woodcock-Johnson Tests of Achievement can be used to determine a child's academic strengths compared with his or her peers and to determine special education eligibility. This is a test that can be used for children aged 2 through adulthood. This test includes specific subtests to identify skill deficits in the areas of reading, writing, and math. Answer A is incorrect because a CogAT test is used to test a student's cognitive ability. Answer C is incorrect because the Myers-Briggs Type Indicator is a personality test. Answer D is incorrect because the SAT is not used to test for learning disabilities.

**87. C:** Unit pretests would typically be considered an example of a diagnostic assessment rather than a formative assessment. Formative assessments are designed to assess students as the learning is occurring, rather than before or after. It is important to informally assess the students while learning occurs in order to determine if the instruction needs to be adjusted. Answer A is incorrect because analyzing student work is a beneficial formative assessment in discovering what the students are capable of. Answer B is incorrect because questioning the students as the learning takes place gives the teacher an understanding of what the students know. Answer D is incorrect because exit tickets can allow the students to demonstrate what they have learned and what they still struggle with at the end of a lesson.

**88. B:** Assessing a student using a diagnostic test is beneficial in providing a baseline score for what the student is able to do. Gerald's baseline score in reading fluency would give the teacher an idea of how fluently he reads and what areas still need to be improved upon. From there, the teacher can develop a lesson plan based on the results of this diagnostic assessment. Answer A is incorrect because progress cannot be measured until the instruction has occurred. Answer C is incorrect because diagnostic assessments typically measure where the individual is rather than comparing them with peers. Answer D is incorrect because a diagnostic assessment likely would not provide information about which accommodations to use.

**89. B:** Although there are many benefits to using curriculum-based assessments (CBAs), they do not always correlate perfectly to the classroom curriculum. Curriculum-based assessments are designed to monitor the progress of student understanding throughout instructional units to help quickly adjust instruction to meet student needs. CBAs are commonly used in conjunction with IEPs as a means of ensuring students with learning disabilities are making progress toward their particular goals. CBAs do not comprehensively measure curriculum mastery but only serve as samples of student comprehension. Answer A is incorrect because curriculum-based assessments can measure the progress of students over a short period of time such as one week. Answer C is incorrect because a teacher's instruction can be informed based on the needs of the student and what they may need to work on. Answer D is incorrect because students can chart their scores and work toward improving them.

**90. B:** In order to be eligible for the developmental delay category, students must be age 9 or younger. There are many impairments that are included within the category, but students must be a certain age. According to IDEA, a student like Mary would likely be eligible in a different category because of her developmental disability. Answer A is incorrect because the developmental delay category does include students with physical impairments. Answer C is incorrect because students with developmental disabilities such as physical or emotional impairments would be eligible for the category if they meet the age requirements. Answer D is incorrect because students younger than age 10 are included in the category.

**91. D:** The purpose of the prereferral process is to put supports in place before obtaining consent for a special education evaluation. Obtaining consent would typically occur after the referral for special education services rather than during the prereferral process. The prereferral process is important in determining whether or not the student needs to be evaluated for special education services. Answer A is incorrect because evaluating a student's strengths and weaknesses is important to determine which supports need to be put into place. Answer B is incorrect because putting accommodations and interventions into place is helpful in evaluating what works for a student and what doesn't. Answer C is incorrect because evaluating the accommodations and interventions is important in deciding if they need to be continued or if another action should take place.

**92. B:** The standard score in an assessment is used to give the student a numbered score in order to compare that number to the average. Many tests will consider 100 to be the average standard score based on the results of the assessments. Students will then be given standard scores that are compared to that average score. Answer A is incorrect because the standard deviation typically determines how spread out the numbers are. Answer C is incorrect because comparing the rank of the score to other students is considered the percentile rank. Answer D is incorrect because the hypothetical range of scores is considered the confidence interval.

**93. A:** In order to assess a student for oral expression abilities, a test to measure their expressive language abilities is most appropriate. Students who struggle with oral expression tend to struggle expressing themselves orally due to many factors. This kind of assessment can guide the data collection needed for instruction in the classroom and skills to work on. Answer B is incorrect because receptive language assessments are more appropriate for students who struggle with language input rather than output. Answer C is incorrect because auditory discrimination tests are used for students who struggle with different sounds. Answer D is incorrect because this kind of assessment would be more appropriate in measuring a student's cognitive abilities.

**94. A:** Although the results of standardized assessments can be valuable tools, it is difficult to monitor the progress of the students when these tests are taken infrequently. It is best to monitor student growth frequently in order to determine if new interventions need to be put in place. When relying on tests that are only taken once or twice per year, it can be difficult to monitor progress. Answer B is incorrect because curriculum-based assessments can be given to students at any time to chart their progress. Answer C is incorrect because classroom observations can be beneficial for evaluating students with behavior goals. Answer D is incorrect because classroom grades can help to determine which subjects a student may struggle with.

**95. B:** Although there can be many benefits of standardized tests for students with disabilities, one of the most useful is in determining class placement. These results show what a student is capable of doing, typically in the areas of reading, writing, and math, and comparing them with their peers. This allows teachers to best determine which instruction they are capable of receiving and what they still need to improve upon. Answer A is incorrect because standardized tests would likely not be able to determine which accommodations a student needs to access. Answer C is incorrect because IEP goals and objectives typically rely more on classroom instruction or achievement test data. State standardized test scores are usually too infrequent to be used as the primary basis for IEP goals. Answer D is incorrect because the least restrictive environment for a student is dependent on many factors, not simply a standardized assessment.

**96. C:** Although it is not always easy or possible to eliminate every bias that a person might have, it is important not to make any assumptions. It is important to be sensitive to student needs especially when working with students with disabilities or from various cultural backgrounds. Assessments should be geared toward the content that students should know rather than the opinions that a teacher may have. Answer A is incorrect because it may not always be possible or realistic to get to know the background of every student in the class. Answer B is incorrect because each assessment will be different, and it may not be possible or the best assessment of student knowledge to include multicultural questions. Answer D is incorrect because it is not appropriate or the best practice to evaluate each student differently.

**97. D:** The child's transition can be eased by visiting the classroom, meeting the teacher and her new classmates, and having the opportunity to ask questions about the change she is about to make. When she is able to visualize what the classroom looks like, meet the people that will become her new educational "family," and have her concerns and questions addressed, she will know what to expect and feel more confident about the transition.

**98. B:** The prereferral stage of the IEP process includes interventions and other activities in the general education classroom to screen students before any formal referral is made for special education. Testing classroom accommodations and modifications for effectiveness is one of these activities. If accommodations, validated teaching methods, instructional modifications, consultation, and help from specialists do not remedy learning problems, the next step is referral. After that, identification (A) is made and eligibility (C) is determined for special education services. Review (D) of the IEP is made after it has been implemented to evaluate progress and, if necessary, change the IEP.

**99. A: By law, a major review of the IEP is required every year. In 2004, an IDEA pilot study attempted to reduce paperwork and administrative duties and some participating states allowed for reviews once every three years. However, it is standard to have an annual IEP review meeting to review a student's services and needs and assess the student's progress toward their goals. As a student's social, behavioral, familial, or health-related factors change, an IEP review may be necessary to address changes in services or needs. Other aspects of a student's eligibility may follow different cycle times, such as eligibility criteria, which may need to be reviewed once every three years, depending on state law.**

**100. A:** A child with intellectual disabilities; hearing, speech, language, visual, orthopedic, or other health impairments; emotional disturbance; autism; brain injury caused by trauma; or specific learning disabilities who needs special education and related services. Children with one or more of these conditions are legally entitled to services and programs designed to help them achieve at the highest level of their ability.

**101. A:** Are results-oriented, includes post-school activities, vocational education, employment support, adult services and considers the individual's strengths, preferences and interests. Additional activities that compose Secondary Transition are instruction, related services, community experiences, the development of employment and other post-school adult living objectives and, if appropriate, acquisition of daily living skills and functional vocational evaluation.

**102. A:** The IDEA annual reports to Congress consistently show that specific learning disability is the most common disability. Recent IDEA annual reports show that speech or language impairment and other health impairment are also among the largest disability categories, but specific learning disability remains the most common.

**103. C:** The teacher should immediately refer him to the counselor. The boy is exhibiting serious emotional distress suggesting depression, trauma, or even abuse at home or elsewhere. While his behavior may seem manipulative, the fact that the boy is unreachable once he's in the highly charged emotional state in which he repeats, "I hate myself" suggests emotional trauma. The fact the child is socializing with peers, playing with them when invited, and not taking rejection personally suggests his emotional distress may be caused by an adult who has convinced him he is unworthy. A trained counselor is the best choice.

**104. C:** There are many items included in an Individual Education Plan. These plans are designed to provide the school and other supporting personnel with enough information to offer the best possible educational experience and support for the student. Most plans include the date of implementation, signatures of the parent and student, health information, equipment the student will need in the classroom, and required personnel for the student. These plans also detail the additional time that the student requires in terms of support or tutoring, test results, goals, objectives, and desired outcomes. However, one item typically not listed in the IEP is the family's medical history or history of disabilities.

**105. A:** The No Child Left Behind Act, signed in 2001, was created to place additional accountability on schools and school districts for the education of today's children. Additionally, this legislation decreased the restrictions on schools' use of federal funding and placed particular emphasis on reading and math. Schools and teachers nationwide were challenged and encouraged to use innovative teaching activities and methods in order to reach all students. This legislation also required schools and school districts to submit progress reports on an annual basis for inclusion in national education databases.

**106. A:** School psychologists are trained to administer IQ tests to students. Although it is possible for the special education teacher to assist in this process, IQ tests are typically administered by the psychologist. Answer B is incorrect because achievement tests are most often administered by the special education teacher. Answer C is incorrect because progress monitoring is completed by the special education case manager. Answer D is incorrect because transition planning inventories are also administered by the special education teacher.

**107. C:** What is true is not that teachers should spend less time or only their own time for professional development, but that teachers should actually spend more time—at least 20% of their work time—in professional study and collaborative work. Professional development is an essential part of teaching, and it is, therefore, legitimate to provide professional development opportunities during work time. Furthermore, it is also reasonable to expect teachers to incorporate continuous learning for themselves during the school day. Option A is what some critics of time spent on professional development say, but it shows a lack of understanding of the complexity and needs of the classroom teacher. Option B is also a common comment of critics of the educational system, but this criticism does not exhibit an understanding of the changes in education that require teachers to need education themselves in order to keep up. Option D is another common complaint from people who resent teachers being out of the classroom for professional development. Such complaints show a lack of understanding about the need for extensive, continuous professional development and a failure to recognize that time restraints might require taking teachers out of the classroom to accommodate the requirement.

**108. B:** Specific learning disability is a disorder that affects a person's ability to listen, think, speak, read, write, spell, or do math. Auditory processing disorder affects a person's ability to listen. Answer A is incorrect because speech or language impairment is its own category of disability. Answers C and D are incorrect because each of these falls under other disability categories and not specific learning disability.

**109. C:** Assessing a young child for learning disabilities often leads to an incorrect conclusion because a student must be taught the subject before it is possible to assess her understanding of it. Intervention teaches the child specific skills to correct her misconceptions. If the intervention fails, assessment is the next step. Because formal diagnoses of specific learning disabilities can be less reliable at very young ages, teachers typically begin with classroom interventions and progress monitoring, referring for a formal evaluation if concerns persist over time.

**110. A:** When parents request an IEE, the testing must be administered by someone who is not employed by the school district. Parents have the right to request an IEE when they do not agree with the results of a special education evaluation. The school must consider the results of this evaluation in order to ensure that it is providing FAPE. Answer B is incorrect because although the IEP team must consider the results of the evaluation, they do not have to accept them. Answer C is incorrect because parents are not automatically required to pay for the IEE. When parents request an IEE, the district must either provide the IEE at public expense or request a due process hearing to defend its evaluation. Answer D is incorrect because an explanation is not required for the parents to request an IEE.

**111. A: If a student is evaluated for special education and later found not to have a disability, the school cannot continue providing the accommodations because eligibility requires documented evidence of a disability. Without such evidence, the student must return to the standard general education program. Answer B is incorrect because accommodations cannot legally be provided without a documented**

**disability or a 504 plan. Answer C is incorrect because the student was found not to have a disability, and Section 504 requires a documented disability. Answer D is incorrect because referring students to outside supports is not necessary unless the evaluation indicates otherwise, which the prompt does not suggest.**

**112. B:** Telling the parents what she suspects and recommending treatment without a formal diagnosis would be inappropriate. This speech language pathologist (SLP) is very observant and has a talent for diagnosis as well as being well-educated about and experienced with autism. And SLPs do work with some autistic individuals. Regardless of these things, she is not qualified to make such a diagnosis. This should be done by a licensed psychologist, behavior specialist, or psychiatrist. Telling the parents what she suspects could alarm them unnecessarily—especially if she turns out to be wrong or if a psychological practitioner disagrees and/or makes a different diagnosis. Therefore, option A is incorrect.

Referring the parents to a clinic for more thorough evaluation by qualified psychological personnel is the right thing to do. If her suspicions are confirmed, the diagnosis will be made by someone with credentials to back it up and who can recommend appropriate interventions. Referring to a free clinic is also helpful since the parents cannot afford to pay a private practitioner. Therefore, option B is correct.

Asking the referring kindergarten teacher to tell the parents is as inappropriate as telling them herself, since the teacher is also not qualified to make such a diagnosis. The SLP would also be evading personal responsibility by diagnosing outside of her role but using the teacher to deliver the information, which is not confirmed. Both actions would be unethical. Therefore, option C is incorrect.

Ruling out other physical or medical conditions is a good idea, and an astute physician may recognize early signs of autism just as the SLP did. But this step in itself is insufficient. To recommend a physical checkup and also refer the parents to a clinic for behavioral evaluation would be an acceptable action plan. Therefore, option D is incorrect.

**113. C:** Giving an IQ test in the midst of a busy, noisy classroom would be distracting to Lee, interfering with his ability to give his best responses. It would also violate confidentiality by giving him no privacy during testing. Omitting the marking and pointing items would leave out valuable test results because, despite being a student with many physical limitations, Lee has the ability to do these things. It would also eliminate an opportunity for him to experience success. Therefore, option A is incorrect.

Asking Kim to make an alternative seating device is not feasible. She has already built the only kind of device that, because of the severe twisting of his spine, Lee can lie on. Anything narrower would cause him pain, injure him, or simply be impossible. Even if such a device were not impossible or harmful, the school's limited funding would prohibit it being made. And with Kim being the only occupational therapist for many students, the extra work would be an unfair, impractical, and unnecessary burden. Therefore, option B is incorrect.

The office area is empty and quiet at the time, so using the hallway outside Gigi's office is a suitable alternative. The test would still be private, and extra time would not be used up transporting Lee to another location. Tom's idea to hold the paper on a clipboard involves no building or spending, and it is a simple and effective solution. Therefore, option C is correct.

Finding a different IQ test is unnecessary in this case. Removing tasks Lee can perform gives him less chance to enjoy success. The hall outside the classroom, unlike the office hallway, is noisy. With students inside the classroom, Lee has no privacy during testing. Therefore, option D is incorrect.

**114. A:** Asking the general education classroom teacher to excuse Frank from spelling tests and not to grade him on spelling would not be in the best interests of Frank's education. He is getting special education instruction to help him work on and overcome his learning disability. Excusing him from tasks that are harder but not impossible for him would do him a disservice. It would also set him apart from other students, who might resent him, and it would call more attention to his disability, thus making it harder for him to fit in with the general education classroom. This is something Ms. Miller should NOT do. Therefore, option A is correct.

Asking Ms. Phillips to highlight Frank's reversed letters and numbers is a useful way to help him focus on his errors. He can bring his highlighted papers to Ms. Miller, and they can work on these together. This is something Ms. Miller should do. Therefore, option B is incorrect.

Allowing Frank additional time to complete in-class reading is not the same as excusing him from spelling tests or grades. This is a more acceptable accommodation. It can be done without calling other students' attention to it, which might provoke envy or resentment. Ms. Phillips can simply allow a slightly longer total time for in-class reading, with instructions for students to begin their comprehension questions when done reading. That way every student works at their own pace. This is something Ms. Miller could do. Therefore, option C is incorrect.

Asking Ms. Phillips to keep Ms. Miller apprised of Frank's progress as well as any areas she would like him to work on more with Ms. Miller is a good idea. It would allow both teachers to help Frank focus on the areas in which he needs more work. This is something Ms. Miller should do. Therefore, option D is incorrect.

**115. D:** Frank has been transitioned from a private residence with a nonprofessional personal caregiver to a group home and a special school. Any training he needs should not be done only in one setting. Therefore, option A is incorrect.

Just as his training should not occur only at the group home, it should also not take place just at the school. Therefore, option B is incorrect.

It is correct that training should be done in both home and school settings; however, caregivers and teachers should not simply start training Frank without any prior planning or documentation. Therefore, option C is incorrect.

Frank's training issues should be addressed by written IEP goals and objectives. This will provide consistency across settings. The IEP objectives should be carried out by both the house parents at his group home and by the teachers at his school. Therefore, option D is correct.

**116. D:** Both former and new teachers need to be involved in transition, but it should not be limited to them. Teachers should collaborate with all those who can contribute to planning. Therefore, option A is incorrect.

The second option omits Sammy's former teacher, who is a valuable source of information. Without his previous teacher's input, a good transition is not likely. Others are omitted as well. Therefore, option B is incorrect.

Both former and new teachers as well as Sammy's parents should definitely be included, so this option is closer to the ideal situation. However, it omits the student himself. Therefore, option C is incorrect.

The teachers, parents, and Sammy himself should all be included in transition planning. There are likely others who could also contribute to this planning. However, this option incorporates more of the people who should be included in planning than do the other three choices. Therefore, option D is correct.

**117. A:** An IQ score one or more standard deviations below the mean, or a score of 85 or lower, is a criterion used in the definition by Heber of the American Association on Mental Deficiency (American Association on Intellectual Disabilities) in 1961. Definitions widely used prior to 1961 did not include this criterion. Therefore, option A is correct.

Social incompetence was included as one of six criteria for the definition of intellectual disabilities by Edgar A. Doll in 1941. (Doll developed the Vineland Social Maturity Scale, now the Vineland Adaptive Behavior Scales.) Therefore, option B is incorrect.

Impaired adaptive behavior was cited in 1937 by Tredgold of Great Britain. Therefore, option C is incorrect.

Being essentially incurable is another one of Doll's 1941 six criteria for the definition of intellectual disabilities. Therefore, option D is incorrect.

**118. C:** Mr. Price's students and their families are not displaying psychological aberrations. They come from various cultures and are displaying different beliefs, traditions, and values; therefore, option A is incorrect.

Mr. Price's students and their families are not displaying dysfunctional family dynamics. They are following their own cultural traditions, beliefs, and values; therefore, option B is incorrect.

Mr. Price has students coming from diverse cultural backgrounds with which he has little or no prior experience. The librarian can suggest various research resources whereby Mr. Price can educate himself regarding these families' different practices and beliefs; therefore, option C is correct. Mr. Price should, however, be aware of when cultural practices violate school rules or state/federal laws. For example, many states prohibit all child marriages, whether arranged or not.

Since Mr. Price has a multicultural class, it is possible that there may not be any other classes with more homogenous demographics. The entire school's population might be similarly diverse. In that case, it would not be possible to reassign him. In addition, rather than Mr. Price avoiding the entire situation, educating himself about his students' diverse cultures would add to his knowledge, make him more versatile as a teacher, enable him to meet his students' needs better, and ultimately benefit both Mr. Price and his students; therefore, option D is incorrect.

**119. C:** one-on-one stuttering therapy will benefit Erin, but keeping her in the same group is not the least restrictive setting for a student with a high IQ and good grades. Therefore, option A is incorrect.

Grouping Erin with other stutterers is more appropriate than grouping her with students who have delayed language development, but it is still not the least restrictive environment. A small group with other stutterers would be appropriate for pull-out speech therapy sessions but not for the whole school day. Therefore, option B is incorrect.

Because Erin has a high IQ and good grades, Donna is right to advocate for her placement in the general classroom. It is commonplace for students who stutter but have good academic achievement to be in the general classroom. Therefore, option C is correct.

Certainly stutterers have been embarrassed and even humiliated when they stuttered in front of large groups. However, this experience also occurs elsewhere in society, not just in school. Students who stutter are typically not segregated in school to protect them from embarrassment, which would still occur outside the classroom. Donna working individually with Erin would not constitute the least restrictive setting. It would also be impractical in terms of the use of Donna's time. Frequent speech therapy sessions with Donna are indicated, along with having Erin spend the majority of the school day in the general classroom. Therefore, option D is incorrect.

**120. D:** A 1998 survey by the National Association of County and City Health Officials (NACCHO) found that 13 states were centralized, 26 states were decentralized, and 11 states had mixed authority. All states do not have centralized organizational structures. Therefore, option A is incorrect.

All states are not decentralized. Therefore, option B is incorrect.

All states do not have mixed or shared authority between the state and the local health department. Therefore, option C is incorrect.

As shown in the survey cited above, some states are centralized, some are decentralized, and some share authority between the state and the local agencies. Therefore, option D is correct.

## Online Resources

Due to our efforts to try to keep this book to a manageable length, we've created a link that will give you access to all of your online resources:

mometrix.com/resources719/gacesegcelemed

# It's Your Moment, Let's Celebrate It!

**Share your story @mometrixtestpreparation**